What's the Matter with White People?

Why We Long for a Golden Age That Never Was

Joan Walsh

WILEY

John Wiley & Sons, Inc.

Lyrics on page 17: From *Fairytale of New York* by Shane MacGowan and Jem Finer. Copyright © 1987 by Shane MacGowan and Jem Finer. Used in the United States by permission of Anderson Literary Management.

Published by John Wiley & Sons, Inc., Hoboken, New Jersey
Published simultaneously in Canada

For general information about our other products and services, please contact our Customer Care Department within the United States at (800) 762-2974, outside the United States at (317) 572-3993 or fax (317) 572-4002.

Wiley also publishes its books in a variety of electronic formats and by print-on-demand. Some content that appears in standard print versions of this book may not be available in other formats. For more information about Wiley products, visit us at www.wiley.com.

Library of congress Cataloging-in-Publication Data:

Walsh, Joan, date.
    What's the matter with white people?: why we long for a golden age that never was / by Joan Walsh.
      p.   cm.
    Includes index.
    ISBN 978-1-118-14106-9 (cloth); ISBN 978-1-118-22544-8 (ebk);
    ISBN 978-1-118-23724-3 (ebk); ISBN 978-1-118-26358-7 (ebk)
      1. United States—Politics and government—20th century.   2. Political culture—
United States—History—20th century.   3. Democratic Party (U.S.)—History—20th century.
4. Irish Americans—Politics and government.   5. Walsh, Joan, 1958– I. Title.
E839.5.W34   2012
973.91—dc23

                                    2011053473

Printed in the United States of America
10 9 8 7 6 5 4 3 2

For my father John Patrick Walsh,
who taught me to debate,
with love.

CONTENTS

PREFACE

A few days after the Occupy Wall Street movement began to stir in September 2011, I walked the narrow streets of the world's financial hub in a light rain, looking for a protest still too small to find.

During the next few weeks, OWS would change the national conversation. The slogan "We are the 99 percent" did what years of complaint by economists and liberals could not: it focused attention on staggering income inequality and "the top 1 percent" who'd enriched themselves phenomenally during the past thirty years. "I am so scared of this anti–Wall Street effort. I'm frightened to death," Frank Luntz, the GOP's master of spin, told a private meeting of Republican governors at the end of 2011. "They're having an impact on the way Americans think about capitalism."

Suddenly, cable news shows that had been obsessing over the deficit "crisis" and President Obama's latest poll numbers were explaining how decades of tax cuts and deregulation unraveled the social contract established in the New Deal. It had been accepted by every American president for thirty years afterward, until Richard Nixon brilliantly divided the New Deal coalition, largely around race. In the early days, polls showed that the Occupy movement's grievances were broadly shared, even by the white working class, which Nixon and then Ronald Reagan had lured to the GOP. Yet how long before the 99 percent would cleave back into the 51 and the 48 percent? I couldn't know. For the moment, though, it was amazing to see such broadly shared political discontent surfacing at all.

As I headed down the dark canyon of Wall Street itself, I decided to climb the steps of Federal Hall to get a better view of blue-helmeted cops behind barricades, waiting for trouble that never came that day. With the famous statue of George Washington to keep me company—our first president gave his first inaugural address on the site—I found myself thinking, and not in a good way, about another historic gathering on those same steps, one that offered important lessons for any American political movement: the Hard Hat Riot of 1970. The violent but little-known skirmish marked the ultimate fracture of the Democratic Party of the twentieth century, a fracture still unhealed in the twenty-first. Would today's protesters be mindful of the sad lessons of protests past? Probably not, because nobody younger than sixty remembers the Hard Hat Riot today.

But I do, even though I was just a kid at the time. My father talked about it for years afterward. An unlikely corporate peacenik, my dad wandered from his office near Wall Street at lunchtime on May 8, 1970, to join a protest denouncing the killing of four antiwar Kent State University students by the Ohio National Guard a few days earlier. Just as he got there, the peaceful gathering was interrupted by flag-wielding construction workers, marching over from the grounds of the World Trade Center they were building a few blocks away. Chanting "All the way, U.S.A." and "Love it or leave it," they broke up the Kent State protest, charging up the steps of Federal Hall to plant American flags on George Washington. Everyone else was rebelling; now the hard hats were, too, paradoxically trying to use disorder to restore social order to a country that had been torn apart by forces nobody entirely understood. Horrified, my father headed back to work, but as he left, he thought he saw one of his brothers, a steamfitter employed on the World Trade Center site, among the angry workers. A few used their iconic hard hats to beat up antiwar students, smashing the remnants of the New Deal coalition at the same time.

Later that month, the head of the rioters' union coalition, Building Trades Council chief Peter Brennan, presented President Richard Nixon with his own hard hat; in 1972, Brennan bolted the Democratic Party to endorse Nixon's reelection. He became Nixon's ineffectual labor secretary in 1973, the same year the World Trade Center opened for business. Labor began a sharp decline that year, as did liberalism. You couldn't blame it all on the Hard Hat Riot—the Democratic Party had begun to unravel years before that event—but the clash further divided the party and the country, and my family, too. Mine wasn't the only working-class Irish Catholic family split that way. A year earlier, *New York* magazine writer Pete Hamill had written a long, anguished feature, "The Revolt of the White Lower Middle Class," about "the growing alienation and paranoia" of a group he claimed as "my people," even as he grappled with their misplaced rage and racism. Yet the violence of the Hard Hat Riot horrified Hamill, and he attacked it in the *New York Post*, writing with a kind of anger that is often borne of shame. I recognized it.

How strange, then, that American dissent began stirring again forty-one years later, at the exact same site, only blocks away from the World Trade Center. Or maybe not strange: terror brought the towers down ten years earlier; the banking crisis that cratered the economy in 2008 was centered there, too. Maybe George Washington created a mysterious vortex of democracy when he addressed his young country at the site more than two centuries earlier. (Alexander Hamilton, the father of American banking, is buried in the Trinity Church yard down the street.) It seems as if we are continually having our attention drawn back to the same spot, trying to get democracy right, as we struggle over America's place in the world. Certainly, democracy seemed to come alive again there, as the movement to wrest control of the country from Wall Street and the wealthiest 1 percent spread to hundreds of American cities and into other Western countries. "We are the 99 percent" became an updated version of *e pluribus unum*, "out of many, one."

I think about the Hard Hat Riot all these years later because it symbolized the culmination of a Republican political strategy that has worked nearly flawlessly for almost my entire life. No matter what's going on in the world, the right can find a cultural issue that will get the left to fight itself, to atomize into little groups, and to give voice to factions that frighten Americans on the sidelines—often, the left-out white middle and working class— and the country winds up the worse for it. Thanks to my roots in that much maligned, misunderstood, and sometimes destructive demographic group, I'm haunted by the mistakes of political movements I barely remember.

In 2011, we began to honestly reckon with the political and social forces that had allowed the rich to sack the country while people in the once-great New Deal coalition fought among themselves. Could we avoid those old battles and meanwhile reach out to attract the anxious folks on the sidelines, rather than repelling them this time? And could those anxious folks, many of them white people—my people—stop longing for a golden age that never was, and help invent a just, multiracial America?

I felt optimistic, yet I had grown up seeing all of the ways my team defeated itself, to the delight and the triumph of conservatives. We can't afford to do that again.

INTRODUCTION

I f America bottomed out politically in May 1970, it did so again in August 2011, and that time it took me with it. I couldn't see that political light was only a month down the tunnel. All summer long, on *Salon* and on television, I had to cover the grim hostage crisis known as the debt-ceiling battle, as Republican extremists—purporting to ride a wave of white middle- and working-class anger—threatened to destroy the world's economy unless President Obama slashed federal spending. When the besieged president finally gave in, a ratings agency downgraded U.S. credit anyway, because the fight exposed the country's broken politics. The president was still learning the hard way that placating extremists only leads to more extremism. Still, I tried to keep my deep pessimism—about Barack Obama's presidency, about our country, about our politics—to myself. As a journalist and a lifelong Democrat, I'm an optimist; I've had to be. This, too, would pass. How long could people badly hurt by the recession continue to support policies that would make things worse? Not forever, right?

I hit my political bottom, oddly, on HBO's anything-goes politics show *Real Time with Bill Maher*. I was having fun until Maher asked me whether Hillary Clinton would have been a better choice for liberals in the 2008 Democratic primary, given the president's struggles. My brain short-circuited; I went mute. I don't think anyone noticed; the brilliant and hilarious astrophysicist Neil DeGrasse Tyson stepped in to save me, answering a resounding *Yes*. "I think she would have been," he told Maher, contending that Clinton would be "a more effective negotiator in the halls of Congress." It turned out to be great television and great politics: the African American scientist backed the white lady Democrat when the white lady pundit would not.

Yet I was left puzzling over how I wound up speechless on a talk show. It wasn't "buyers' remorse" over Obama, as Maher framed it. I'd supported Clinton in the bitter 2008 primaries, but I knew the country's mess was too spectacular to clean up by trading one Democrat for another. Besides, I'd proudly backed Obama in the general election, defending him in the pages of *Salon* and on TV, too. On Election Day, almost 70 million Americans voted with me, as the African American Democrat won the largest share of the popular vote of any nonincumbent president or vice president since General Dwight Eisenhower in 1952. It was what had happened since then—the stunning, racially tinged anti-Obama backlash that thwarted desperately needed economic reform, restored Republicans to Congress, and forced beleaguered Democrats to accept GOP definitions of what was politically possible—that had me tongue-tied, with no ready answers.

I had to admit that Democratic infighting over the president's troubles had thrown me back to that fractious 2008 primary, when identity politics paralyzed the party for a while, to the exclusion of what should have been urgent questions about class and inequality. In some precincts of the left, if you backed Clinton, you weren't just wrong; you were racist. If you backed Obama, you faced the charge of sexism, of cruelly ignoring a track record of political success just because it wore pumps and pastel pants suits. Some Obama supporters dismissed Clinton's white working-class support as a Hard Hat Riot at the ballot box, bashing the dream of a black president. The late Geraldine Ferraro embarrassed herself by attributing Obama's success to his race (and maleness) and blaming Clinton's woes on her gender. It was a great relief for me, personally and politically, when the nation moved on from primary-season infighting, and we elected our first black president.

Yet as his presidency hit hard times, I discovered a vexing Obama paradox: Electing our first black president provoked a genuine and appalling racial backlash—but not all of Obama's troubles could be blamed on a resurgence of racism. And parsing out what was real prejudice and what was valid political disagreement wasn't always easy. Obama certainly made political mistakes, and the sputtering economy magnified their importance and frustrated even some ardent supporters. The backlash was giving me whiplash: one day I'd be on TV blasting the racist fringe of the Tea Party, whose most extreme supporters depicted our dignified president as an African witch doctor, a watermelon-eating simpleton, a character from *Planet of the Apes*, and, on its "birther" extreme, as a Kenyan Muslim who was ineligible to be president. But the next day I'd critique the president's cautious, conciliating moves as the economy worsened and Republicans doubled down on their opposition to him—only to find myself called a racist, or more gently, someone who couldn't acknowledge the leadership of our first black president.

In the *New York Times*, author Ishmael Reed compared Obama's white critics to spoiled children. "Unlike white progressives," Reed intoned, "blacks and Latinos are not used to getting it all. They know how it feels to be unemployed and unable to buy your children Christmas presents. They know when not to shout." Nine months later, in the *Nation*, scholar Melissa Harris-Perry asked whether Obama's white liberal critics were exhibiting "an insidious form of racism" because they held him to a higher standard, she believed, than they did President Bill Clinton.

Were progressives being unfair to the first black president? Was I? Or were we all falling victim to the same kind of dead-end infighting that had split the forces of social justice since the sixties and the seventies? Could it possibly be that the Republicans had again dug the Democrats a political grave, then watched in amusement as they eagerly pushed their own allies into it? I began to believe that the long American decline that began in the 1970s could be traced back to just these kinds of battles among people who ought to be partners. Suddenly, at the nadir of that dismal summer of 2011, I was doubting myself, pulling my punches, biting my tongue.

After a lifetime on the fractious American left, I felt stranded on the sidelines without a side: a civil rights integrationist stuck in a world of narrow boxes; a working-class Irish Catholic San Franciscan jousting with Beltway and Ivy League elites; an American who loves my country fighting charges that I'm un-American from an increasingly vicious right. One party, my own, had lost its spine; the other lost its mind. I knew that change lay in a broader definition of common ground, and I saw hope in the rising realization that "We are the 99 percent."

Yet if we are the 99 percent, why do we so often fail to get a majority of the country to listen to us?

I had the broad outlines of an answer, as others had put much of the evidence together before me. I'd seen it over and over. Democrats do best when they can unite around a vision of economic improvement for everybody; they get derailed when Republicans toss culture war grenades or play on race. Then Democrats attack one another, and the party's agenda gets framed in a way that makes a lot of people—particularly white middle- and working-class men—protective of their shrinking resources and diminishing status. Democrats lose the public opinion battle, and their chance to make things better; the GOP comes in, protecting the interests of the top 1 percent, and makes everything worse for the rest of us. With the bark of a demagogue into a microphone, whether it's Father Charles Coughlin in my grandparents' day or Rush Limbaugh in mine, the class war is turned into a culture war, burning ever hotter, all heat, no light.

And yet, first in the Obama coalition and then in the Occupy Wall Street eruption, I saw a national yearning to create a new social compact based on more broadly shared opportunity and prosperity. A hallmark of American exceptionalism—that each generation does better than the next, that social class isn't a barrier to climbing here—had ceased to be true: Most countries in "Old Europe," where opportunity was supposedly strangled by a sclerotic class system and a big welfare state, now offered their citizens a greater chance to climb economically than the United States did. The top 1 percent of Americans, who received 9 percent of the income in the mid-'70s, got a quarter of it in 2007; they own 40 percent of the nation's wealth. Economic inequality is worse than it's been since the eve of the Great Depression. Finally, though, more Americans seemed to realize that the 1 percent were able to grab all of the economic rewards of the past thirty years at least partly because the 99 percent were fighting among themselves.

The 2012 Republican presidential primary helped raise the issue even higher. Mitt Romney, the presumptive nominee, looked like the poster child for the top 1 percent, a cross between Richie Rich and Thurston Howell III from *Gilligan's Island*. When Romney released 2010 tax returns showing that while he made $21 million off investments, he only paid a 13.9 percent tax rate—a lower rate than middle-class workers—he offered the nation a crash course in our plutocratic tax policy. Unfortunately, some of the politicians who'd worked hardest to protect Romney's low investment tax rate were Democrats, a complication that hinders the party's attempt to channel the interests of the 99 percent.

Even some of the white working class, the group Ronald Reagan had turned into Reagan Democrats by railing against "welfare queens" everyone knew were black, seemed to be waking up. Right-wing author Charles Murray, who in the 1980s blamed government for encouraging sloth and single parenthood in the black community, published a best seller that said the same thing about the white "lower class": they were suffering from declining wages and higher unemployment not because of a changed economy, but because they had come to prefer slacking and shacking up to hard work and marriage.

Suddenly, when today's Republicans attacked moochers, slackers, and welfare queens, they included some working-class whites—cops and nurses, firefighters and teachers, the public employees who formed the backbone of what grew into the American middle class. When Sandra Fluke, a young white law student, defended President Obama's mandate that insurance companies provide contraception cost-free, Rush Limbaugh attacked her in obscene, misogynistic terms; more genteel right-wingers called her a "welfare queen" for demanding taxpayer-funded contraception. As people took to the streets from Madison, Wisconsin, to Wall Street to Davis, California, a new spirit of political courage and curiosity spread.

Republicans tried to demonize the protests, to scare Middle America, all to make us forget that, like it or not, social change requires agitation—or in Frederick Douglass's words, "Power concedes nothing without a demand." The New Deal wasn't handed to us; it took decades of fighting, including strikes and civil disobedience, to get government's and business's attention. The civil rights movement likewise involved strife and turmoil and jail time for its leaders. I was thrilled to see the new activism. Maybe we were finally realizing we're all in this together.

Maybe.

But the old ways take time to be unlearned. Though the Occupy movement transformed the political debate, emblazoning the issue of income inequality high on the national agenda, many of its local satellites fell back into '60s style infighting—over property destruction and violence, relations with police, and race and gender. Too many Democrats judged the new activism only on the grounds of whether it was good or bad for President Obama and the party's congressional leadership. Republicans did what Republicans do: they revived the culture wars, crusading, rather unbelievably, against contraception; questioning the work ethic of poor people (even suggesting that poor kids work as school janitors); labeling Spanish a "ghetto language."

Yet, in a daring new flourish, some Republicans joined Charles Murray in attacking the morality of the white working class, which apparently, according to Republicans, had begun to share the lamentable attitudes toward work and family once associated with "welfare queens," a variety of political scapegoat that used to only come in black. What is the matter with white people, indeed?

Sometimes I found myself hopeful: Maybe the white working class would realize that the GOP was talking about *them* now, while hoping they'd only notice the nasty things they said about the other guys. At other times, we seemed condemned to relive those battles of the '60s and '70s, battles that weren't dead; in Faulkner's words, they weren't even past.

And occasionally, I confess, I found myself thinking, Maybe the problem is me. Maybe I'm stuck on what happened forty years ago. Maybe I'm the one with a faulty understanding of left and right, black and white, the cleavages of race and class, why this country comes together, and why, more often, it comes apart. Over the past four years I've spent a lot of time searching my personal history, my family history, and American history to understand how I got here. I particularly wanted to understand the divisive clash between race and class, a destructive wedge often manufactured, or at least encouraged, by politicians, and one that I once believed I had a rare capacity to identify and deflect. Now I felt like the wedge was coming right at me.

I had to start by examining the lessons I learned in my family, most of them handed down to me by my father, an Irish Catholic liberal dreamer. The son of poor Irish immigrants, born in the Bronx, New York, on the eve of the Great Depression, he was the person who taught me that you could trace the decline of the Democratic Party and of the movement for economic inclusion and fairness to the brutal tensions that surfaced in the strange Hard Hat Riot that split his family but that nobody my age even knew about.

My father set me on an eccentric political path early, back before kindergarten, with a fractured Irish fairytale. Against the galvanizing moral backdrop of the civil rights movement, which my parents supported fervently, my father confided that dark-haired Irish such as he and I—my mother was a pretty redhead, my little brother had blond curls—were called "black Irish," and it wasn't just because of our chestnut hair and hazel eyes. Some people thought the black Irish were offspring of Spaniards and Moors mixing with fair-skinned Celts many centuries ago, he told me. Who knew but if many generations back, we might have black ancestry, too?

It was a perfect fable for 1963, and it worked. A driven little Catholic girl—I wanted to be a nun, then a missionary, then a saint—I shared my parents' belief that the civil rights movement was the moral issue of our time, good versus evil, played out literally in black and white. In my father's version of history, black people were just the latest group of Americans to struggle for rights and freedom. Our people, the Irish, had also faced cruel prejudice and endured their own share of suffering. For my parents and all of our Irish Catholic relatives, the election of John F. Kennedy in 1960 proved that we'd left steerage, although status anxiety persisted throughout my childhood, as we fought not to seem "shanty Irish" on Long Island. President Kennedy, my dad explained, was working hard to bring black people into the Promised Land of full citizenship in America, where we had only recently arrived. (Yes, as I learned very early, he exaggerated Kennedy's civil rights exertions a bit.)

The most unique aspect of my father's political worldview, though, was that his civil rights passion coexisted with a deep commitment to the rights of working-class people: cops and firefighters, steamfitters and utility workers, men like his father, brothers, and brothers-in-law; women like my grandmother and her sisters, all of whom had to work back when women supposedly didn't. Sadly, we lived in a time and a place where those two sets of values were dangerously colliding, when those who cared passionately about the lasting injustice of racism had trouble relating to the fears and struggles of the increasingly alienated and often manipulated white working class, and vice versa. Historian Rick Perlstein labeled that era "Nixonland," a time when divided Americans began to believe not merely that the other side was wrong, but that they couldn't share the same country, a besieged state of mind encouraged by our thirty-seventh president. I grew up in Nixonland, with family on both sides of the divide. It forged my political identity—and led to my midlife political identity crisis.

The Obama campaign wasn't the first time I realized I didn't live in my father's dream world. On the left as I grew up, identity politics had far more energy than did economic populism, on almost every front. The troubles of the white working class got blamed on the white working class itself, which did in fact let racism and fear drive its political decisions too often. For a while, my father's comparing the sufferings of Irish Catholic immigrants to the black experience seemed naïve, maybe even racist, a way to dodge the much greater injustice, and perhaps the guilt, of slavery. Besides, colleagues on the left insisted that the Irish weren't freedom fighters; they were reactionaries. I can't count the times people recommended to me the shrill "whiteness studies" tome *How the Irish Became White* (the Spark Notes version: by kicking black people every chance they got). New lefty scholars declared my people the uniquely racist enforcers of white supremacy.

I watched one area of common ground emerge on the left: more and more observers seemed to believe that so-called people of color—a bewildering expression linking folks as disparate as African American investment bankers, Cuban teachers, Laotian refugees, Caribbean entrepreneurs, Salvadoran doctors, Chinese cops, and fourth-generation Mexican real estate moguls—shared more interests with one another than with any white Americans. That magical thinking became the operating assumption of many of my left-wing allies. I saw it in the Obama movement, when his backers dismissed Clinton's white working-class supporters as racist and insisted their candidate could win without them. I disagreed. "What's the matter with white people?" I found myself asking—in a different way—as in, "Aren't we part of your multiracial future, too?"

The loneliness of my position hit me hard one day as I debated the emerging Tea Party with Pat Buchanan, a fellow Irish Catholic and one of Nixon's henchmen, on *Hardball*. When I noted the prominence of birthers within the Tea Party, the wily Buchanan quickly dragged me into Nixonland. "Do you know why you lose these people?" he asked, his voice rising. "Because you show contempt for them! You call them birthers. You call them names. All they want, Joan, is respect. And you liberals never give it to them. No wonder they go over to the Republican Party!"

Ouch. I partly agreed with Buchanan. Lefty scorn for the working class helped push it right; I knew from experience that my team threw around the term *racist* too easily. No matter what kinds of coalitions the Democrats can assemble to win an election, it will be harder for them to restore America's economic potential without the support of the white middle and working class.

Not a minute later, however, Buchanan approvingly compared the Tea Party to the supporters of George Wallace—the segregationist Alabama governor who drew blue-collar whites in two presidential runs with an anti-integration appeal—whom Buchanan helped win over for Nixon in 1972. So he could link the Tea Party to that earlier white backlash, but I couldn't suggest there was a racial tinge to their Obama-hate?

The other irony was Buchanan labeling me an elitist who had "contempt" for the common people, when in fact I came from those people, and he did not. The son of a prosperous accountant, Buchanan went to Georgetown and Columbia University. My father was raised by poor Irish immigrants, who sent him away to a Christian Brothers boarding school at age thirteen; I went to the great land-grant college the University of Wisconsin. But I'm the elitist snob and he's the man of the people? I pushed back. "Pat, that's unfair," I told him. "I'm a working-class Irish Catholic. I don't like the demonization of the president." I wasn't going to let Buchanan pit me against my people, any of them: black people or the Irish. Buchanan and his allies had widened these divides for way too long.

When I began researching this book, I knew I wanted to write about the sixties and the seventies, with a particular focus on why

Americans have let our nation decline in almost every measurable way since then—and sometimes even cheered on those who engineered that decline. I wanted to tell it the way I saw it growing up, watching many of my working-class Irish relatives forsake the Democrats, a party they saw as forsaking them. Yet my family's story, and that of the Democratic Party, turned out to be more complicated. I thought I could look back to an earlier time of unity and surface lessons for the present, but there was no such time. So I had to go farther back in history than I'd anticipated.

First, I had to explore the black-Irish conflict that my father so ingeniously resolved for me with his fairytale of fusion. In fact, the African American–Irish Catholic divide is one of the fundamental fractures at the core of the Democratic Party and American politics today, and understanding it can illuminate the way the politics of race can so often clash with the politics of class. This is the gap I've been trying to bridge throughout my political and personal life, to make my father's fairytale real, with little success. I once blamed the conflict solely on wealthy capitalists and their politician-servants such as Nixon and Buchanan, pitting two groups at the bottom against each other. In this book, however, I explore the role played by my side—the forces of social justice, the liberal reformers and do-gooders—as well.

I also had to look more closely at my extended family, how they climbed out of poverty into the working and then middle class. From what did they benefit, and what were the costs? We were lucky, all of us, and yet the climb involved fracture and loss. Growing up in Nixonland, I had a father who stayed the course of civil rights liberalism, and a mother who had the same values but who reacted to the chaos of the era with fear and who drifted back to the law-and-order security of the past. I saw the New York of liberal Republican John Lindsay become the city of conservative Democrat Ed Koch, all before I turned twenty, as bitter battles over race, education, unions, cops, and crime shattered the city that had been a laboratory of the New Deal.

Then I had to unpack my own baggage, accumulated by my coming to adulthood in the Reagan era, watching the society in which my family had risen be dismantled, with the support of many of my relatives and others like them. I'd been raised to change the world, but the great movements of the sixties had either self-destructed or morphed dutifully into do-goodism, which I quickly joined. I found meaning in a new generation of antipoverty work, but I learned that my black-and-white civil rights paradigm didn't quite fit the multiracial California in which I was raising my Irish-Jewish daughter.

Finally, I had to go back to the most painful political experience in my recent life: the 2008 election and its aftermath, when clashes over race and class once again marred what should have been a renewal of the Democratic Party. When I first came out of the "closet," so to speak, as a working-class Irish Catholic (and as a white person, too, I suppose), it was to challenge the Pat Buchanans of the world. Then I realized I was also challenging a multiracial world of liberal political elites in which "white working class" is either a political anachronism or worse, code for a wide swatch of voters viewed as unreachable, too stupid or racist to know they should be voting for Democratic politicians (who often ignore or condescend to them). And yet despite our crucial and admirable focus on eradicating racism, only a slightly smaller proportion of African Americans live in poverty than when Dr. King tried to launch a Poor People's Campaign. It's not that our necessary effort to fight racism and discrimination led to that outcome, but it certainly didn't prevent it. We took our eye off the prize of economic inclusion, for everyone; we left the poor, disproportionately African American though still a majority white, to fend for themselves.

When I began this book, I thought the fracture at the heart of the American experiment was disturbing, but paradoxically, I came to find it liberating. Even some liberals believe that we used to be one big happy European-immigrant family, *one white nation, indivisible*, and that it was only when we began to try to reckon with racial difference and injustice that things fell apart. That isn't true: we've always struggled to live up to our country's founding ideals, particularly the notion of *e pluribus unum*. We scapegoated many generations of white immigrants, as well as the white poor. We have never lived up to our grand promises—but there's still time.

I don't say any of that to deny that racial discrimination has been more persistent and debilitating, especially to African Americans, than the prejudice faced by any white immigrant group, including Irish Catholics. Still, when we insist that our current struggle can't be placed on a continuum with America's long history of exclusion and injustice, and then a reckoning to right those wrongs; when we suggest that there's something uniquely troublesome about building a strong, united, multiracial America, maybe even impossible—Pat Buchanan wins. That's what he thinks.

That's not what I think. That's not what most of us believe—not even white people. As the right wing gives up on America because it's changed beyond their recognition, we're the ones who can make the American Dream real, for everyone this time.

PART I

Fact-Checking a Fractured Irish Fairy Tale

1

They've got cars big as bars,
They've got rivers of gold
                    —The Pogues, "Fairytale of New York"

In my earliest memories, New York is a landscape of graceful bridges spanning shimmering rivers and landmarks soaring above crowded sidewalks, glimpsed through the window of a boxy, blue '55 Chevy as my father ferried us around to visit our large family. A lot of those bridges and landmarks came with a story about our relatives. The Statue of Liberty welcomed my grandparents from Cork, Ireland, to Ellis Island. The Empire State Building provided my Irish grandfather, a steamfitter, with his first real job. My mother's Irish grandfather painted the Brooklyn Bridge. My grandmother still worked at Macy's in Herald Square, which was, back then, the world's largest store. They were all proud of their work, as if those landmarks belonged to them a little bit, and I grew up feeling that way, too.

My father also made sure that I saw the scaffolding beneath our family, the help they had climbing out of poverty. I knew we were responsible to help those coming up behind us. In New York, the capital of liberalism, strong unions, churches, neighborhood groups, and extended family helped my grandparents rise. In my parents' generation, the invisible hand of government felt like wind at our backs, guiding all of us gently but steadily into the middle class.

It turned out that I was growing up at the dreamiest moment of the American Dream. My family's move to Long Island—to the

17

humble town of Oceanside, used by Tom Wolfe to symbolize down-scale suburban dowdiness in his tales of radical chic—was subsidized by a government-powered building boom and highway construction. Government helped my parents and aunts and uncles buy homes; my father and uncles, almost all of them veterans, benefited from the GI Bill. The oldest commuter train system in the country, the Long Island Railroad, shuttled my father to and from work.

I went to great public schools, as well as Catholic schools. I paid almost no tuition to get a fantastic college education at the University of Wisconsin. Having started school on the eve of the Great Society, I graduated in the age of Ronald Reagan. I'm part of the last generation of young people to whom the nation kept its promises, but we didn't know that as I was growing up.

I was raised to understand that government helped my family rise, that the nation, led by Democrats, made political decisions to spread prosperity and build the middle class. Sometimes I think that knowledge itself makes me unusual. I didn't grow up seeing the American Dream as some modern-day Garden of Eden, from which we've now been cast; we built it. That makes me think we can do it again.

The fact is, on the eve of the Great Depression, we had historic income inequality (which was matched only in 2007, on the eve of the Wall Street crash), and for a long time people drew the conclusion that such radical economic disparities were dangerous, for everyone. From 1947 through 1973, we had tax policies that flattened income inequality. It was a political decision. The earnings of people at the bottom and in the middle grew faster than those at the top. That progressive tax policy brought in the public resources to pay for the scaffolding of the American Dream that helped my family and created the middle class.

The white middle class, anyway.

Going back to the New Deal, from Social Security to the Wagner Act empowering unions and continuing with the GI Bill, few, if any, new programs to build the middle class prohibited racial discrimination; many openly or cagily excluded people who weren't white. FDR's great reforms didn't cover agricultural workers, another way African Americans were left out. Then, as the great white middle class grew and left the cities, banks redlined minority neighborhoods and kept residents from borrowing, while restrictive covenants kept black people out of many suburbs. (I am mainly talking about the American North here; the Jim Crow South had crueler and more obvious methods to lock out African Americans.)

Our failure to understand how government built the middle class creates two big political problems for us. First, too many white people think they didn't have help, that they did everything on their own. Then, predictably, they reject the idea that they got something African Americans and Latinos didn't get. It makes a kind of sense: If I believe I didn't get help, how can you say you didn't get something I don't even know that I got?

We have to talk about that.

I took another practical political lesson from my childhood immersion in American liberalism: I can tell you from experience that it was genuinely terrifying when the country began to come apart in the 1960s, starting with the assassination of John F. Kennedy. The nation is still coping politically with the decade's trauma today.

Kennedy was a shining hero to my family, to millions of Irish Catholics, and to millions more beyond our clan. Clearly, my father's black-Irish history lesson exaggerated Kennedy's civil rights activism. The canny Irish pol balanced the moral imperative to put the federal government on the side of black people, as Southern racism got more violent, against his political need to keep Southerners on the side of the Democrats. Kennedy did eventually move, with a rousing civil rights speech five months before he died, declaring: "We preach freedom around the world, and we mean it, and we cherish our freedom here at home, but are we to say to the world, and much more importantly, to each other that this is the land of the free except for the Negroes; that we have no second-class citizens except Negroes; that we have no class or caste system, no ghettoes, no master race except with respect to Negroes?"

It was Lyndon Johnson who won the era's great civil rights and antipoverty reforms, partly in Kennedy's memory. Johnson presided over the greatest expansion of government in history, with the Civil Rights Act and the Voting Rights Act, Medicare and Medicaid, the Economic Opportunity Act, and much more. That's when all hell broke loose, or so it seemed. At least, that is the point in my life when America seemed to splinter, and the long-standing race and working-class conflicts that would so affect my political identity began to make themselves known to me.

Just five days after Johnson signed the Voting Rights Act, my family watched on television as the low-income African American neighborhood of Watts in Los Angeles exploded in days of rioting. There was no connection between Johnson's long-overdue civil rights measures and the chaos that followed, first in Watts, then in almost every major American city during the next few years. Yet right away, the right and even some conservative Democrats tried to fuse them. L.A.'s notorious police chief, William Parker, claimed the Watts violence became unavoidable once "you keep telling people they are unfairly treated." The problem wasn't racism, poverty, and police brutality, in the conservative view; it was people *talking about* racism. The right argued that the chaos resulted from Johnson doing too much, too soon; in fact, we did too little, too late.

New York, our home, became ground zero for liberalism's implosion. Driving around the five boroughs to visit family, we couldn't miss the crime and poverty: vacant lots strewn with garbage in Brooklyn, my father's family homes charred by the arson that blighted the Bronx; idle men on street corners, in a world where blue-collar jobs were disappearing. Most of my working-class family drifted to the right, including my mother. Her two brothers, a cop and a firefighter, still worked in the decaying, dangerous city. She flinched and said a prayer every time she heard a siren, though we lived far from her brothers' threatening beats.

Eventually, my mother, who had adored John F. Kennedy, became a reluctant convert to the law-and-order politics of Richard Nixon. She made me understand that "Nixonland," the state of fracture over which our divisive president proudly reigned, was defined by genuine fear, not merely by racism. My father stayed the course with civil rights liberalism, but he watched appalled as the nonviolent multiracial civil rights and antiwar movements gave way to Black Power, separatism, and violence. He did not hold "our side" blameless in the unraveling of liberalism. We did too much shouting and not enough listening to the people who disagreed with what we had to say.

Because Democrats were in charge when the country came undone in the 1960s, Democrats got blamed. Since then, I've watched a parade of party leaders try to outdo one another in denouncing their party's past—and the causes and commitments that I grew up believing in. "Big government" became the enemy as Democrats fumbled to rewrite their own history and erase their liberalism. In 1974, "New Democrat" senator Gary Hart declared "the end of the New Deal." President Jimmy Carter proclaimed that "government cannot solve our problems, it can't set our goals, it cannot define our mission." Bill Clinton famously announced, "The era of big government is over," although he stealthily used the tax code to provide credits that made millions of low-wage workers better off and helped many more families afford college.

Barack Obama stated flatly during the 2008 campaign, "I come from a new generation of Americans. I don't want to fight the battles of the sixties." After the crushing 2011 debt-ceiling battle, as Obama tried to sell the deal of slashing public spending to the American public, he announced that it would bring the United States to "the lowest level of annual domestic spending since Dwight Eisenhower was president."

Dwight Eisenhower: the Republican who was president in the 1950s, when I was born. Our first black president was taking us back to the soothing fifties, back before the Civil Rights or Voting Rights Acts; the Clean Air, Clean Water, or Occupational Safety and Health Acts; the Economic Opportunity Act; Medicare and Medicaid. Back before the country came unraveled, and Democrats got the blame.

I understand why Democratic leaders ran from the destruction of the sixties, as though they sought a witness protection program that would change their identities and keep them alive.

I also know that it didn't work. The GOP continues to make white voters believe Democrats are the party of big government—a corrupt big government that doesn't work for white people, only for undeserving minorities. Forty years of running hasn't left those lies behind.

Democrats have been left with two versions of their own history, a pair of too-simplistic stories of their party's legacy. They have attempted to either obliterate the sixties or depict it as a thrilling time, when we fought racism, sexism, and an unjust war and made everything right. What they don't do is acknowledge how scary it was for most Americans back then, how liberalism seemed to lead to chaos or worse. Republicans seized the day and used that fear for their own divisive purposes, but it was a fear that was very real, very much a part of my earliest political consciousness, and very much at the heart of my extended family's turn to the right.

I saw three presidents toppled before I turned sixteen: Kennedy by an assassin, Johnson by a mostly peaceful but sometimes violent antiwar movement, and Nixon by his own paranoia and lawlessness in Watergate. How did the unraveling start? No one knows exactly why, but 1965, when I turned seven, was not only the year of the Voting Rights Act and the Watts riots; it was also the year crime and divorce rates began to steadily rise and membership in mainline churches declined, along with Americans' affiliation with political parties, according to Bill Bishop's *The Big Sort: Why the Clustering of Like-Minded America Is Tearing Us Apart*. Trust in government plummeted. The trauma of the mid- to late 1960s—riots and crime, drugs and divorce, black and white faux-revolutionaries taking up arms, the assassinations of President Kennedy, Malcolm X, Martin Luther King Jr., and Bobby Kennedy—scared the hell out of a lot of people, not only racist reactionaries. We are living in the shadow of that fear to this day.

Republicans seized our anxiety about change, shaped it, manipulated it, and stoked it into rage, all to drive people apart. Meanwhile, the economy began to sputter. Asking the white working class to share what it had with others might have worked in a time of affluence—the very sort of time, in fact, during which the Great Society was designed and launched. Yet it proved painfully divisive as the economy began to rattle and then go off the rails in the 1970s. Wily Republicans depicted those economic dislocations as having a lot to do with race, too—they didn't, as I will explore in the coming pages—and drove a wedge between the beleaguered working class and its old party, the Democrats, which the GOP now depicted as the party of everyone but white workers. I watched these old tensions arise again during the 2008 campaign, but we've hesitated to examine their roots for so long, we have only one word for them: *racism*.

I have been a witness, during my political coming of age, to Democrats running away from the sixties, from the truth and accomplishments of their own story. It's a story of how government, under Democrats, expanded economic equality and built the white middle class—and how we just might be able to do it again. Yet we Democrats have sold ourselves out, helped dirty the image of liberalism, and, in the process, have helped enable Americans, particularly the middle class, to live in a dream world where their rise was entirely their own making: real Americans don't get government help. But my parents did, and so did their entire generation. So did my generation, at least until now. The result of this dysfunctional strategy is a practical and political impotence that's been particularly debilitating since 2008, as the country has struggled to emerge from economic catastrophe, yet for a while President Obama resisted both the language as well as the measures used by FDR and those who came after him, to show how government can fix the economy and fix itself.

And by the way, none of this maneuvering succeeded. Conflict reigns; manufactured battles dominate the political landscape, and polls show that despite the revisionism of a generation of Democrats, Americans still consider them the party of overgrown, ineffective government that is bigger than ever—and that still hasn't fixed the economy. Running away from the truth has robbed my party of its accomplishments—and made us look sneaky as well as incompetent.

. . .

The most important thing I learned, as I examined the myths and the truths about my childhood political indoctrination: Our troubles didn't start in the sixties, anyway; they go all the way back to our founding. Rick Perlstein's wisdom about "Nixonland" aside, Americans didn't start hating one another in the sixties; Nixon just updated hate for the twentieth century. Enmity was baked into the American experiment by Founders who disagreed with one another about crucial issues—slavery, religion, equality, freedom—but made common cause around independence from England. They left an awful lot of problems to be solved by those of us who came after them.

By ceding American history to the right wing, the left looks as if its conceding their claim that we're un-American or not proud of our country. In fact, they're the ones who have given up on some core beliefs: that this is where the people of the world come together, to make a nation that's stronger than the sum of its parts; that diversity and tolerance make us exceptional; that we can afford to create opportunity for everyone. Their Tea Party pageantry and "constitutional conservatism" represent the right's crisis of faith: that our flesh-and-blood Founders, flaws and all, left us not a tablet of Ten Commandments, nor a fully formed and perfect union, but an unfinished American experiment.

If the right seems to be giving up on that experiment, the rest of us have to rise to the challenge. But first we have to understand how we got here. It turns out that my father's black-Irish fairytale was misleading, to say the least. At the same time, I still believe he was on to something.

2

How unique in all of the world, that one nation . . . was the resting point for people, groups all across the world. It didn't matter the color of their skin, it didn't matter their language, it didn't matter their economic status. Once you got here, we were all the same. Isn't that remarkable?

—2012 GOP presidential candidate
Michele Bachmann

Now, that's a fairy tale.

I first heard Bachmann's crackpot version of *e pluribus unum* through a tiny speaker in my ear, getting ready to do *Hardball*, in early 2011. Host Chris Matthews takes credit, or blame, for bringing Bachmann to national attention. It was on *Hardball*, at the height of the 2008 fall campaign, that she urged the media to investigate the "anti-American" beliefs of congressional Democrats, most notably Barack Obama. Our twenty-first-century Joe McCarthy had arrived, wearing lipstick, ready to lead the Tea Party.

Just as Democrats have, ineffectively, tried to rewrite their own history since the 1960s, so the GOP and now the Tea Party have rewritten everyone's history—since the 1700s. As Bachmann geared up her preposterous run for president, she showcased her "remarkable" whitewashed version of the Founders' accomplishments in Iowa, the first caucus state. Even as she declared, "It didn't matter the color of their skin," Bachmann acknowledged the "scourge" of slavery to her Iowa audience. Yet she insisted that

America's Founders "worked tirelessly until slavery was no more in the United States," singling out John Quincy Adams for particular praise—even though John Quincy Adams was the *son* of a Founder, and a boy in 1776.

Bachmann's recounting of the past is characteristic of the simplification and the distortion that let Republicans demonize their opponents. To talk honestly about the Founders, their flaws as well as their genius, is to hate America! Conservatism is ostensibly about preserving the world as it is. Really, though, it is about returning the world to a lost state of grace, to some early time when things were nearly perfect. Being a Republican in America means believing the period from the founding until the day LBJ was sworn in (or FDR, in some tellings) was defined by the march of freedom and prosperity. The few detours from that path can be easily explained as the work of un-American Democrats, which Republicans managed to fix.

Despite this, the very roots of our racial divide and class conflicts lie with the Founders. Of course, they didn't work to end slavery, not tirelessly or any other way. Some owned slaves, the Constitution they wrote made slavery legal, and even those who were coming to realize its immorality left it alone, to keep slaveholding states part of the union. Slavery wasn't abolished in the United States until after the Civil War. "Once you got here, we were all the same" wasn't true for white people, either. Most white immigrants, who came as indentured servants, couldn't vote. There wasn't universal male suffrage in every state until 1830. And we know women didn't get the franchise until 1920. I believe American history has a lot to inspire us, but it's hardly a story of "once you got here, we were all the same." Why can't we talk about our past truthfully?

The Founders became pawns in the Tea Party effort to downplay America's history of racism and play up the Democrats as the anti-American foes of freedom. Even beyond the slavery issue, their whitewashed history lessons are nonsense. The Founders didn't magically and unanimously form a perfect union; they disagreed about almost everything except independence from Britain. They struggled with how to balance the rights and responsibilities of "the few and the many," in the words of Alexander Hamilton. Every faction worried that the government they formed would impose the other guys' values, and power, on them. (You might describe it as a marriage in which each partner secretly believes he or she can change the other.)

The union they formed represented a balance of trust and fear, and that's why the pendulum of American history swings between optimism and pessimism. Our story is one of slowly gaining confidence that other Americans—white men without property; new immigrants; black men; finally, women of every race—are as worthy of self-government as we are. We expand the idea of who's fit for this grand experiment only gradually, as we either gain that trust or are forced to fake it. Yet that sometimes reluctant extension of trust leaves Americans suspicious and on the lookout for those who don't deserve freedom and equal rights, the slackers and the moochers, the "welfare queens," the people who don't want to work as hard as the rest of us do, who will only take advantage.

This is the fear that Republicans have so successfully exploited, especially since the 1960s, when the country began to try to bring in the economically and politically excluded at the precise moment the economy was beginning to sputter. It is sad but true that a people renowned for the notion that America is an idea, created and shared by different ethnicities and religions and classes, turned out to be obsessed with defining who is "un-American" and thus unfit for this great experiment, from the country's founding to today.

From the beginning, almost every American political faction believed that democracy wasn't for just anyone. The men around Hamilton were the most frank about tying political power to wealth and property; the men around Jefferson were more comfortable with broader suffrage and rights, but only for white men. Both groups believed that certain people didn't have what it took to be part of this new experiment: To the early Federalists and their Whig and Republican descendants, those people turned out to be my people, Catholic immigrants, particularly Irish Catholics.

For the Democratic Party that descended from Jefferson, it was African Americans, who were kept from exercising not merely voting rights but also any rights.

That was the first problem with my father's well-intentioned but fractured "black Irish" fairytale: politicians, religious leaders, and reformers have pitted the Irish against black people since the nation's founding and maybe even before, in specific and gruesome ways that we don't learn about in American history classes.

Strangely, it wasn't until adulthood that I learned there are actual "black Irish" people in the Caribbean, and I didn't hear about them from my father, but from another Joan Walsh, a black Jamaican woman who once checked me into a New York hotel. We both smiled at the coincidence, and then I got a little bit shy. It's beyond presumptuous for whites to greet blacks who share a surname as "kin," because the lineage of their name more often derives from slavery than love and marriage. Yet the Jamaican Joan Walsh joked with me and invited me home to meet "our" family sometime. When I mentioned the coincidence to a colleague, a devoted scholar and a champion of the American working class, he chuckled and said, "Well, she could be right." Seventeenth-century British crusader Oliver Cromwell, he told me, banished the Irish not just "to hell or Connaught," but to the West Indies. They worked on sugar plantations, "like slaves," he said. Some wound up in Jamaica.

"Like slaves"—but were they slaves? In fact, the status of these early ancestors of the real "black Irish" becomes the first contentious question about black-Irish relations in America and one of the hidden histories that I've come to believe still haunts American politics to this day.

We know that the Irish Catholics who landed in the West Indies and in the colonies in the seventeenth century were poor and landless; the vast majority were indentured servants. Some were former anti-Cromwell soldiers and/or their families, as well as paupers, vagabonds, and criminals "sentenced" to work in the West Indies or the colonies indefinitely, often permanently. British historians of the era sometimes referred to those banished Irish as "slaves." Thousands more were kidnapped and transported to Barbados as indentured labor; the practice was so common the Irish had a verb for it, to be "Barbadosed." Perhaps the most famous Irish servant, or slave, in the New World was Ann Glover, the last woman hung as a witch in Salem, Massachusetts, denounced by Cotton Mather as "a scandalous old Irishwoman, very poor, a Roman Catholic and obstinate in idolatry." She'd been banished to Barbados as a young woman and later made her way to Boston as a servant.

Tragically, or maybe farcically, in our own time the topic of Irish "slavery" has been dominated by white nationalists trying to argue that in the seventeenth century, at least, there were more Irish than black slaves in America, and that they were worked harder, were beaten more, and were all around worse off than Africans. The revisionist "history" book *They Were White and They Were Slaves* spawned a website devoted to the encouragement of white supremacy. I found "Celtic Pride" websites and message boards that dramatically exaggerate the extent and duration of Irish bondage. Sadly, like so many other experiences Irish Americans had in common with African Americans, this one, too, leads to bickering and, for many, Irish supremacy, not solidarity.

The political lesson for today starts with this: there was once some solidarity between the two groups; my father's fairytale was true for a time, in the colonies, at least. They worked and lived side by side, with little apparent discomfort with difference. "The Negro and white servants of the seventeenth century seemed to be remarkably unconcerned about their visible physical differences," the noted slavery historian Kenneth Stampp wrote. "They toiled together in the fields, fraternized during leisure hours, and, in and out of wedlock, collaborated in siring a numerous progeny." They also collaborated in rebellion. In their "unhappiness and alienation," wrote Irish American historian Kerby Miller, Irish Catholic servants "frequently ran away from their masters. . . . [C]olonial officials in Newfoundland, Nova Scotia, New York and the West Indies feared that Irish 'papists' were plotting insurrection with Negro slaves or foreign enemies."

And they were. Irish and Africans joined to revolt in the colonies and the West Indies many times in the seventeenth century, in Barbados, St. Kitts, Montserrat, and Gloucester County, Virginia. The most famous is Bacon's Rebellion of 1676, when several thousand English, Irish, and African indentured servants, slaves, and freedmen formed an army that fought local Indian tribes (alas, it wasn't fully multiracial) and the planting class aristocracy. They torched Jamestown and drove out the colonial government, but they were ultimately defeated and the last twenty-three holdouts were executed by hanging.

After that Virginia politicians and wealthy landowners began enacting slave codes to divide poor whites and Africans. In the late seventeenth and early eighteenth centuries Southern colonies began imposing a strict color line, making Africans slaves for life, while reminding white indentured servants that their bondage was temporary. The codes prohibited intermarriage and policed and punished romance harshly. Virginia's slave codes gave freed white servants land, food, and guns; big planters paid them to join slave patrols, looking for runaways and bringing them back. The slave codes didn't end black-white or black-Irish collaboration entirely, but a stark color line, drawn and redrawn, mostly kept them on different sides.

This may be the first recorded episode of American elites realizing they could pit poor whites against blacks to protect their own interests, but it certainly wasn't the last.

President Obama himself shined a spotlight on the next great historic attempt at black-Irish unity when he traveled in 2011 to Moneygall, Ireland, where he'd traced a great-great-great grandfather on his mother's side (making the president black Irish, too). As he hailed the bonds between Ireland and America in his 2011 visit, President Obama recalled that Frederick Douglass, a former slave and a brave abolitionist, received a hero's welcome on his visits to Ireland. (A monument to Douglass stands in Cork, my ancestral home.) Douglass famously said that in Ireland, he felt liberated: "Lo! the chattel becomes man." The president also pointed to "the unlikely friendship" between Douglass and Ireland's "Great Liberator" Daniel O'Connell, who crusaded for the abolition of slavery, as well as for Irish independence. New York's Abyssinian Baptist Church honored O'Connell in 1833 as "the friend of oppressed Africans and their descendents, and the unadulterated rights of man."

Yet Obama left out one disappointing dimension to their inspiring "unlikely friendship": When Douglass and other abolitionists tried to use O'Connell's popularity with Irish Americans to win them to the antislavery cause, they failed. Miserably.

In 1841, seventy thousand Irish men and women, including O'Connell, signed an "Address from the People of Ireland to their Countrymen and Countrywomen in America," beseeching Irish Americans to "cling by the abolitionists" and join their fight to eradicate slavery. Yet the message didn't sell. That failed coalition is central to "whiteness studies" scholarship—it's a pivot point for Noel Ignatiev's shrill *How the Irish Became White*, and it figured prominently and one-sidedly in David Roediger's *The Wages of Whiteness* and Nell Irvin Painter's otherwise astute *The History of White People*—showing how the Irish chose whiteness over justice. The doomed attempt at alliance is much more complicated, with lessons about black-Irish tensions that reverberate to this day.

The abortive Douglass-O'Connell coalition had two core problems. It took place against the backdrop of rising, brutal nativism, as Protestants attacked Catholics, particularly Irish Catholics, as servile, superstitious subjects of the dastardly Vatican, thoroughly unfit for democracy. The attacks weren't just rhetoric; they involved riots and the destruction of Catholic churches, convents, businesses, and homes. Struggling fiercely for acceptance, even survival, Irish Catholics were unlikely to join the abolitionist cause, which was the far political frontier of the antislavery effort. Even many slavery opponents considered abolitionists too radical.

The second problem was, some prominent abolitionists and antislavery activists were also virulently nativist and particularly anti–Irish Catholic. Religious abolitionism had roots in the Second Protestant Awakening, which also inspired the temperance movement and the campaign to make Sunday a day of prayer, not partying. Both crusades stigmatized rowdy Irish Catholics. Clearly, the abolitionists were on the right side of history when it came to slavery, and thus we think of them as if they were the nineteenth century's Freedom Riders. Yet the fact is, some of them were elitist, nativist haters of all things Irish Catholic. Thus were my people pitted against one another, not merely in some theoretical, job-competition kind of way, but with a deep and bitter specificity. The very folks who tried to help blacks often hated and persecuted Irish Catholics, and vice versa.

Members of the storied Beecher clan preached a fiery nativism, from Lyman Beecher (the father of *Uncle Tom's Cabin* author Harriett Beecher Stowe), whose days of anti-Catholic sermons and crusading formed the cultural backdrop to the 1834 torching of an Ursuline convent in Charlestown, Massachusetts, through Henry Ward Beecher, an abolitionist who denounced the Irish as "the most admirable race that ever abominated the earth" and the "destroyers" of many nations. Abolitionist martyr Elijah Lovejoy, murdered by an Illinois mob inflamed by his antislavery newspaper, crusaded against Catholicism almost as stridently as against slavery. Massachusetts abolitionist congressman Anson Burlingame got elected on the anti–Irish Catholic Know-Nothing Party ticket. As historian Peter Kolchin notes, "Some abolitionists managed to combine a passionate belief in the goodness and intellectual potential of black people with an equally passionate conviction of the unworthiness of the Irish. . . . Many nativists saw little difficulty in moving from the anti-Irish Know-Nothing Party into the antislavery Republican Party."

Sadly, even Frederick Douglass himself sometimes expressed the anti–Irish Catholic attitudes of his white abolitionist allies. His liberating trip to Ireland was sponsored by wealthy Irish Protestant abolitionists at the start of the tragic famine, and while he expressed sympathy for poor Irish Catholics on many occasions, he seemed to pick up some of his hosts' notions about the causes for their poverty. Although he famously compared the plight of Ireland's landless poor to African American slaves—"these people lacked only a black skin and wooly hair, to complete their likeness to the plantation negro," he wrote—he blamed much of their plight on drunkenness as well as on Catholicism. "The immediate, and it may be the main cause of the extreme poverty and beggary in Ireland, is intemperance," Douglass wrote. "Drunkenness is still rife in Ireland." At home, he joined Protestant Yankee abolitionists in blaming the misery of the immigrant Irish on Catholicism. "The poverty, ignorance, misery and sin" that blighted the Irish community could be traced to the "domination of a most-crushing religious system," he explained.

Seeing so many of their enemies among O'Connell's abolitionist friends, most (though not all) Irish Catholics rejected the Liberator's appeal. Certainly, racism played some role, but in first-person reactions to O'Connell's abolitionist address recounted in Angela Murphy's *American Slavery, Irish Freedom: Abolitionism, American Citizenship and the Transatlantic Movement for Irish Repeal*, many told the Liberator that to "cling by the abolitionists" was dangerous for America's white scapegoats—and that some leading abolitionists made the Irish scapegoats in the first place. O'Connell kept crusading to build Irish American opposition to slavery nonetheless, though he acknowledged that "there are amongst the abolitionists many wicked and calumniating enemies of Catholicity and the Irish." He even suggested the need for "an Irish Address in reverse": an "Address to the Abolitionists" that would ask them to "cooperate in the spread of Christian charity with the Irishmen and Catholics in America, and obtain their assistance."

No such cooperation ever materialized. Although some individual abolitionists were antinativist, the abolitionist movement neither embraced the cause of Irish Catholics nor worked to counter nativism. For rejecting O'Connell's appeal to join the

abolitionists, the Irish went down in much of left-wing history—
well, at least in whiteness studies tomes—as backward racists.
Yet I'm not sure why anybody would expect one downtrodden
people (the Irish) to rise up and help another downtrodden people (African Americans). Wouldn't that be like criticizing the
African American poor for failing to rise up and defend the rights
of undocumented Mexican immigrants, or vice versa? The fact is,
colliding at the bottom of industrializing American society in the
mid-1800s, the Irish and African Americans had different enemies and different friends. The poorly understood legacy of being
pitted against one another persists to this day.

Sadly, though, the only people less interested than whiteness
studies scholars in finding Irish-black common ground happen to
be conservative Irish Catholics. I saw that personally, in my own
family, as the 1960s exploded.

3

People are saying that the Irish had their problems . . .
but that they didn't turn to civil disobedience.
                    —Pennsylvania representative Frank Clark,
                                    after the 1965 Watts riots

As my family watched Watts go up in flames on the evening news, my father missed a once-in-a-lifetime opportunity to point out a direct but little-known parallel between the black and the Irish poor: before Watts, the largest domestic insurrection in American history had been the awful New York City Draft Riots of July 1863, when hundreds of furious Irish took to the streets to protest Civil War conscription. It's very possible my father didn't know about them; the Draft Riots are hidden history for most of us. The riots show the Irish their place at the very bottom of New York society, and the savagery they used to rebel against their oppression. Once you know about the Draft Riots, it's hard to argue, as some Irish Americans did, that the urban violence of the 1960s meant that African Americans were uniquely depraved.

For three days, a mostly Irish crowd rampaged through New York, attacking draft-board workers, local and federal officials, wealthy Republican industrialists, black New Yorkers, the Irish wives of black men, and even Irish cops and soldiers who tried to stop them. Nominally protesting the nation's first draft—which mainly hit low-income men; the wealthy could buy their way out of the army for $300—the draft unrest became much more: a race riot, a labor insurrection, a religious uprising, and proto-class warfare, all in one.

As the economy lurched from boom to panic in the 1850s, New York featured some of the earliest American debates about dealing with urban poverty and about the "deserving" and "undeserving" poor, an idea that has come to dominate our modern discussions about the economy. In this earlier go-round, Irish Catholics played the role later assigned to African Americans: a proto-underclass, stigmatized as poor and lazy, unable or unwilling to conform to the mores of the emerging nineteenth-century industrial society.

Especially after the potato famine, which the British used as a tool of ethnic cleansing, destitute Irish Catholics teemed into the slums of the East Coast. Many of the overcrowded, dilapidated "coffin ships" that carried the desperate famine emigrants were retooled slave ships, and in both Atlantic crossings, their cargo endured unimaginable suffering and an unconscionable casualty rate. One-third of the Irish who sailed to North America in 1847 died during the crossing. Remember that anti-Irish nativism preceded the famine; the estimated two million Irish who came to the United States between 1845 and 1855 triggered an even more furious reaction.

Many reformers believed the Irish corrupted the African Americans who lived beside them in New York's poorest neighborhoods. An emerging Republican elite blamed Democrats for coddling the slackers and encouraging their immorality and indolence. When Tammany Democratic mayor Fernando Wood proposed a public works program for the unemployed, Republicans blasted him as a "pseudo-philanthropist" whose indiscriminate aid hurt the poor, rather than helped them, while also making them reliable Democratic voters. Sound familiar?

The new elites of the Union League Club, a rising cadre of industrialists and reformers, particularly loathed Wood's program. They backed the Protestant charity sponsored by the Association for Improving the Condition of the Poor (AICP), which ministered to New York's needy but conditioned its aid on good working-class behavior—temperance, monogamy, school attendance for kids, punctuality, and, of course, hard work. Those who didn't comply simply didn't get help. The AICP turned down three-quarters of the requests for aid it received during the brutal winter of 1857–1858, a time of financial panic marked by soaring unemployment and bread riots. Yet elite New Yorkers began to side with the AICP approach. In 1860, Republicans knocked out Wood and took over City Hall.

Appalled by the apparent depravity of the Irish, those elites were more sympathetic to the black poor and working class, with whom they at least shared a Protestant religion and culture. Union League Club founder Frederick Law Olmsted, the architect known for New York's Central Park and San Francisco's Golden Gate Park, urged wealthy New Yorkers "to deal justly and mercifully with the colored people in [their] midst," whom he praised as having "the virtues and graces of the Christian and the gentleman." Union League Club officer Jonathan Sturges agreed: "Those who know our colored people of this city can testify to their being peaceable, industrious people, having their own churches, Sunday schools and charitable societies and that as a class they seldom depend upon charity."

Unlike the Irish.

In fact, the growing phalanx of missionaries and other do-gooders marching into New York's slums, most notably the poverty-racked Five Points neighborhood in the Sixth Ward, widely believed the Irish dragged down the black population there. "Where blacks were found by themselves, we generally encountered tidiness and some sincere attempt at industry and honest self-support," wrote one reformer quoted in Leslie Hughes's remarkable history *In the Shadow of Slavery: African Americans in New York, 1626 to 1963*. Another missionary observed, "The negroes of the Five Points are fifty percent in advance of the Irish as to sobriety and decency."

Some black and white abolitionists worked hard to keep free black workers from forming unions and other alliances with Irish workers. They wanted to make sure the emerging black working class maintained a strong work ethic and good relations with employers and resisted the debauchery of the Irish. When New York's black and Irish waiters joined together in 1853 to form a fledgling union, black abolitionists tried to form a rival race-based organization. The United Association of Colored Waiters emphasized "the harmony of interest between employers and employees and encouraged black waiters to take pride in moral reform rather than manual labor," Hughes observed. The black waiters rejected the race-based pitch and stuck with the Irish, a rare example of workplace cooperation.

Despite attempts to pit the two groups against each other, there were fascinating pockets of black-Irish community, most notably in the impoverished Sixth Ward. Charles Dickens made Five Points world famous when he visited in 1842 and found blacks and the Irish living and sleeping side by side in filth and poverty. Though appalled by the degradation, Dickens was entranced by Five Points nightlife, particularly the dancing of Master Juba, who regularly competed with Irish dancers. What became tap dancing may have had its roots there, the mulatto offspring of amalgamation between Irish and African step dancing.

In 1850, George Foster, a reporter for Horace Greeley's *New York Tribune*, followed Dickens with *Five Points by Gaslight*, a tour of Irish-black underclass nightlife. Foster's wanderings commenced after midnight, and he titillated his middle-class readers with tales of poor blacks and Irish living together in the Old Brewery tenement. At a Five Points bar, white women, mostly Irish, danced naked with "shiny buck negroes." Foster marveled at the frequency of intermarriage between black men and Irish women, who seemed to find their husbands "desirable companions and lovers." One missionary's tour of Five Points found an Irish woman who'd produced an infant by a black man he called just "Sambo." The black-Irish child would have "rum its first medicine, theft its first lesson, a prison its first house and Potter's Field its final resting place," the missionary concluded.

Daylight in the Sixth Ward showed evidence of community: Irish boarders living with black families, blacks in boarding-houses run by the Irish, the two groups starting small businesses side by side. Significantly, during the three days of the Draft Riots in 1863, the Sixth Ward was the only one spared Irish-on-black violence. Irish neighbors protected black businesses and shielded black men and their Irish wives from the mob.

Such stories were rare.

The Draft Riots didn't start out as an Irish-only affair. On the first day, the disturbance had support from German workers and others who couldn't afford the $300 it cost to get out of the draft. But once the rioters shut down draft offices and other mechanisms of conscription, most groups drifted away; their work to block the draft was done. Not the Irish. The riots became an uprising against Republicans, industrialists, wealthy Protestant abolitionists, and, most savagely, African Americans. The Irish shut down factories, burned the homes of Republicans, and looted Brooks Brothers. Yet they attacked black homes, churches, businesses, and individuals with particular cruelty and intent.

A mob burned down the Colored Orphan Asylum (the children were swept to safety at a nearby police station) and the Aged Colored Women's Home. They murdered the Irish wife of a black man who tried to save her mixed-race son from the mob (the boy escaped; she did not). The attacks on black men had a particular savagery that can only be described as sexual. Some were castrated; others were burned, then doused in water, in what looked like an unconscious ritual of purification by the sexually and spiritually tortured Irish. Clearly, some in the crowd were inflamed by "amalgamation" between Irish women and black men; they attacked brothels where white prostitutes (most of them Irish) served black customers, as well as white women with black husbands. It's probably no accident that a writer of Irish descent, David Croly, coined the term *miscegenation* in 1863, and depicted it as a nefarious abolitionist plot.

The Irish rioters beat their own as well. Police chief John Kennedy was almost killed by rioters the first day; accounts of the conflict find officers named Kiernan and Eagan and Caffrey and O'Brien brutalized by the overwhelmingly Irish mob. A young Irish immigrant named Paddy McCafferty went down in history for helping to save the black children when the Colored Orphan Asylum went up in flames. Irish men were represented disproportionately among thousands of police officers, National Guardsmen, and military who fought the rioters, yet that can't erase the riot's ugly ethnic legacy.

Far from making the Irish "white"—the goal that drove them to scorn alliances with blacks in favor of intimidation, according to the whiteness studies analysis—the Draft Riots led to a new wave of nativism and a demonization of the Irish as "animals" and "savages." Many Irish New Yorkers responded to the trauma by becoming flag-waving super-patriots, to live down the shame of their community's racist and treasonous resistance to the war.

Meanwhile, after the war some Republicans' passion for helping the former slaves waned, although many abolitionists threw themselves into projects to educate and otherwise prepare the former slaves for full citizenship. Henry Ward Beecher took up the cause of low-wage Chinese workers, defending them as better Americans than the lazy Irish (some of whom were doing everything they could to oppress the Chinese in California, it must be noted). Abolitionist Horace Greeley, who once crusaded against slavery and pushed Lincoln to move faster on emancipation, now featured "exposés" of Reconstruction in his *New York Tribune*, focusing on tales of black "corruption" and political incompetence. New York recoiled at the Boss Tweed corruption scandal of 1870; the *New York Times* used it as "an example of the Irish Catholic despotism that rules the City of New York." Around the same time, the paper blamed "ignorant Negroes" for the corruption in South Carolina's statehouse, which had, of course, predated black suffrage and would survive it.

There's no better symbol of the transformation of Northern abolitionist sentiment after the Civil War than the work of cartoonist Thomas Nast: The pro-Union Harper's artist once graphically depicted the perfidy of Confederates and championed civil rights for slaves. Yet his most famous cartoon, from 1876, depicted Irish Catholics and African Americans—two simian creatures labeled "Paddy" and "Sambo"—as "The Ignorant Vote." The Grand Army of the Republic, the leading organization of Union Civil War veterans, excluded both black and Irish soldiers from membership. Still, the two groups mostly failed to make common cause against the elites who despised them.

But maybe it's crazy to expect that they would have. The whiteness studies version of history distorts our understanding of the uneven, unpredictable way the American movement for social justice evolved. It also "runs the risk of blaming one victim (the Irish) for the greater misfortunes of another (African Americans)," in the words of historian Kevin Kenny. "The American Irish did not create the social and racial hierarchy into which they came, and to expect them to have overturned this hierarchy in the course of putting food on their tables is surely unrealistic."

You can agree with Kenny—and I do—and still find the missed opportunity for coalition tragic, with ramifications that haunt us today.

4

Practically all the things we've done in the federal government are the things Al Smith did as governor of New York.

—Franklin Delano Roosevelt, 1936

Irish Americans might be better known for progressive, rather than reactionary, politics if the story of Al Smith was more widely remembered. Smith's role as a Progressive era leader is often underplayed in popular accounts of that moment in history. But the father of the New Deal helped erase himself from the Progressive pantheon after losing the presidency in 1928 and failing to get the Democratic nomination in 1932. He started to chip away at the so-called New Deal coalition almost as soon as he helped assemble it, pulling some white working-class ethnics, particularly Irish Catholics, out of the party they helped build.

Smith moved steadily to the political right as soon as Franklin Delano Roosevelt won the nomination with what was essentially Smith's platform—a familiar tale of understandable Irish resentment mixed with corrosive self-pity. Many of his Irish supporters seethed that the country elected the Harvard-educated, high-WASP FDR, while rejecting the same appeal when an Irish Catholic had made it four years earlier. That Roosevelt ran for president three years into a terrifying Great Depression was much more responsible for his success than his elite breeding was, but the Irish are stubborn, and the idea persisted. Yet Smith deserves credit he rarely receives for assembling the New Deal coalition, even if he would later reject it.

The half-Irish working-class son of the Lower East Side, Smith was propelled from state Assembly majority leader to national renown by the galvanizing tragedy of the Progressive era: the Triangle Shirtwaist Company fire of March 1911. He would become a pivotal figure in the creation of New Deal policy as well as New Deal politics. FDR's labor secretary, Frances Perkins, called the day of the Triangle fire "the day the New Deal began," pointing to social welfare legislation Smith pioneered in the aftermath of the tragedy. Roosevelt himself famously said that "practically all" of his New Deal policies "are the things Al Smith did as governor of New York."

Traumatized by the Triangle fire, the loyal Irish Tammany pol reached out to the disaster's mostly Jewish and Italian survivors, visiting their homes and even the morgue to comfort them as they identified loved ones. The New York Democrat began to assemble the urban New Deal coalition by courting Italians and Jews who'd long been neglected by Tammany. The activism around the fire challenged Tammany's traditional reliance on a formula that combined patronage for immigrants and workers with indulgence of the excesses of business, even when business ran roughshod over those immigrant workers. Triangle showed Tammany Democrats that they might win votes by actually representing workers' interests, not merely with their time-tested machine politics of cronyism and patronage. It could help them fend off Socialists, who were making inroads with the growing working class.

Smith headed the commission that investigated the fire with Robert Wagner, who went on to become a senator from New York and to sponsor the New Deal labor rights legislation that unleashed modern unionism. During a remarkable four-year period, they examined conditions at a wide swath of city sweatshops and passed a stunning wave of strong prolabor legislation, creating new health and safety codes, as well as restricting child labor and shortening the workweek for women (to fifty-four hours). Smith rode his Triangle fame to the governor's mansion in 1918.

"Immigrants and city dwellers recognized that he was some-one in his politics who stood up for them, accepted them as equals and above all, who gave them respectability," Smith's biographer Robert Slayton wrote. Triangle fire historian David Von Drehle concluded that thanks to Smith's outreach and reform legisla-tion, "in the generation after the Triangle fire, Democrats became America's working class, progressive party." In his run for presi-dent, Smith's opposition to the Ku Klux Klan, as well as intermit-tent attempts to woo black voters, paid off, even after he chose an Arkansas running mate to appease the "Solid South."

Black newspapers such as the *Baltimore African American* and the *Chicago Defender* endorsed Smith, the NAACP's Walter White personally (if tepidly) backed him, and a young civil rights organizer named Bayard Rustin volunteered for him as well. GOP support among black voters declined 15 percent from 1924 to 1928, and Smith captured a larger share of the black vote in key cities, including Chicago and Philadelphia, than did prior Democratic presidential candidates. It was the first sign that African American voters might someday wind up Democrats, even though that had been the party of slavery and remained the party of Jim Crow in the South. Smith's candidacy galvanized the New York Irish; his theme song "Sidewalks of New York" became the anthem of their rise in the city that once shunned them.

But if Smith was the right man to pull together what would become the Northern Democratic base for the next thirty-five years, most of the nation wasn't yet ready for an Irish Catholic president. Smith opposed Prohibition, which was still the law of the land, and he was widely depicted as an Irish drunk. Anti-Smith leaflets and jingles blanketed America: "Popery in the Public Schools," "Crimes of the Pope," and "Convent Life Unveiled." An election-day flyer proclaimed:

A vote for Al is a vote for rum,
A vote to empower America's scum. . .
Let Historians write, "Smith also ran."
Now it's time to support the Ku Klux Klan.

Antipathy against Smith wasn't confined to KKK backers. Progressive movement editor William Allen White, who had himself fought the Klan in Kansas, warned, "The whole Puritan civilization which has built a sturdy, orderly nation is threatened by Smith." Outside of New York City, it seemed, the country rejected the notion of Irish Catholic leadership overwhelmingly.

Smith wanted the Democratic nomination again four years later, but it went to FDR, and Smith began moving right. He fulminated against what he saw as Roosevelt's efforts "to stir up the bitterness of the rich against the poor and of the poor against the rich." At a 1936 dinner for the American Liberty League, an elite organization of wealthy conservatives implacably opposed to Roosevelt, he attacked his former ally as a tool of Moscow, foreshadowing the red-baiting he and others would use to split Irish Catholics from the Democrats. (It was in a fit of pique at Smith's betrayal, not a moment of admiration, that Roosevelt told his liberal labor secretary, Frances Perkins, that "practically all the things we've done in the federal government are the things Al Smith did as governor of New York." Then he asked, "What in the world is the matter?" Perkins had no answer.)

Smith wasn't the only one embittered by his 1928 defeat. For New York's Irish Catholics, Samuel G. Freedman later wrote, the Depression began a year earlier than for the rest of the country, with Smith's disappointing loss. In *Beyond the Melting Pot*, Daniel Patrick Moynihan explained the impact this way:

> The bitter anti-Catholicism and the crushing defeat of the 1928 campaign came as a blow. The New York Irish had been running their city for a long time, or so it seemed. They did not think of themselves as immigrants and interlopers with an alien religion; it was a shock to find that so much of the country did. Worse yet, in 1932, when the chance came to redress this wrong, the Democrats, instead of renominating Smith, turned instead to a Hudson Valley aristocrat with a Harvard accent.

The well-to-do Irish turned on Harvard and Roosevelt; the lower classes fell prey to Father Charles Coughlin, who early on fought the Ku Klux Klan in Michigan, backed Smith and FDR, and called the New Deal "Christ's deal"—and then became a reactionary anti-Semite railing against Roosevelt, the Jews, and Wall Street.

Pat Buchanan's father, William, a Washington, DC, accountant, followed the Irish Catholic Smith out of the Democratic Party. He and many others would later embrace another Irish politician, Joe McCarthy, who fused their Catholic fear of communism with their Irish resentment of elitist Ivy Leaguers such as those alleged State Department subversives. A young Irish Catholic lawyer named Robert F. Kennedy got his start on McCarthy's staff in 1953. His father, Joe Kennedy, was a Roosevelt Democrat who moved right; he thought association with his pal McCarthy would keep his sons in the good graces of the senator's many Irish-American devotees. Senator John F. Kennedy's refusal to censure McCarthy remained a strike against him for liberals until his election. Communism split the American left in ways too numerous to detail here; it also split the left from American Catholics, most of whom saw communism as the most dangerous enemy of God, family, and their church.

I grew up believing that both sides of my extended Irish family had been true-blue Democrats until the disorder of the 1960s made them look again at Richard Nixon. In fact, many in the older generation worshipped Al Smith—and quite a few of them followed him out of his party, the way Pat Buchanan's father did. When a young Daniel Patrick Moynihan joined the Kennedy campaign in 1960, he noticed that Adlai Stevenson had failed to carry formerly Democratic strongholds such as the Bronx and Brooklyn against Dwight Eisenhower, and he hoped that an Irish Catholic could lure them back to their party. But not even Kennedy could lure some of my relatives in 1960; a lot of my mother's family, especially, voted for Richard Nixon.

That made their story more typically Irish American than my father's romanticized version. It's as if the Irish radar about power relations and snobbery got warped by American politics, so that the enemy became self-righteous liberals who seem to think they're better than everybody else, rather than the actual ruling class. Then, as some of them got rich doing the elites' work, their antiliberal bias became a self-interested class bias as well. That was certainly the story in Pat Buchanan's family—but not so much in mine.

5

The greatest generation was also the statist generation. . . . The middle decades of the twentieth century were an entirely anomalous period in American history. Never had the state been so strong, never had people submitted as uncomplainingly, never had the country been more economically equal, never had it been more ethnically homogeneous, seldom was its political consensus more overpowering.
 —David Frum, *How We Got Here*, 2000

My Irish immigrant grandfather owed his first American job, in a way, to Al Smith, who became the president of Empire State Building Inc. after he lost his historic bid to become our first Catholic president. Construction began on March 17, 1930 (yes, that's St. Patrick's Day), as decreed by Smith, and the building went up in an astonishing thirteen months.

My father's parents had come from the County Cork village of Blarney (yes, that Blarney, home of Blarney Castle and the Blarney Stone, the kissing of which imparts "the gift of gab"— and yes, I've kissed it). It was 1928, the year of Smith's sad loss, on the eve of the Great Depression. My mother's Irish family had arrived a generation earlier and settled in Brooklyn.

Ironically, something else that helped my father's family was the 1921 Immigration Act, tailored mostly to keep out southern Europeans (and Jews). But it limited immigration from all countries, and that helped the American working class rise in the next decades. Their wages weren't always being flattened by an influx of more desperate newcomers, and the ethnic differences that had long thwarted unionization and working class solidarity eased a little bit with familiarity.

Thanks to my father's stories about the Irish struggle, I thought for a long time that his parents' poverty when they came to America had to do with their Irish-immigrant status. In fact, it had to do with being poor people who had lots of kids during the Great Depression. They were decades past "No Irish Need Apply" signs; in the Bronx, being Irish probably gave them a leg up. They settled in the Highbridge neighborhood, which was named for the famous landmark where Edgar Allan Poe regularly strolled during his sad Bronx sojourn. Highbridge was a little Irish village on this side of the Atlantic when my grandparents arrived. They pledged allegiance to District 9 of the Ancient Order of Hibernians, the conservative Irish Catholic benevolent association, and Sacred Heart Parish, and in turn they got a lot of help.

My father's mother had come to the United States first, cleaning houses for the rich at the Jersey shore before returning to Blarney for my grandfather. Her decision to strike out on her own was a common Irish story: women drove the Irish diaspora, coming to the United States alone or with reluctant husbands, working as domestics, married late (if at all) and widowed early, and were quite likely to wind up raising children alone, yet another echo of the African American experience in New York.

In the New York that Al Smith built, being Irish had advantages. On my father's birth certificate, not even a year after his parents cleared Ellis Island, my grandfather's occupation is already listed as "steamfitter." He had been a driver at Blarney Woolen Mills before he left Cork; somehow he'd gotten into the Irish-controlled Steamfitters' Union almost immediately. After his first big job on Smith's Empire State Building, work was scarce again for my grandfather, for a while. My grandmother took in laundry and made a little raisin wine during Prohibition to bring in extra money, while my grandfather labored as a barber and a cabdriver.

The cheerful version of my father's family's up-from-poverty story is the American Dream: poor immigrants get help from their family, their neighborhood, their church, and, back in the day, their labor union. The American-born kids do better than their immigrant parents, making everyone's struggle worthwhile. It worked for my family. The way my father's siblings talked about their childhood sometimes, you could see shamrocks and shillelaghs and those Irish eyes, always smiling.

One sunny November day in 2010, my Uncle Gene took me, my daughter, my sister, and his youngest son on a Highbridge tour and showed us an idyllic version of the Walsh childhood. On a busy corner where a gas station now stands, there used to be a tavern where the boys fetched their father a "pail" of beer on Sunday after church and ate pretzels while they waited. I have a picture of my father and Uncle Gene standing in front of white latticework in the tavern's outdoor courtyard. It looks like a suburban backyard, not the inner city. Over on Ogden Avenue was the apartment where my grandmother made raisin wine. (Uncle Gene gave me her recipe.) As an infant, my Aunt Peggy apparently fell out of an upstairs window, but she was caught by a neighbor coming over to buy our Irish moonshine. Lots of family stories ended that way, tragedy averted, the punch line of a funny Irish story served up where heartbreak might have been, glory be. The three boys slept in one bed, horizontally, so their feet hung over the side as they grew taller.

My uncle took us out to an overlook clogged with the freeway clover leafs that make driving in the Bronx hair-raising. From there, we could see both Yankee Stadium and the site of the old Polo Grounds, where the New York Giants once played. He had worked in both stadiums for Harry M. Stevens's famous concessions. Uncle Gene had a replica of a "No Irish Need Apply" sign in his family room, but he knew being Irish helped him as a kid. He remembered going into Manhattan, to the Henry Hudson Hotel, where he mentioned the Hibernians, "and a Maureen Mulcahy typed up my Teamster card," he recalled with a smile.

My grandfather prospered in the 1940s by serving on steamfitter "efficiency teams" that traveled to defense plants around the country, to accelerate the completion of military building projects by providing a round-the-clock workforce. (African Americans, I should note, were excluded from the Steamfitters Union entirely during World War II.) He sent his paychecks home to my grandmother—he got his room and board on the job—and when he returned, they bought their first house. They went from desperate poverty to homeownership in fewer than twenty years.

That's the happy story, the one many folks in my family still wish I'd stick to. Yet my father told another story, about a childhood marked by deprivation, as much emotional as material. My plucky grandmother, the one who came to America alone, cleaned houses on the Jersey shore, and found a place for her boyfriend, collapsed for a while under the strain of having four children in five years during the Great Depression. She was hospitalized with a "breakdown," but no one knows where or for how long; my father and his three siblings were sent to live with relatives for at least a year.

No one could tell us exactly what happened; we only know the family was reunited in time for my grandmother to conceive her youngest sons, twins, in 1938. At that point, the family was complete: five boys and one girl. I didn't know my grandmother; she died a day before my first birthday, of pneumonia she caught on a trip back to Ireland. I didn't know about my father's being sent to live with relatives during her "breakdown" until I was grown. Even then, he talked about it quietly, as if it had been a shameful exile.

At age thirteen, he was exiled for good: He was found to have a "vocation," like his older cousin Jack Twomey, a De La Salle Christian Brother. So he went away to St. Joseph's Normal Institute, ninety miles from the Bronx in rural Barrytown, New York, to prepare to join the order. His closest brother, my Uncle Connie, joined him when he turned thirteen, two years later. In an early essay about my Irish family, I judgmentally called my father and my uncle's Christian Brothers boarding school education "foster care for the Irish poor," and several aunts and uncles disowned me briefly for the insult. "They had *vocations*!" one aunt told me tearfully. "They were *thirteen*!" I argued back.

The truth was somewhere in between my aunt's sentimental memory and my materialist scorn. My father loved his cousin Jack, and he did think for a time he might have a vocation. On the other hand, his struggling parents were quick to act on a thirteen-year-old's desire to leave his home and join a monastic, celibate teaching order for life. In fact, a Christian Brother the neighborhood kids nicknamed "Felix the Kidnapper" was in charge of identifying boys with "vocations" who might want to study at Barrytown and getting parents to sign them over. In New York at the time, almost all of them were poor Irish kids from Brooklyn and the Bronx. The story of Brother Felix made me think of the "spirits" who lured or kidnapped children from the streets of Dublin in the seventeenth century and sold them to colonial masters in the West Indies or America.

My father would, of course, eventually leave the Brothers, or else I would not be sharing this story with you. Uncle Connie left, too, but later. My Uncle Gene went to join the Carmelites, but he later left and joined the air force, getting his college education that way. My father always said Aunt Peggy was the smartest one in the family, but without a vocation, girls especially didn't go on to college, so she took a secretarial job, married a cop and raised four kids, and made sure they went to college. My father's two youngest brothers, the ones who didn't join religious orders, became steamfitters like my grandfather. The pathway to the middle class for my family involved religious service, or marriage to a public worker, or a blue-collar unionized job.

My father never recovered from being sent away by his parents in childhood. It made him a sort of exile, forced to find belonging in a larger community because he didn't quite fit in the one he came from. That's what drove his politics, to a degree. One of the last things he told me before he died was about the time his father saved him from a tenement fire when he was six months old, a story he'd only recently heard from his father's sister, Auntie Hannah, when she found out he was ill. It was like a gift she'd been saving his whole life, until he needed it.

His parents fled the fire in terror, Auntie Hannah recalled, each thinking the other held the baby, and they reconnected outside their apartment on West 167th Street, only to realize my infant father was inside. My grandfather defied the flames and the firefighters to save him. My father told the story over and over again as he lay dying, as if he finally had evidence that he'd once been a loved and cherished child, before loving and cherishing children became a luxury his parents couldn't afford.

6

To be an exile, to choose exile, is to put oneself among a group of people who will always have to struggle to understand one, to put oneself in a situation where one's gestures are not readily legible, where one is not given away by a word, a look, a tone of voice. To be permanently in exile is to be permanently in disguise; it is an extreme form of self-protection. And self-protection is an Irish obsession.

—Mary Gordon, *New York Times*,
October 1988

A picture of my father in his Christian Brothers garb, broad white bib on a black cassock, sat on a shelf in a cabinet when I was little. I didn't exactly know what it meant. For a while I thought he had been a beginner priest, maybe even a beginner saint. I linked my father's liberalism, as well as his exile status, to his time with the Christian Brothers, as a saint-in-training. It was actually his college education, which helped him rise out of the working class, that enabled his political views. A cynic might view my father's civil rights liberalism (and mine) as a kind of class privilege. He—we—left those old New York neighborhoods long before they became forbidding and dangerous.

I knew my family owed an enormous debt to the Christian Brothers; my father got a college education at a time when most kids from Highbridge didn't. St. Joseph's in Barrytown sat high on a cliff above the Hudson River. The Unification Church bought it in the 1970s, so the Steely Dan song "Barrytown," describing its odd inhabitants, "I can see by what you carry that you come from Barrytown," wasn't about the Christian Brothers, though I always heard it that way. Surrounded by books and classical music and men of learning, my father played baseball and basketball and ice hockey. He was an editor and a writer for his senior yearbook and a correspondent and an editor on his high school newspaper. He thought he wanted to write as well as teach.

My father got his concern for the issue of poverty at least partly from the Christian Brothers, a French order founded in 1680 by Jean Baptiste De La Salle expressly to teach the poor. Like priests, the Brothers took vows of poverty, obedience, and chastity, but they didn't administer the sacraments or lead parishes; De La Salle wanted them to devote their lives to teaching instead. They took an additional vow promising to educate the poor for the rest of their lives.

I knew that my father's time with the Brothers helped develop his personal identification with the oppressed, because he told me that, directly. He remembered often being hungry and getting a little extra tea and maybe some bread, if he complained. The boys drank "scallion milk" in the spring—the cows ate the scallions that grew on the hillside, and the milk the Brothers used for tea and cereal smelled and tasted strongly of onions. My father was always cold in the winter. Once, shivering in a thin cloth Barrytown-issued overcoat on a brutal winter day, he passed a higher-up wearing a warm coat with a thick fur collar. "I wondered if we'd both taken the same vow of poverty," he told me when I was a teenager.

Even the college education for which he was grateful didn't turn out to be what he'd been promised. In the post–World War II years, some young "novitiates" were forced to leave Catholic University in three, not four, years, because there weren't enough teachers for the growing network of Catholic schools in postwar New York. He was brought back from Washington, DC, to finish at the Christian Brothers' Manhattan College on nights and weekends, while he taught English and coached basketball at Brooklyn's famous Bishop Loughlin Memorial High School (notable alums include Rudy Giuliani and rapper Biggie Smalls, then known as Christopher Wallace). Sometimes I thought of my father and his classmates as a cheap labor force for the Catholic Church. His experience bred a skepticism of Catholic hierarchy that he passed on to me, but he remained devoutly Catholic, too. He recognized that his were just another set of sacrifices, of little losses, required to climb out of poverty. Some people had it much harder. But everyone gave up something.

Whatever the reasons my father had for finally leaving the Brothers, and I never fully understood them, everyone in my family made it simple: he left because he'd fallen for my mother. A Christian Brothers colleague at Bishop Loughlin knew my mother and my grandmother, as the story goes, and one night he brought the handsome young Brother Cosmas Maurice to dinner at their home. No one knows when or exactly how my parents connected. Their song was Doris Day's "Secret Love," implying that something secretly began before he left the Brothers. My Irish grandparents were crushed that their son lost his "vocation."

They married on October 1, 1955, my father's twenty-seventh birthday, in the middle of the World Series. Theirs was a mixed marriage—my father's entire Bronx family rooted for the Yankees, while my mother's clan cheered for the Brooklyn Dodgers. On the day of their wedding ceremony, the two teams met in Game Four of the World Series, at Brooklyn's Ebbets Field, only a few miles away from St. Agatha's Church, where they were married. The World Series blared from television sets in color for the very first time but not at the wedding. It turned out to be the only year the Brooklyn Dodgers would beat the Yankees to become world champions.

Baseball loyalties aside, my mother's Irish family had a little disdain for my father's immigrant family, whom they found cold and slightly eccentric. The decision to send their young sons away to find their "vocations" was one reason for their disapproval of their new "Harp" (or fresh-off-the-boat Irish) in-laws. "What parent sends away a thirteen-year-old?" my mother's Aunt

Agnes would ask. She would resist her own son's insistence that he wanted to become a priest, until he was out of high school and decided for himself.

Although they were at least a couple of generations removed from Ireland, my mother's Irish family, the extended Hardiman clan, was not really entitled to lace curtain pretensions or condescension to my father's poor Harp parents. My grandmother and her sisters' formal education stopped early. Two years after the Triangle factory fire, my grandmother left eighth grade to look for work. She, too, found it in the garment industry. On the 1920 census, the four oldest Hardiman girls are listed as "winders" in a silk mill, charged with winding the silk from silkworm cocoons onto bobbins. Much later, after her alcoholic (German American) husband left the family, my grandmother got a job at Macy's; her widowed sisters were already working, one at Saks Fifth Avenue, one at the old S. Klein's on Union Square. For a while, I thought being a grandma meant working in a big retail store in Manhattan.

Clearly, my grandmother wasn't lace-curtain Irish; she called the refrigerator the "icebox" and talked with the famous Brooklyn accent in which I'd be *berled* in *erl* if I ever left the Catholic Church, *Jesus, Mary, and Joseph*! She and my mother worried about seeming "shanty Irish" to our new suburban neighbors after we left Brooklyn for Long Island. Seeming "shanty Irish" apparently involved two things: my mother and my grandmother couldn't just yell out the window to get us to come home, as people did in Brooklyn, and we could never bring a pot or a pan directly to the table to serve food; everything had to be on a plate or in a serving bowl, including second helpings.

"Only the shanty Irish eat out of the pot!" my grandmother once shrieked at me, when I carried mashed potatoes directly from the stove to the dining room to give my father another serving.

I remember my father just smiling at his wife's and mother-in-law's fixations about "shanty Irish"; I never heard him rebuke them, even though he probably knew they were talking about his side of the family. I couldn't understand the snobbery. My father and two of his brothers had college degrees, after all, when my mother and her siblings did not; one brother joined the New York Police Department, the other the New York Fire Department. I loved my mother's family dearly but I couldn't see why they were better than the Walshes.

Almost no one in my mother's extended clan of cousins attended college, except for two: her cousin Jack McMahon, later an NBA player and a coach, went to St. John's University on a basketball scholarship, and her youngest cousin, Bill, completed Manhattan College with Rudy Giuliani, while studying for the priesthood, and became a social worker. On both sides of the family, it took sports, religion, or the military to get a college education— another echo of the African American experience that no one but my father and I tended to discuss. The central political fact of my childhood was that those college-educated men were Democrats; everyone who didn't go to college wound up Republicans. I never thought of that as a matter of intelligence but opportunity. Even so, I'm sure I exuded a kind of snobbery about my father's and my family's enlightened views to both sides of our extended family, for which I'm still ashamed.

There was another echo of the black experience, on my mother's side at least: my grandmother and her sisters lived in an Irish matriarchy. The three who lost their husbands young raised all of their children together in a big Bay Ridge three-flat; my grandmother, before and after my grandfather left, spent all of her time there. Men died young or they were disabled by alcohol or both. My mother and her brothers were raised so close to that house full of seven first cousins they were like siblings.

That's the family my father married into: solidly part of the laboring masses, with all of their own troubles, yet still able to look down a little on his immigrant Irish family. The comfort of the American working class, of every color: there's always someone beneath you. But that means there's also someone who might rise above you, and it is this fact that Republicans learned to manipulate, to the disadvantage of Democrats.

Despite the richness of their lives and heritage, both sides of my Irish family seemed to share a sense of being outsiders, along with an inability or a reluctance to articulate exactly why. My father thought he knew why: they'd been at the bottom of society, vying with African Americans and Puerto Ricans for wretchedness. Yet nobody talked about that. In fact, nobody believed it. My mother's Bay Ridge neighborhood had begun to change before she left it, as low-income Puerto Ricans moved in. She spoke Spanish, and my charming redheaded mother always made the neighborhood change sound like an adventure, her own personal *West Side Story*. But she left before crime began to rise and her aunts and cousins' next-door neighbors turned their house into a brothel.

Years later, one of my mother's cousins would try to explain her anger: "It wasn't that they were Puerto Ricans, they were the *worst* Puerto Ricans—they were the Puerto Ricans even the Puerto Ricans didn't want!" (I resisted noting that Anglo New Yorkers were convinced they had to put up with the *worst* Irish imaginable a century earlier.) They threw their garbage out the windows, she said, and let their kids stay up late at night. And she resented the notion that the newcomers' poverty or isolation was somehow unique. "Don't tell me I don't know what it's like to live in a ghetto—we lived in an Irish ghetto!" she told me.

"I could go around that neighborhood *today* and show you," she continued. "In that house the husband didn't work, in that one he drank, in that one he beat his wife and kids—in that one, the man did all three! In a lot of houses there were no men. We had one whole apartment house full of families on welfare. Mothers, we almost never saw fathers, went to school for teacher conferences in their housecoats. My mother and my aunts dressed up for everything," she said proudly.

Yet familiarity with the troubles of "ghetto" life bred no solidarity with the Puerto Ricans and the African Americans who came later. My aunt spoke for a lot of people when she insisted, "We worked for everything we had; some people had things handed to them."

I don't know why it was so hard for so many of my people to see that blacks and Puerto Ricans were playing the role the Irish had before them, filling in the bottom rungs of society, as the white working class climbed. They were buoyed by unions that were often hostile or even closed to minorities, buying houses with government lending programs that didn't prohibit discrimination by race, in suburbs sometimes closed to blacks—even the government-built roads they traveled to get to their new Long Island homes discriminated by race. The master builder Robert Moses made sure that the system of parkways he pioneered had overpasses too low for public buses, to keep the minority poor away from his parks and beaches and suburbs. Yet the idea that some people had no help, while others "had things handed to them," is still widely shared. It became a founding tenet of the modern Republican Party, a core belief in Nixonland.

PART II

GROWING UP IN NIXONLAND

7

Wounded but not dead.
                    —Motto on the Walsh coat of arms

Most of my childhood talks with my father are set in our tiny dining room, a place of Formica furniture, not wood, with doilies of plastic, not lace, in a china cabinet that held inexpensive dishes from Sears Roebuck, not fine china. There are two plaques on the wall. One held the Walsh coat of arms, a swan with an arrow piercing its chest, above the words *"Transfixus sed non mortuus,"* which translates from the Latin as "Wounded but not dead," a motto that horrified me as a child. When I grew up, I learned there were other Walsh crests with more inspiring mottos, such as *"Veritas et virtus vincunt,"* meaning "Truth and virtue prevail." Why couldn't we have that one? In adulthood, I came to appreciate ours.

The other plaque I remember from our dining room held two praying hands above the Serenity Prayer, adopted by Alcoholics Anonymous. Sometime after my parents got married, my father fell to the Irish curse, alcoholism. He spent most of my early years trying to get sober. As I got closer to kindergarten, I'd follow him around as if I were afraid to lose him. In the morning, I'd wake up with him, and we'd sometimes sneak to early Mass. He'd drop me off at home on his way to the train station. At Mass, I'd pray that he would come back that night.

I was born in Brooklyn about eighteen months after my father's discharge from the army; my brother, not quite my Irish twin, just fourteen months later. Conceived the month Walter O'Malley

63

announced that the Dodgers were leaving Brooklyn, I always wondered if my mother needed a new love to take their place (in fact, a December 1957 subway strike figured prominently in stories about my conception, which may account for my lifelong soft spot for public employees' unions). The week I was born, *Life* magazine featured a story on school desegregation, "Integration goes on—but with ugly incidents," and a photo of Rev. Martin Luther King Jr. being jailed in Alabama. The same month, September 1958, the devout Irish Catholic turned devout American socialist Michael Harrington would begin the US tour that inspired his searing exposé of the hidden poor, *The Other America*, which helped drive the Johnson administration's War on Poverty.

After getting married, my father went to work as a writer and an editor at the nation's oldest and largest Catholic textbook company, William H. Sadlier (cofounded by novelist Mary Anne Sadlier, who wrote novels to instruct and uplift Irish Catholic immigrants and was considered an Irish American counterpart to Harriet Beecher Stowe). Sadlier was located on Park Place, near Wall Street. His work had nothing to do with "the street," but I knew he was working in the seat of American power. His boss's name was actually Mr. Power; I'm not making that up, it's a fine Irish name. When he got a promotion into the higher-paying sales department, his official writing and editing career ended for good, although I still have a sales brochure he wrote for a new Sadlier series. My mother kept it in her hope chest, along with hundreds of love letters and poems he'd written to her while in the army.

In 1960, we moved to suburbia, to Oceanside, Long Island, and my father joined that male migration back to the city on the Long Island Railroad. In some of my earliest memories, he just didn't come home. I remember my brother and me in pajamas, two chubby toddlers, keeping my mother company behind our not-lace polyester curtains, waiting for him. I learned later that she threatened to leave my father if he didn't stop drinking. But if she did, she told him, she would leave me with him and take only my brother. When I first heard that story as a child, it made sense; I was clearly already Daddy's girl. As a teenager, I began to wonder how she could think of leaving a small child with an alcoholic who regularly didn't come home at night. Maybe she thought responsibility would sober him up.

And he did sober up, comparatively early. He quit drinking on October 1, 1963, on his thirty-fifth birthday and their eighth wedding anniversary. That's when the praying hands plaque appeared on the dining room wall. I memorized the Serenity Prayer almost as early as the Hail Mary:

> God grant me the serenity
> To accept the things I cannot change;
> The courage to change the things I can, and
> The wisdom to know the difference.

Once my father joined AA, my parents had a second honeymoon and a third child, my little sister. Oceanside was a white-ethnic melting pot: we had a sweet Jewish couple on one side of our house and argumentative Russians on the other; nice Catholic Poles across the street and friendly Italians next to them. Across another street, there was forbidding old Mr. Shipley (ethnicity and first name uncertain) in a ramshackle house with a junkyard dog that barked and snarled if we crossed the street. We shopped and dined at Lincoln Shopping Center, feasting on the world's cuisines at Ho King and Zion Deli and Five Star Bakery and Capri Pizza a block away. Much of my mother's extended family made the migration to Long Island with us.

Our lives in Oceanside were organized around St. Anthony's Parish, which had been home to an underground shrine touted nationally for miracles during the 1940s and 1950s, before a fire destroyed it in March 1960. I spent most of my childhood attending Mass in the school auditorium while they rebuilt what they could of the old church. They never rebuilt the shrine; it's buried under the church parking lot, and I grew up haunted that I'd missed miracles there. An amazing thirteen Hardiman-descended cousins went to St. Anthony's. Some of them would later claim it was because Jews dominated the public schools. I'm not sure that's true; all of our parents had gone to Catholic schools. I don't think they were fleeing Jews so much as gravitating toward what they knew—which later would come to seem like the same thing. For a long time, it was all I knew, and I loved it. Being Irish Catholic was something to be proud of. On St. Patrick's Day at St. Anthony's, the nuns would attach an O' or a Mc to the names of the kids who weren't Irish. Years later, I learned that after the famine, Irish immigrants used to drop the Mc and the O to de-Irishize their names, but I knew none of that growing up.

Suburbia had its downside, mainly isolation. For a while, my grandmother would bring a folding chair out on the tiny stoop on the steps to our front door. She could barely fit. The stoop was nothing like the capacious landings outside even modest homes in Brooklyn, where families would gather to kibitz with neighbors and keep an eye on the kids. Finally, she gave up. She might have worried that it looked shanty Irish.

In his epochal *New York* magazine article "Lenny Bernstein and the Radical Chic," Tom Wolfe would use Oceanside as an example of the no-class middle-class people whom Bernstein's wealthy crowd shunned while they embraced the dashing, leather-clad Black Panthers. He described my townsfolk as "those fantastically dowdy herds roaming past Bonwit's and Tiffany's at dead noon in the sandstone sun-broil, 92 degrees, daddies from Long Island in balloon-seat Bermuda shorts bought at the Times Square Store in Oceanside." As always with Wolfe, it's not clear whether he was sending up the snobbery of his subjects or sharing in it. Probably both. We shopped at that Times Square Store, by the way.

Tom Wolfe's scorn aside, this is when things were best for the white American worker. He—and it was still usually a he—could afford a home for his family, a car, a vacation, and the occasional summer day window-shopping in the big city, even if he couldn't actually patronize Bonwit's or Tiffany's. So much of New York life had always been spectacle, anyway, even for the working class: the symbols of a wealth and power beyond your grasp sparkled above you, but as long as you were climbing higher, you were moving toward that light. We were happy with our Times Square Store outfits, as long as we could have new ones, not hand-me-downs, for every holiday.

And yet white suburban middle-class life wasn't entirely happy. Looking back, I've come to believe that some of the anger of my people covered guilt. My family didn't have to flee the lovely Flatbush neighborhood where I was born. There was no crime or violence or disorder there. They were doing what everyone did: lighting out for the suburban territories, for the yard and the garage, and the bedroom for every kid. There was a certain sadness attached to that migration, leaving behind the churches and the big stoops, the cluster and the comforting density of urban life. I think for some people it got disguised as anger. So many acted as though they were pushed out of their urban enclaves, as if they hadn't left voluntarily, even when it wasn't true. Then they tried to re-create their tribal clusters in suburbia, but it was impossible.

My mother was never entirely happy in Oceanside. For one thing, she was that rare suburban mom who couldn't drive, and she often felt lonely and isolated. If my father made me a feminist, by pouring his stunted ambition into me and encouraging my every intellectual pursuit, my mother made me a bad, guilty feminist, because I knew from an early age I didn't want a life like hers. She'd been a bright and ambitious student, senior class president of her high school, a basketball star, though only 5′2.″ Then she marched off to New York's Hunter College in 1948. Without her father, she had to work to help support her family, and she became executive secretary to a General Motors vice president. Her boss became a mentor, and he gently counseled her to discontinue night classes; women didn't need to go to college! When she got pregnant with me, she wrote not a letter of resignation, but a request for a one-year maternity leave. I don't know whether it was denied; I only know she never went back to work. Years later, she'd still boast that when she left GM, she was making more money than my father at Sadlier. I have her last paycheck.

I was only five when Betty Friedan famously diagnosed "the problem that had no name" in *The Feminine Mystique*, but I already knew the problem well. Friedan's picture of bored and depressed housewives who traded jobs for vacuum cleaners was eerily familiar; it was as if she'd been taking notes in our kitchen. My father lived his greater ambitions through me, but my mother's feelings about my drive and my limitless future seemed unresolved and ambivalent. She tired of my endless questions, which my father enjoyed. Why not? She was home all day, and he wasn't. When debates began to rage over whether working mothers harmed children, I knew that it was the opposite: having a mother who wanted to work but didn't wasn't the best thing for children, either.

For a while, though, my mother thrived in the sixties. Both of my parents did. They seemed different, even liberated, by all of the change. My father's sideburns grew an inch longer during the decade, my mother's skirts got an inch shorter. My father's favorite comedian, Irish Catholic rebel George Carlin, was making a similar transition from harmless jokes about the "hippie-dippie weatherman" to pointed social commentary about racism and the war. My father was changing in similar ways but without the drugs.

The liberalism of Pope John XXIII was as important as the Kennedy presidency in the particular ways my parents opened up to the world. The Mass changed entirely—the priest was suddenly facing the people, and we prayed in English, not Latin. My family started attending a new "folk Mass" for a while, where my brother played guitar and we sang "Kumbaya," for real. My parents started going to "ecumenical meetings" and interreligious Seders at Oceanside's Temple Avodah, because Pope John preached ecumenism and engagement with the world's other religions.

I first learned that Catholics don't always practice what the Church preaches about contraception when I was pretty young. It was my job to help my mother with the laundry. One day while putting my father's socks away, I found a box of condoms at the back of his sock drawer. After a few awkward attempts at conversation, my parents came clean. They had only three kids, and almost all of our relatives had comparably small families, because most Catholics planned their families, too. The Church was a wonderful institution, my parents said, but it was very old, and it sometimes took a while to catch up with the times. Kind of like the way Grandma still said "icebox" for "refrigerator."

When I made my first Jewish friend, I couldn't sleep the first night, wondering how Elissa and her family, who were wonderful to me, could possibly go to heaven if they weren't Catholic. My father cracked the walls of our religious ghetto by telling me all good people go to heaven, whatever their religion; heaven was not a country club, he said.

Once those walls were cracked, however, it was only a matter of time before I started slipping out regularly.

8

I don't think there's any point in being Irish if you
don't know that the world is going to break your heart
eventually.
—Daniel Patrick Moynihan after JFK's assassination

Aside from my parents' shy ventures into our local Jewish
community, my family watched most of the social revolution
of the sixties on television. The civil rights struggle transfixed us.
Crowded around the black-and-white screen, we saw billy clubs
and police dogs turned on men and women, young and old, even
on children who looked as small as I was. Sometimes my mother
wanted to turn off the television, but my father, when he was
home, insisted we watch.

I was obsessed with the civil rights battles I watched on TV.
I was in my phase of reading books only about saints and mar-
tyrs. Try being a devout Catholic girl named Joan and *not* thinking about how you might have to lead an army as a teenager
and be burned at the stake at nineteen to save Catholic France,
or maybe just New York. I had gotten the idea in my head that
I might be asked to die for my faith someday, and I worried
about my own courage.

My father pointed to the Serenity Prayer, though he made
clear that "accepting the things I cannot change" wasn't an option
when it came to social injustice. He knew I'd find the courage to
do whatever my religion demanded of me; it just wasn't time yet.

In November 1963, another Catholic martyr claimed our
prayers. On the day of JFK's assassination, my mother raced to

school at midday, in tears, to pick me up from kindergarten; my father came home from work early. We watched the news about Kennedy's murder all that weekend on television, on that same glowing box that showed us the courage and the violence of the civil rights movement. They were fused for me, Kennedy's murder and the turmoil over civil rights—wasn't Dallas in the South? Even as an adult, I've never entirely pulled the two things apart. I remember Jackie Kennedy in her blood-stained suit. Yet it wasn't garish in black and white; her raw grief was far more shattering than the signs of carnage. We watched Lee Harvey Oswald's perp walk and then his murder, and that was scary. But my mother wasn't even trying to turn off the television anymore.

Almost fifty years later, in memory I'm less shaken by the scenes of blood than by the symbols of grief and absence: the riderless horse, the fatherless children, three-year-old John-John's brave salute. And my parents' shock: they were deeply sad and they seemed a little bit afraid. They were right to be afraid. The bullet that took down JFK was only the first shot in a decade that promised such great change but produced so many divisions, misunderstandings, revisions, heartbreaks, and lies.

My parents tried to transfer their love for Kennedy to Lyndon Johnson, trusting him to make Kennedy's shining civil rights vision a reality. During most of Kennedy's tragically short term, civil rights leaders debated how hard to push him, while the administration debated how hard to push the segregationist Democrats who ran the South.

Even the 1963 March on Washington, that victory for peaceful protest, featured infighting over whether to tolerate criticism of the president. The administration tried to squelch the march from the beginning. Washington archbishop Patrick O'Boyle threatened to back out of delivering its invocation when he learned about one particularly fiery passage in Student Non-Violent Coordinating Committee (SNCC) leader John L. Lewis's draft speech, vowing that black civil rights leaders would "pursue our own 'scorched earth' policy and burn Jim Crow to the ground—nonviolently." An Irish Catholic leader blessing this outpouring of peaceful democratic protest would send a powerful message; O'Boyle backing out would have been a blow. Labor leaders and administration allies ultimately got Lewis to excise the controversial passage from his speech, and O'Boyle blessed the gathering.

In retrospect, what's probably most surprising about the march is not the infighting, but that its leaders got beyond it. Only the decency and diplomacy of the black leaders kept it from falling apart. American Federation of Labor and Congress of Industrial Organizations (AFL-CIO) president George Meany flat-out refused to back the march, while liberals such as the United Auto Workers' Walter Reuther gave time and money. Yet in exchange, labor demanded a say in how far the march would go in denouncing the administration's civil rights sluggishness. Still, conservatives didn't know enough about the new movement to figure out how drive a wedge between the forces of change—yet.

Few people today remember the extent to which the early civil rights movement came out of a movement for labor rights. King went down in history as the struggle's prophetic leader, but A. Philip Randolph, the cofounder of the influential Brotherhood of Sleeping Car Porters, stands next to King in the pantheon of early civil rights heroes. It was Randolph who threatened FDR with a wartime March on Washington in 1941 and Randolph who got Roosevelt to issue his executive order banning racial discrimination in the defense industry. Randolph and the Negro American Labor Council proposed the 1963 march and went to King, seeking his backing.

Looking at an old handbill advertising the 1963 march, I was struck by the multiracial, economic focus of its call to action:

> America faces a crisis . . .
> Millions of Negroes are denied freedom . . .
> Millions of citizens, black and white, are unemployed . . .

It absolutely was about helping all of us, although many of us—particularly white working-class people—weren't paying attention.

Its second two demands, after "Meaningful Civil Rights Laws," were "Full and Fair Employment" and a "Massive Federal Works Program." The latter would turn out to be the road not taken, in any of the major attempts to address poverty and exclusion (black or otherwise) during the next fifty years.

Lyndon Johnson would largely deliver on the first demand with the Civil Rights Act of 1964 and the Voting Rights Act of 1965, but his War on Poverty played at the margins of the labor market. At first, a strong and growing economy seemed to make concerns about jobs passé; unemployment was dropping. What few people noticed, though, was the decline in jobs for people without higher education, the result of automation and offshoring. Johnson's spending on the war would also make a big jobs initiative fiscally impossible.

It's not that no one proposed one. Inside the administration, *The Other America* author Michael Harrington teamed up with another Irish Catholic, Daniel Patrick Moynihan, who'd gone to work in the Labor Department, to push a jobs thrust in the new poverty programs. "If there is any single dominant problem of poverty in the U.S., it is that of unemployment," they wrote in a memo to Johnson's labor secretary, W. Willard Wirtz.

Harrington and Moynihan proposed a public works program, which Wirtz supported. But the Labor Department's public works jobs proposals all carried price tags of $3 billion to $5 billion; Johnson couldn't spend anything like that, with war spending climbing. In fact, the budget he submitted for 1965, the year he launched the War on Poverty, actually contained a slight cut to poverty programs. Instead, he chose Sargent Shriver's approach—"a hand up, not a handout"—with programs such as job training and education, legal services, and Head Start, intended to ready the poor to take advantage of opportunity, rather than creating opportunities for them. Harrington and Moynihan's idea for a public works program was rejected; Harrington left his consultancy with the Labor Department; Moynihan stayed on.

Fatefully, the next year, Moynihan would seek to bolster his argument for an employment focus with an epic report, *The Negro Family: The Case for National Action*, which became known simply, and notoriously, as "The Moynihan Report."

Moynihan became a fascinating figure to me as I worked on this book.

All that most people remember about "The Moynihan Report" (if they remember it at all) is that it identified a "tangle of pathology"—single-parent households, teen pregnancy, high school dropouts, rising crime—as part of the "Negro problem." Yet Moynihan's attitudes were more complicated than the left's lasting caricature. His statements about the black family had a lot in common with some of what he wrote and said about his own people, Irish Catholics. When he agreed to write the Irish Catholic chapter in *Beyond the Melting Pot*, the 1963 book on race and ethnicity he coauthored with Nathan Glazer, he confessed to Glazer that "for a good while I was interested in the subject only as it provided an explanation for the things that were wrong with the way I was brought up." I could relate to that.

Born in Tulsa, Oklahoma, he spent his early childhood in relative comfort in Greenwich Village, until his alcoholic journalist father abandoned the family. Then he bounced around with his mother, who struggled to support her children during the Depression and briefly relied on welfare, according to Moynihan. The family returned to the middle class when his mother remarried, but fell out of it again for a while when she divorced again. Moving from school to school, working shining shoes and stocking shelves, and finally helping his mother run a bar in New York's Hell's Kitchen, he saw a lot of what he later identified in poor black families in his own Irish family and neighbors. "I know what this life is like," he told an interviewer after he became an expert on poverty, albeit a notorious one.

Moynihan's chapter on New York Irish Catholics in *Beyond the Melting Pot* describe a forlorn people who have underachieved in a land of opportunity. "Drink has been their curse," he wrote, sounding like Frederick Douglass a century earlier. "It is the principal fact of Irishness that they have not been able to shake." Relatedly, he concluded, Irish Catholics had poor attitudes toward hard work, their educational institutions were mediocre, and even the educated Irish clumped in fields that "offer more security albeit less prestige and income."

It's fascinating that as late as 1963, during the Kennedy administration, an Irish Catholic Democrat was theorizing that his people were unable to excel in modern America because they drank too much, lacked ambition, and chose security over ambition and excellence.

So when Moynihan zeroed in on the "pathology" of the black family, he wasn't saying much that he wouldn't say about his own people. He wasn't blaming black families themselves or even a "culture of poverty," as many would later claim. He attributed the problems of the black family first to slavery, then to Jim Crow and the almost forced black rural migration north. He compared their troubles to those experienced by the rural Irish exiled to American cities a hundred years earlier. "It was this abrupt transition that produced the wild Irish slums of the 19th Century Northeast. Drunkenness, crime, corruption, discrimination, family disorganization, juvenile delinquency were the routine of that era," Moynihan noted.

Despite his attempts to compare black poverty to that of the Irish a century earlier, he sometimes comes across as an awkward anthropologist studying the customs and trends of a tribe, *the Negro*, whose odd behavior sometimes obscures its common humanity. He is frankly patriarchal, yet he tries to nod to possible feminist objections by arguing that he's describing, not prescribing: "There is, presumably, no special reason why a society in which males are dominant in family relationships is to be preferred to a matriarchal arrangement. However, it is clearly a disadvantage for a minority group to be operating on one principle, while the great majority of the population, and the one with the most advantages to begin with, is operating on another. This is the present situation of the Negro."

In a private memo to Johnson, Moynihan was more dogmatic and judgmental about the problems of single motherhood, but he tied it not to culture but to black male unemployment and the push for welfare rights, not jobs. "During times when jobs were reasonably plentiful (although at no time during this period, save perhaps the first two years, did the unemployment rate for Negro males drop to anything like a reasonable level) the Negro family became stronger and more stable. As jobs became more and more difficult to find, the stability of the family became more and more difficult to maintain."

Yet Moynihan became a pariah on the left for "blaming the victim." In his book of the same name, clinical psychologist William Ryan attacked Moynihan's arguments, misrepresenting his research, as well as his recommendations, with self-contradictory arguments. Things weren't as bad in "the Negro family" as Moynihan believed—and if they were, it was all due to racism. It's true, and lamentable, that Moynihan's report included few policy prescriptions, but it wasn't because he didn't have any. Around the same time, he wrote Johnson's famous Howard University speech on race, which committed the country not merely to equality of opportunity but demanded efforts to achieve a much more controversial "equality of results." As Johnson memorably intoned:

> Freedom is not enough. You do not wipe away the scars of centuries by saying: Now you are free to go where you want, and do as you desire, and choose the leaders you please. You do not take a person who, for years, has been hobbled by chains and liberate him, bring him up to the starting line of a race and then say, "you are free to compete with all the others," and still justly believe that you have been completely fair. Thus it is not enough just to open the gates of opportunity. All our citizens must have the ability to walk through those gates.

Working for Johnson, Moynihan proposed public works jobs and affirmative action measures, as well as a guaranteed national income, to lift black families, whether they were headed by one or two parents, out of poverty.

The biggest problem with Moynihan's report was its timing. Written before the Watts conflagration, it was leaked around the same time, and Washington pundits and politicians found in it an excuse to exonerate white America for the urban rebellions that would soon ignite coast to coast. *Those people* didn't want to help themselves; they just wanted to demand help from the (white) taxpayer. It gave Americans an excuse to do nothing. Twenty years later, when a new generation of community activists began working on African American poverty issues, I heard advocates make almost every single point Moynihan raised, as they argued for programs to focus on black men and boys. They advocated for special attention to the toll that slavery, Jim Crow, and persistent unemployment took on black men, and the way women—wives, mothers, and welfare-system social workers—tried to address the problem but sometimes made things worse. Poverty scholar William Julius Wilson would complain that "the controversy surrounding the Moynihan report had the effect of curtailing serious research on minority problems in the inner city for over a decade." When researchers began looking again, the African American scholar found, "they were dumbfounded by the magnitude of the changes that had taken place."

Reading Moynihan from a distance of almost fifty years, I was struck less by his judgmental prose than by his attempt at empathy with the black poor, which was unfashionable at a time when activists were beginning to argue that American racism made comparison between black people and white immigrants impossible. He genuinely believed that his low-income Irish origins gave him the sympathy and standing to have an opinion about poor black people. His sin was partly to have the wrong opinion, but it was also the audacity to have an opinion at all.

Stung by the hostility to his "case for national action" on behalf of the black family, Moynihan continued to make it privately, arguing that employment should be the focus of antipoverty programs. "It will be a good deal easier to pension the Negroes off, as it were, than to accept the major, wrenching changes in our way of doing things that will be required if we are going to bring them into the larger community," he wrote to Wirtz. Johnson didn't listen; meanwhile, the left got behind "welfare rights organizing," assisting poor women in signing up for public assistance. The number of children on AFDC doubled from 1960 to 1968, to more than six million, while the cost more than quadrupled. The proportion of welfare families who were black rose from 41 to 47 percent in those same years. With hindsight, the idea that poor black women could be "pensioned off" without having to work, when women in the rest of society were surging (or being driven) into the workforce, whether they wanted to or not, seems naive at best. But very few people were publicly asking those kinds of questions back then.

9

If you were bright and Jewish and you wanted the Irish teacher's job, you didn't lock her up in the bathroom and demand "Jew Power."
—Striking teacher, Ocean Hill/Brownsville, 1968

The New York World's Fair of 1964–1965 represented the city's zenith, for me, anyway. It may have been the high-water mark for American liberal optimism as well. It confirmed my view of my birthplace as the center of the universe—the whole world came to *us*—and my family's place in the center of New York. From the Uffizi in Florence came Michelangelo's incomparable Pietà, the statue of the dead Jesus Christ on his mother's lap, revered by devout Catholics and passionate art lovers alike. Disneyland left California for New York, with its schmaltzy global village pavilion "It's a Small World After All."

My mother's venerated old employer, General Motors, sponsored an exhibit called Futurama 2, updating Norman Bel Geddes's vision of a glorious highway-linked American future that had stunned the 1939–1940 New York World's Fair. In this new Futurama, the entire world is linked by global highways that cut through oceans, rain forests, mountains, polar ice caps, and even outer space (all traveled by presumably GM-made vehicles). The exhibit culminated in the city of the future, and Futurama seemed to be trying to reassure us that the urban experiment would work out in the end. "Its traditions and its faiths preserved, there is a new beauty and new strength in the city of tomorrow," the confident narrator told us. And we believed him.

79

At the end of the day my parents, my little brother, and I climbed into a tiny, swaying carriage and rode in an enormous Goodyear tire, a giant Ferris wheel that was, like Futurama, a great big ad. From there, we could see Shea Stadium, the brand-new home of the Mets. We had a panoramic view of the city we loved. Luckily, we couldn't see the actual future.

As the battles of civil rights and the culture wars that ensued grew more violent and bitter, the white working class grew more alienated, more certain than ever that what some called progress was destabilizing the world they had built. Social upheaval fueled fears they had never relinquished and intensified the feeling that they were unimportant, overlooked, less powerful than either "people of color" or the educated elite who championed their causes. All of that was about to become very clear with the election of John Lindsay as New York's mayor.

My father liked Lindsay, even though the mayor was a Republican (he later became a Democrat), so I liked him, too. In memory, I see those iconic Kennedyesque photos of a youngish white man in shirtsleeves, walking through Harlem. A boarding school patrician who met his wife at a Bush family wedding, Lindsay represented New York's so-called silk stocking district, and he was emblematic of a now-extinct species of northeastern liberal Republican.

He would become a Rorschach test for how one saw New York in the sixties and the seventies; maybe even for how one saw the sixties and the seventies, period. Liberals tend to admire him as an urban innovator who did his best to make the city live up to its promise of opportunity for everyone. Conservatives despise him as someone who caved to black "militants," as well as to white union leaders, and destroyed New York. Some see him as a dangerous naïf rolled by the city he was supposed to govern.

Liberal journalist Jack Newfield, who loved him, summed it up this way in a Lindsay obituary in 2000: "Lindsay was great on race, but not so great on class. He lacked a certain empathy for the white ethnic communities of the city. . . . The mayor who wanted reconciliation so deeply accidentally created contention and white backlash." That could be the epitaph of the Democratic Party somewhere around the same time.

We watched from Long Island with optimism as the mayor vowed to unite the city. By the mid-1960s, New York had already become two New Yorks: one for upwardly mobile white-collar workers, and one for the declining working class of every race. My family had a foot in each. In 1945, New York had been solidly blue collar across all five boroughs, giving my working-class family its boost into the middle class. Yet Manhattan, where my father wore a suit and a tie to work, was becoming overwhelmingly white collar by 1965, and Lindsay was most definitely the mayor of white-collar Manhattan. Between 1945 and Lindsay's second term, in the early 1970s, New York lost almost half of its manufacturing jobs.

In many ways, Lindsay catalyzed a worst-of-all-worlds backlash: he drew white union members' ire by talking tough to them; he drew taxpayer ire by caving to the unions; and his racial liberalism united the white working class and the outer boroughs against him. His first term began with a subway strike that lasted twelve days but still resulted in big wage concessions. Lindsay tried a racial appeal against the strikers, arguing that the strike disproportionately hurt black and Latino workers, who did in fact have fewer cars and relied more on public transit. That enraged Transport Workers Union leader Mike Quill, an Irish immigrant radical and an ally of Dr. King's who had organized across racial lines for much of his career. There they go again, those silk-stocking do-gooders, pitting the Irish against the blacks.

Lindsay also took on another union, the Patrolmen's Benevolent Association—a less progressive union, for sure—as part of his admirable effort to curb police abuses. Early in 1966, he appointed a civilian review board to examine claims of police brutality and other infractions, which were growing louder in the black community. From the *New York Times* to liberal GOP senator Jacob

Javits, the idea had wide support, though William F. Buckley Jr. demagogued against it in his maverick 1965 campaign for mayor, denying police wrongdoing in the black community and mocking liberals who believed "that Negro crime is any less criminal."

With cops in my family, I listened as the anti-Lindsay rhetoric went through the roof. They had signed up to be the good guys, they were now policing a city whose crime rate had soared, their lives had gotten more dangerous—and they should submit to civilian review as if *they* were the bad guys? Some of them were the bad guys, of course, taking every excuse to abuse the rights of blacks and Puerto Ricans.

All grievances were becoming racial. My uncles came home from their jobs as cops and firefighters and steamfitters, in Manhattan, Brooklyn, and the Bronx, with endless stories of crime and arson. And the crime rate was rising in New York City. Though robbery rates had been stable up to that point in the twentieth century, they jumped fivefold between 1962 and 1967 and doubled again between 1967 and 1972.

The Patrolmen's Benevolent Association backers put a measure on the 1966 ballot to abolish Lindsay's civilian review board, and to the shock of liberal Manhattan, it passed in a landslide, thanks to an alliance of outer-borough Jews and so-called white ethnic Catholics: 83 percent of white Catholics backed the measure, but so did 55 percent of Jews, shocking the proreview forces. It was a vote on behalf of the police and against rising crime.

My mother seemed frightened, too. I partly remember the sixties as a series of weekly *Life* magazine covers, bringing us stories of valiant civil rights struggles but also, increasingly, chaos. The iconic covers now regularly displayed scenes of urban violence: a bombed-out mosque after Malcolm X's murder in 1965, the ruins of the Watts riots that same year. A June 1966 cover graced by a gorgeous Elizabeth Taylor, who was said to be shattering "the rules of censorship" in *Who's Afraid of Virginia Woolf?*, also carried the squib "Plot to Get Whitey: Red-Hot Young Negroes Plan Ghetto War." The next month we learned "Watts Still Seething." The government's efforts to address black poverty weren't quelling black rage; in fact, they might seem to be making every-thing worse.

There were scary dispatches from the impending culture wars: "LSD: The Exploding Threat of the Mind Drug That Got Out of Control," a March 1966 cover screamed, and "LSD Art" a few months later. There were terrifying crime stories, with covers on nurses-killer Richard Speck and Texas sniper Charles Whitman (both of them white, by the way) just two weeks apart in August 1966. And many, many sad, scary Vietnam covers: maimed American soldiers, a wounded marine, a crippled Buddhist lying in the street.

My mother saw the coming storm and went inside for shelter: inside the home, the family, the Church. She watched less television and began teaching Sunday school. My father tried to make sense of the chaos, including the rising clamor of anger and even separatism among black people. One of my favorite but most puzzling memories is of him reading *The Autobiography of Malcolm X* on his way to and from work. I still have his yellowed, dog-eared paperback copy. I can't imagine there were a lot of white men in suits heading to Wall Street, heads deep in that story. The first thing my father told me about Malcolm X was that he'd moved away from his "blue-eyed devils" rhetoric before he was murdered, embracing a multiracial version of Islam. But it bothered me: *that* Malcolm, the one who crossed racial lines, had been assassinated; the angry, separatist Malcolm had been left alone? I didn't know what to make of that, and I still don't.

It's common to argue that what we think of as "the sixties" ended with the tragedies of 1968, but in some ways they ended in 1966. There was New York's overwhelming rejection of the civilian police review board, of course. In August of that year, King brought his crusade against racism and poverty north, to Mayor Richard Daley's Chicago, and he was defeated by Daley's wily brutality and white Chicago's militant racism. Marching in white neighborhoods, demanding integration, King and his allies were beset by white mobs who bloodied them with sticks and bricks and fists. "I think the people from Mississippi ought to come to Chicago to learn how to hate," a bewildered King remarked.

It wasn't just Chicago; the entire country was learning that the civil rights revolution wasn't going to stop with voting rights in the South. Undoing the legacy of racism and segregation required big change in the North as well. Fair housing laws and school busing orders provoked a huge backlash, as whites resisted integration— sometimes violently, as in Chicago, and sometimes stealthily, with the destructive guerrilla tactic known as "white flight." Those efforts at integration were necessary, however painful. Once again, though, they had the greatest impact on the whites who had the least, who felt that their piece of the American Dream was already so small, they shouldn't be asked to share it. For the most part, the politicians and the judges who imposed housing and busing laws didn't live in the neighborhoods they were changing.

King's Chicago defeat emboldened a growing Black Power movement that was tiring of the preacher's message of nonviolence and integration. It was futile: whites didn't want to integrate, and they were happy to use violence to prevent it. Nineteen sixty-five began with the multiracial Selma march; it ended with Stokely Carmichael taking over as head of the crucial civil rights organization SNCC, the Student Nonviolent Coordinating Committee, defeating Selma hero John L. Lewis. Carmichael expelled SNCC's white members and denounced integration as "a subterfuge for the maintenance of white supremacy" that forced blacks to accept a dominating, yet inferior, "white culture."

Across the country, a liberal turned conservative named Ronald Reagan defeated California governor Edmund G. Brown on a platform of law and order, mocking Brown for coddling black criminals in Watts and white radicals in Berkeley. Reagan vanquished liberalism, in the person of the good Irish Catholic Pat Brown, and liberalism "never really recovered," historian Robert Dallek wrote. The year 1966 was also when Republicans swept Congress in a Great Society backlash: Democrats lost 3 Senate seats, 47 House seats, and 477 spots in state legislatures across the country. Nine of 10 new governors were Republican.

Newsweek declared that on Election Day 1966 "the thousand-day reign of Lyndon I came to an end."

In New York, we watched all of those issues explode the next year in the devastating Ocean Hill/Brownsville conflict, when black parents in that poverty-stricken, heavily black Brooklyn neighborhood demanded community control over their low-achieving schools, including the right to hire and fire teachers. The Jewish-dominated United Federation of Teachers (UFT) fought them, while Lindsay backed the parents, and the battle raged under a national spotlight, through multiple teachers' strikes, for nearly two years. The teachers believed they were fighting for old liberal values: hiring teachers by seniority and testing, not cronyism, and standing up for the free expression of ideas. Michael Harrington later lamented that the conflict prefigured "the split in the liberal-labor-black movement, which was the precondition of Republican presidential power for the next two decades," according to his biographer Maurice Isserman. It was the first political battle my father couldn't clearly explain to me.

City elites from the *New York Times* to the Ford Foundation backed the black parents, but UFT president Albert Shanker, who had marched in Selma, had support from a surprising number of civil rights leaders, including A. Philip Randolph, King confidant Bayard Rustin, and even King himself. Rustin compared calls for community control to "states' rights."

That King, Rustin, and Randolph supported Shanker isn't surprising; they were fighting similar battles within their own movement—and losing, to a new generation of young black leaders impatient with integration and disdainful of the majority American culture they were expected to join. They dismissed that culture as not only alien to theirs, but morally inferior: individualist, conformist, and materialist. In New York, the growing African American Teachers' Association was openly rejecting what it saw as the UFT's cultural chauvinism in pushing "white middle-class values" on black kids. For its part, Shanker's UFT failed to acknowledge that its hiring and promotion protocols had the effect of stifling black and Latino advancement within the school district. Shanker relied on his Selma marching to deflect charges of racial bias way past the time when it might have seemed relevant.

On May 8, 1968, the community school board representing the black parents terminated nineteen teachers and administrators deemed "unacceptable," almost all of them Jewish. Hell broke loose, with daily pickets and counterpickets at local schools and City Hall. Anti-Semitism surfaced. Picketers shouted "Jew pigs!" at protesting teachers. The black teachers' magazine *African American Teachers' Forum* asked in an editorial, "How long shall the Black and Puerto Rican communities be forced to sit back and allow the Jewish-dominated United Federation of Teachers destroy our every effort to rescue our children from incompetent teachers whose only goal—aside from receiving fat paychecks—is stifling our children's intellectual growth? . . . The Jew, our liberal friend of yesterday . . . is now our exploiter."

After three separate strikes, the UFT mostly prevailed: the fired teachers got their jobs back, and Rhody McCoy, the African American educator running the experiment, was replaced by a trustee. In an interview with *Ebony*, as he was being relieved of his duties, McCoy gave a depressing summation of the conflict: "Everyone else has failed; we want the right to fail for ourselves."

And they did: Ocean Hill/Brownsville schools remained among the worst in Brooklyn. Yet the conflict helped tear apart the liberal coalition for good, while cementing the alliance between Jews and white Catholics that surfaced in the opposition to the civilian police review board in 1966. It had one other under-noticed effect that to this day divides the movement for education reform. The city's monied elites made common cause with black parents rightly angry at the system's failure to educate their kids, a conflict that now plays out in the charter school movement. With different values and motives, both sides blamed teachers. According to his *New York Times* obituary, Lindsay would later say that the community control experiment in Ocean Hill/Brownsville was his greatest regret.

10

The working-class white man feels trapped and, even worse, in a society that purports to be democratic, ignored. . . . He is beginning to look for someone to blame. That someone is almost certainly going to be the black man.

—Pete Hamill, *New York* magazine, April 1969

So many forces fractured liberalism and the country in 1968, as my parents watched, anguished and fearful. It was the moment when Americans began to associate social change with violent upheaval and the Democrats with both. For decades, the Democrats would run from the association. Images of urban riots, teachers' strikes, and a rising, if always marginal, Black Power movement replaced the scenes of nonviolent multiracial protest that once symbolized the civil rights movement. The growing chaos frightened even some liberals, the group whose tolerance had, in the eyes of many Americans, enabled the radical fringe.

The Vietnam War, which my father had come to oppose, was more divisive than even race—and it, too, managed to split educated liberals such as my father from working-class men like his brothers. Maybe it was partly the legacy of the Civil War Draft Riots; Irish workers became the super-patriots, enraged at what seemed like the treason of liberal elites. They watched as their heroes became society's villains: first urban cops, then American soldiers in Vietnam. Yet it wasn't only the Irish: the patriotic working-class sons of immigrants didn't like seeing their flag disrespected, especially by an ungrateful younger generation that enjoyed unprecedented freedom and privilege.

One town over from Oceanside, Allard Lowenstein, a white civil rights supporter turned antiwar leader, was plotting a run for Congress, and my father backed him. Lowenstein had been an organizer of Mississippi's Freedom Summer, helping to recruit white college students to challenge the state's violent segregation. He fell out with the Student Nonviolent Coordinating Committee as it moved toward radicalism and separatism, and he became a leader of the "dump Johnson" movement, trying to build support for a Democratic primary challenger to LBJ, most likely Senator Eugene McCarthy.

In the windup to the presidential race, liberalism cracked for good. Labor and old-fashioned civil rights leaders found themselves left behind as the dizzying pace of change still couldn't keep up with impatience to correct society's many wrongs. They began feuding with New Left organizers over the morality of the Vietnam War, as well as with the movement to dump President Johnson over the war's widening. Rick Perlstein recounts a 1967 Americans for Democratic Action meeting where Gus Tyler of the International Ladies' Garment Workers' Union (which was on the left of the labor movement) accused the New Left of trying to hijack the party "away from economics to ethics and aesthetics, to morality and culture" with its dump Johnson crusade. Tyler warned Lowenstein prophetically that if the left mortally wounded the Democratic president who had given the nation the Civil Rights Act and the Great Society, it would throw America's poor "to the Republican wolves" in November.

As the factions swirled, some leaders of the civil rights movement took Tyler's side. The left-wing crusader Bayard Rustin, one of my civil rights heroes, fell out with Lowenstein over the dump Johnson crusade. Rustin warned that abandoning Johnson over the war could be "distinctly unprofitable and possibly suicidal" for the movement toward black equality. Rev. Martin Luther King Jr. agonized. He came out strongly against the war, but he told his advisers he didn't want to be seen as part of the move to dump Johnson.

Not even King could have resolved all of those tensions: black against white, integrationists against separatists, LBJ vs. an anti-war primary challenger. Yet there would have been less bitter fracture had it not been for King's assassination, which devastated his followers. As the zealots took over from the voices of reason, Americans watched as King's murder triggered another wave of the urban riots that either terrified or angered most members of my working-class family. My mother, nostalgic for what used to be and perceiving change as, increasingly, something scary, fought back tears as prime-time television was interrupted to broadcast news of King's killing. She put my brother and sister and me to bed and made us say our prayers for Dr. King's family, five kids just about our age. There was no rioting in Harlem, where John Lindsay walked the streets to calm the crowds, nor in Indianapolis, Indiana, where a grieving Robert Kennedy broke the news to a heavily black crowd on a campaign stop.

The Irish Catholic Kennedy had moved steadily left after his brother's assassination. Yet his political roots enabled him to assemble a remarkable coalition of white working-class ethnics, black activists, the emerging Chicano community, and even some union leaders behind his presidential bid. On the night of King's murder, he reached into own suffering to counsel the Indianapolis crowd away from vengeance. "What we need in the United States is not division; what we need in the United States is not hatred; what we need in the United States is not violence and lawlessness, but is love, and wisdom, and compassion toward one another, and a feeling of justice toward those who still suffer within our country, whether they be white or whether they be black." Would his vision have won back the working-class voters lost to the Republicans since his brother's time? We will never know. Two months later, Kennedy himself would be murdered, further confirmation to working-class voters and many other people that the country was out of control.

With King and Kennedy gone, the United States lost its chance at a New Left coalition that included the white poor and working class, along with women, minorities, and students. As he tried to galvanize a new Poor People's Movement, King had insisted, to the discomfort of some old allies, that "When I say poor people, I am not only talking about black people." The month before he died, King convened a multiracial group of seventy-five community leaders, American Indian Movement and United Farm Workers leaders, Appalachian mine workers, and the daughter of a Klansman, Peggy Terry, who organized poor whites in Chicago's Uptown district, to explore a multiracial movement of the poor.

In those same months, Kennedy's 1968 presidential campaign was uniting poor whites, blacks, self-described Chicanos in California, and Puerto Ricans in New York. Author Robert Coles praised Kennedy's ability "to do the miraculous: attract the support of frightened, impoverished desperate blacks, and their angry insistent spokesmen, and, as well, working class white people." No one knows where Kennedy's coalition would have gone; frustrated by labor's conservatism, he once suggested Democrats should "write off the unions." All we can say for sure is that no one since has pulled together the broad coalition he did. "Our best political leaders were part of memory now, not hope," wrote Jack Newfield after the assassinations of King and Kennedy. "The stone was at the bottom of the hill and we were alone."

My father tried to hold on to hope. McCarthy's antiwar candidacy, too associated with radicals for the working class, seemed unlikely to prevail as the 1968 Democratic Convention opened in Chicago. But the antiwar left despised Johnson's vice president, Hubert Humphrey. That in itself was a picture of the party's fracture: Humphrey had been one of the most reliable voices on civil rights and labor rights. He gave the speech supporting the controversial civil rights plank at the 1948 Democratic Convention, telling delegates, "The time has arrived in America for the Democratic Party to get out of the shadow of states' rights and to walk forthrightly into the bright sunshine of human rights." Strom Thurmond and his Dixiecrats walked forthrightly, all right—out of the convention and eventually into the Republican Party.

As long as I could remember, my parents watched both party conventions gavel to gavel, back when the networks covered them all day and night, none of the truncated prime-time celebrity focus we have today. This time we watched with a sense of foreboding. The 1968 convention happened to feature an Irish Catholic bad guy, Mayor Richard Daley, with a team of heavily Irish Catholic accessories, the Chicago cops. My father didn't like Daley, but neither did he like the way the New Left targeted and taunted cops as the enemy. (Of course, the cops often targeted them first.) With police officers on both sides of our family, even he seemed to reach some limit when it came to demonizing the entire police force, though he acknowledged that some bad apples brutalized the black community.

He also saw something ugly, a class-based snobbery, in the way the student left baited the police. "Pigs" was an Irish slur, he believed, fusing the stereotypical image of angry, chubby-faced Irish cops with the historic association of the Irish as "pigs." During the Columbia University occupation in 1968, one student leader made the connection explicit: "What we are dealing with is a certain kind of Irish Catholic prudery. They're the kind of guys who have a hard time with sex, they have a hard time getting hard is what I mean."

Chicago's most militant demonstrators provoked police every way they could. There were widespread but ultimately debunked reports that some threw bags of human excrement at the cops, but my normally fact-loyal father believed the story, and seized on the image as the most nihilistic move he could imagine, disgusting and politically stupid as well. Demonstrators chanted, "The whole world is watching," and that was true. Watching—and coming away horrified at the Democratic infighting on display. Instead of being appalled by Daley and the cops' brutality, many Americans watched them standing up to anarchy and applauded. My father didn't applaud, but he was disgusted by the excesses of the protest.

Though he backed McCarthy and resented Humphrey's refusal to commit to ending the war, my father supported the Democratic nominee after the divided convention. A Humphrey-Muskie button replaced McCarthy-Lowenstein on his suit lapel. But most leading antiwar Democrats delayed in backing Humphrey, until it was too late. After Johnson announced a halt to his bombing campaign on October 31 (a move Humphrey had already pledged he'd make if elected president, in a break with Johnson), McCarthy and Lowenstein tepidly endorsed their party's nominee. Humphrey jumped in the polls, but he still lost. Too many had forsaken the Democrats, a party that was about to forsake itself. Against all odds, Nixon made a comeback; the man JFK defeated eight years earlier was going to become our president and with a significant number of Irish Catholic votes, too.

Lowenstein won his race for Congress, though he'd be gerrymandered out of his seat after one term. Yet my father took no comfort in that; he was furious at the antiwar leader's refusal to back Humphrey when it might have mattered. He took one of his McCarthy-Lowenstein buttons and mailed it to the new congressman's office. "Congratulations: Your candidate—Nixon—won."

My father wasn't the only working-class Irish Catholic liberal worried that rising New Left insurgents left out their families, guys such as their brothers and brothers-in-law, the men most of my cousins were growing up to be. Just a few months after Nixon's inauguration, in April 1969, *New York* magazine writer Pete Hamill set out to explain their grievances with sympathy in a long, anguished feature, "The Revolt of the White Lower Middle Class." He labeled the malcontents "my people," even as he grappled with their graphically quoted racism about "spades" and "niggers," and he warned darkly, "It is imperative that New York politicians begin to deal with the growing alienation and paranoia of these people. They can't wait much longer; it's almost the point of no return."

Yet Hamill didn't have much to recommend that politicians do. I don't say that to criticize him; I look back with hindsight and wonder what could have been done to tether the working-class voters who departed from the Democrats in those years. Hamill talked to guys like my uncles, who worked hard, played by the rules, and still couldn't keep up, guys who were taking second jobs and seething as their wives, like my aunts, were forced to go to work. Irish Catholic Brooklyn Democrat Hugh Carey, who later became governor, put the problem this way: "The black man has hope, because no matter what some of the militants say, his life is slowly getting better in a number of ways. The white man who makes $7,000 a year, who is 40, knows that he is never going to earn much more than that for the rest of his life, and he sees things getting worse, more hopeless."

Carey and Hamill were watching an economy change; we all were, but none of us knew it at the time. Hamill warned in closing, "The next round of race riots might not be between people and property, but between people and people. And that could be the end of us."

Those warnings about white rage didn't come true right away. By mid-1969, in fact, Nixon looked weaker, with the economy sliding and opposition to the war growing. My father joined two million Americans who participated in the nationwide antiwar moratorium on October 15, 1969, marching with John Lindsay down near Bryant Park while a quarter of a million people gathered in Washington, DC. But the next May featured something a little bit like what Hamill was describing: the white working-class revolt that went down in history as the "Hard Hat Riot."

Sympathetic to guys like this a year earlier, Pete Hamill recoiled, especially at the apparent collusion between cops and the construction workers, as the hard hats beat protesters with little interference from police. "The police collaborated with the construction workers in the same way that Southern sheriffs used to collaborate with the rednecks when the rednecks were beating up freedom riders," he wrote in the *New York Post*. Like my uncle, many of the rioters were Irish Americans, who still dominated the building trades. Construction trades council president Peter Brennan staunchly praised his members' patriotism. Some accused Brennan of instigating the riot, perhaps with Nixon's help, which Brennan denied. Many of the cops, accused of going easy on the rioters, were Irish as well.

The Irish were rioting again, along with other white working-class brethren, but this time to support the ruling class. Whether I liked it or not, looking at the seventies I had to admit: a whole lot of my own people tore apart the New Deal coalition they had helped build. And the right swooped in to take advantage.

11

What kind of delegation is this? They've got six open fags and only three AFL-CIO representatives!

—AFL-CIO head George Meany, on the New York delegation to the 1972 Democratic National Convention

My loving father despised Richard Nixon, and he handed that hate down to me. But in adulthood, I had to admit that the Nixon who got elected in 1968 seemed to be a different candidate than the guy who ran in 1972. Sure, his first campaign played off white ethnic fears about rising crime, the counterculture, and racial unrest. Yet he had rejected explicitly racial appeals. Although Pat Buchanan would later brag to me about capturing George Wallace voters in 1972, in 1968 Nixon attacked Wallace repeatedly, charging him with waging "a calculated campaign to divide this nation, to deliberately inflame the fears, frustrations, and prejudices of our people." He called Wallace "the creature of the most reactionary underground forces in American life."

No doubt, some of Nixon's criticism came from his fear that Wallace's third-party candidacy could cost him law-and-order, white-ethnic votes. By 1972, Nixon would be the one deliberately inflaming "the fears, frustrations, and prejudices of our people," with a campaign to play on anxiety about racial change and social disorder to create a lasting Republican majority. And he succeeded. Watergate would bring Nixon down, but the politics he pioneered are with us today.

By today's policy standards, of course, Nixon looks like a liberal. He tapped Moynihan as the executive secretary of a newly created "Urban Affairs Council," and the isolated Democrat crafted a "Family Assistance Plan" to replace welfare, which forty years later looks like socialism. It would have created a nationwide guaranteed income and provided payments to families with a father at home, reversing the incentives for family split-up he saw in traditional welfare programs. No less a liberal than Ted Kennedy would eventually lament turning down Nixon's proposals for national health-care reform, which were arguably more far-reaching than the law enacted under President Obama forty years later.

The Nixon administration pioneered affirmative action, with its 1969 "Revised Philadelphia Plan," a proposal to integrate the city's white building trades while providing government contracts to minority businesses. George Meany's plumbers and my grandfather's steamfitters were among the most segregated unions, with "apprenticeships" passed from father to son, uncle to nephew, in an unbroken white chalk line. Black advocates targeted the building trades for integration understandably: providing middle-class wages to workers without college degrees, they had offered a pathway out of poverty for white immigrants before them. Black Philadelphians galvanized one of the strongest local movements to integrate the building trades, and Secretary of Labor, George Shultz proposed a plan to set "goals" and "timetables" to increase black employment in government building projects there.

Shultz's plan had the effect of inflaming tension between two already warring core Democratic constituencies, blacks and labor—particularly the Irish trade unions. John Ehrlichman praised the Philadelphia Plan for its "great style" in pitting the AFL-CIO against the NAACP and leaving the GOP in "the sweet, reasonable middle."

Labor howled on cue. "We still find the Building Trades being singled out as being 'lily white' as they say, and some fellow the other day said it was 'the last bastion of discrimination,'" George Meany complained. "Now this is an amazing statement, when you figure how small participation of Negroes and other minorities is in, for instance, the banks in this country, the press. . . . I resent the action of government officials—no matter what department they are coming from—who are trying to make a whipping boy out of the Building Trades."

There they were again, those elite do-gooders, trying to help blacks at the expense of white workers, with remedies that didn't touch their own privilege. At the same time, it was getting hard to ignore that blacks and Latinos were having a hard time grabbing a rung of the ladder of middle-class opportunity that blue-collar unionized work provided to generations of white ethnics. And when they did get ahold of a rung, a workboot often came down on their fingers to kick them off.

Despite Meany's bluster, Nixon's Philadelphia Plan spread, mainly in the form of government regulations mandating a percentage of contracts for black-owned and later women-owned businesses. But the president never pushed the parts of the plan intended to integrate the building trades. Nixon and his team, guys such as Buchanan and Kevin Phillips and Chuck Colson— were paying much more attention to the complaints of the white working class. Where FDR had railed against wealthy elites in the 1930s, famously telling the nation "I welcome their hatred," Nixon welcomed the hatred of cultural elites, and he made common cause with a generation of working-class whites who were identifying those elites as their enemy, too.

Nixon liked Pete Hamill's piece "The Revolt of the White Lower Middle Class" so much, he had it xeroxed for his cabinet. The Hard Hat Riot of May 1970, the one my uncle supposedly joined, while my father watched in sadness, buoyed the president, too. Peter Brennan led a second protest in the same spot just a few weeks later, explicitly to support the Vietnam War. At the end of May, Brennan made a hero's visit to the White House, carrying a hard hat specially made for Nixon.

After Brennan's visit, Nixon gave Chuck Colson the go-ahead to work on a plan for courting labor in his 1972 reelection campaign. Colson's portfolio would also include responsibility for dirty tricks and "ratfucking" that would encompass much more than his outreach to organized labor in reelecting the president, although the two activities sometimes overlapped.

• • •

Pat Buchanan left a road map of Nixon's plans in his infamous 1971 memo "Dividing the Democrats." He told Nixon the "guiding political principle" of his 1972 campaign should be to "focus on those issues that divide the Democrats, not those that unite Republicans." To that end, "top level consideration should be given to ways and means to promote, assist and fund" the political activities of "the Left Democrats and/or the Black Democrats."

The campaign should look for ways to "champion the cause of blacks within the Democratic Party," but also to convince African Americans that "the Power Elite within the Party is denying them effective participation." Put simply: Nixon's operatives would look for ways to make the white working class think the Democrats were slavishly serving black people, while making black people think the Democrats were ignoring their rights and concerns. (This worked only because both sides already had begun to think that way.) Buchanan advised that "bumper stickers calling for black Presidential and especially Vice Presidential candidates should be spread out in the ghettoes of the country." A successful racial strategy could "cut the Democratic Party and country in half; my view is that we would have by far the larger half," he confidently concluded.

Clearly, Buchanan worried that the existing strife in the Democratic Party wasn't enough to split blacks and working-class whites; they needed some Nixonian tricks to turn up the heat—and they'd get them. Chuck Colson helped organize a walkout of black delegates to the National Youth Caucus in 1971. When Nixon got word of a movement of black Democrats to form a third party in Alabama, he wrote to H. R. Haldeman: "Get this subsidized now."

Another crucial part of Nixon's "dividing the Democrats" strategy involved making sure George Wallace ran in the Democratic primaries in 1972, rather than as an independent, as he had in 1968. To that end, Nixon met with the Alabama governor in the summer of 1971, and then a couple of things happened: the grand jury investigating Wallace's brother Gerald on tax fraud dissolved, and the Justice Department gave its seal of approval to Alabama's less-than-impressive civil rights enforcement plan, calling it "a much better plan than many states'." Nixon got his wish: Wallace declared himself a candidate for the Democratic presidential nomination in early 1972.

Where Buchanan and Colson were economic conservatives, recommending a strategy of "cultural recognition" for the white working class but not practical government support, Kevin Phillips was more of an economic populist. He backed New Deal programs and more, favoring national health insurance, for instance. Phillips would later denounce the Republican Party that his strategies enabled to take over the country, for the way the modern GOP allowed wealth to undermine democracy. But in the 1960s, his enemy was liberal Democrats who let race trump class.

In *The Emerging Republican Majority*, he showed how the GOP drew New Deal coalition members from "the Catholic sidewalks of New York," not merely from the South. He hailed "the Lawrence Welkish masses" as if he was looking through my family's not-lace-curtained windows every Saturday night, when we watched Lawrence Welk religiously. "The principal force which broke up the Democratic (New Deal) coalition is the Negro socioeconomic revolution and liberal Democratic ideological inability to cope with it," he wrote. "Democratic Great Society programs aligned that party with many Negro demands, but the party was unable to defuse the racial tension sundering the nation." Phillips's plans contained no measures to defuse that tension, of course.

Where Roosevelt's New Deal succeeded "by taxing the few on behalf of the many," Phillips argued, the Great Society was now "taxing the many on behalf of the few." Phillips denounced "silk-stocking" liberals who "send their kids 2,000 miles to look for poverty in Mississippi but won't travel one subway stop to help poor whites working for $1,800 a year." He decried "the Toryhood of change," a line of elite do-gooders that likely went all the way back to the abolitionists, who somehow never included the white working class on the list of unfortunates needing help. What Phillips couldn't know was that he was helping nudge forward a boulder that would take off uncontrollably down a hill, setting off a forty-year downhill decline in the living standards of the white working class he purported to care about.

Buchanan and Phillips only intensified the trouble in the Democratic base; they didn't create it. The progressives who wove the innovative New Deal safety net had themselves left the loose threads that Nixon and Co. used to unravel the coalition thirty years later. To win the support of Southern Democrats, FDR left agricultural and service workers out of crucial New Deal reforms, from Social Security to the National Labor Relations Act (NLRA), excluding many African Americans as well as women. The NAACP tried to push to make the NLRA include racial discrimination but failed. When you look closely at the political, social, and moral contradictions of a "coalition" that included both African Americans and Southern segregationists, it's a wonder the New Deal base stayed intact as long as it did.

Southerners weren't the only problem. As we saw clearly when King took his crusade to Chicago, many northern Democrats resisted demands to integrate schools and neighborhoods, too. Even progressive labor leaders were slow to tackle racial discrimination within their own unions. In fact, rather like the banking and media "elites" Meany would attack for pushing integration on the building trades, rather than integrating their own ranks, labor union leaders supported civil rights measures most fervently when they didn't encroach on their own power and status or that of their members.

The other way the New Deal undermined the New Deal coalition was by succeeding. The wave of labor organizing unleashed by the NLRA drove the number of union members from 3.5 million to 17 million between 1935 and 1955, and it helped create the vast American middle class. Between 1947 and 1972, the weekly earnings of nonsupervisorial employees jumped 62 percent. By the mid-1960s, pollster Samuel Lubell observed, "The inner dynamics of the Roosevelt coalition have shifted from those of getting to those of keeping." Unions themselves became less militant and more interested in helping management maintain productivity and profits.

The prosperity built by the New Deal coalition unraveled it in one final way: it helped create the New Left, which I was too young to officially join, but whose political, social, and cultural goals I supported once I came of political age. The largest cohort in history was attending college, and many became foot soldiers in a movement to attack the system that made their lives possible. In 1946, two million Americans attended college or university, representing only one in eight college-age students; by 1970, there were eight million undergraduates, one in three in that age group. Much of the student left took for granted the affluent society that stifled their dreams and made them mere cogs of capitalism but that also made their protest possible.

They weren't alone. McGovern strategist Fred Dutton, who worked for Johnson and both John and Robert F. Kennedy, began talking about a "New Politics" uniting students, feminists, minorities, and elite knowledge workers, leaving big union leaders on the sidelines. In the affluent, postmaterial age of "individual purpose" that Dutton and other "New Politics" Democrats believed had finally arrived, union members didn't deserve a special place at the Democrats' table anymore.

In short, prosperity undermined the New Deal coalition, giving white workers the freedom to believe their enemy was black protesters and white hippies, while providing the New Left with the dream it could create a progressive majority coalition without big labor. The two groups suddenly had the luxury of hating each other, of focusing on their cultural differences, because their economic battles seemed to have been won.

If, as my father believed, an intransigent New Left bore some responsibility for electing Nixon in 1968 because of its disdain for labor-favorite Hubert Humphrey, labor would get its self-destructive payback in 1972. Some conservative labor leaders such as Brennan endorsed Nixon; Meany flirted with the president but kept the AFL-CIO officially neutral, which was almost as destructive to the dying New Deal coalition, refusing to endorse the most prolabor presidential candidate in Democratic Party history, George McGovern, and helping to brand the South Dakota senator a dangerous radical. The 1972 Democratic National Convention wasn't disrupted by the rioting and repression that destroyed Chicago in 1968, but it was almost as disastrous.

My family watched the 1972 political conventions, as we always did, with one big change: we were viewing them from a new home, in Shorewood, Wisconsin, a suburb of Milwaukee. My parents had done something fundamentally American: my father had gotten a better job at another Catholic education company, in Milwaukee, this time as president. We traveled from lower middle to upper middle class on a two-hour Northwest Airlines flight from New York to Milwaukee that February, to explore the American frontier, or so it seemed to me at the time. I knew nothing about Wisconsin, except that I'd be free. Or so I thought.

There was one other notable change in our family's political convention viewing in 1972: as we watched the GOP gather in Miami a month after the Democrats' convention disaster, my mother, the Kennedy lover, seemed to be rooting for Nixon.

My mother was my personal guide to the transformation of the white working class from Kennedy Democrats to Nixon voters. She idolized Kennedy; we had Kennedy plates and Kennedy key rings and magazine commemorative books all over the house. Yet by the late sixties, she was changing, expressing fear about the decay of the New York around her and the chaos set loose in the country. In 1970, she had been diagnosed with breast cancer, and that, too, seemed part of why she and my father wanted a new start somewhere else.

With hindsight, my father's decision to uproot all of us seems strange. Just as he'd been exiled from his own family at thirteen to join the Christian Brothers, which he remembered with pain, he exiled me from my extended New York family at the same age. My brother and my little sister resented it, but I saw opportunity. I knew my life would be smaller if we stayed on Long Island. A true American, I sensed I could start over and be anything I wanted. And the last thing I wanted to be was working-class Irish Catholic.

Except that's exactly what I was in my new upper-middle-class world, at least for a while. With a Brooklyn-inflected accent like mine, everyone expected me to be a dumb thug-girl. All over suburban Milwaukee at the time, white girls were either aping fifties greasers or wearing their moms' pearls, Lilly Pulitzer sweaters and shirts and dresses, and pastel Pappagallo shoes. I had my first pangs of personal class consciousness: I knew in my soul that wealthy suburban kids had absolutely nothing on my friends and cousins in New York. They weren't smarter or harder working. They'd simply been born into the upper middle class, a few into the real upper class, and most were just coasting and would coast ever upward. Safety nets of wealth and family connections caught the few who would fall.

I didn't know it at the time, but by America's standards, we were now in the upper class, too. My father got a big raise, and given the Midwest's lower cost of living, our lives felt hugely different. And yet I could feel a keen difference between my arriviste family, which now had income but no "wealth"—no real estate, no stock, no savings—and my wealthier peers, who had all of those.

But my father had been right: just as his own exile to the Christian Brothers allowed him to jump a social class beyond most of the rest of his family, our move to suburban Milwaukee did the same thing for me and my siblings. A few funny things symbolize that leap for me. Now, instead of opening a can of corn or splurging on a box of frozen Green Giant peas in butter, complete with a "boil-in bag," my mother walked to a nearby produce store and bought fresh fruit and vegetables. I had never tasted a fresh (not frozen) strawberry until 1972. Suddenly we lived in a world of museums and lectures and the liberal-minded sorts who ran them and patronized them. I took a rigorous, life-changing poetry class, because I had a crush on a boy who was taking it, and moved on to advanced literary criticism because my new friends did.

While suburban Milwaukee inspired my rising class-consciousness, I loved the egalitarian optimism of Wisconsin and its progressive history. Milwaukee had Socialist mayors, most recently Frank Zeidler, from 1948 to 1960. I actually knew his daughter, through friends in my father's office. Father James Groppi, a white priest who had led local civil rights demonstrations and marched with King in Selma, was no longer active but still a legend, although the city is to this day one of the most segregated in the country. As important as New York was to the New Deal, Wisconsin had its own proud progressive legacy, and even more than in New York, that legacy still seemed alive.

Paradoxically, my upper-class Milwaukee life was more racially diverse than my lower-middle-class Long Island life had been. It turned out that our high school was a sponsor of the "A Better Chance" (ABC) program, the pioneering project to put black kids in white schools. (It was less a sign of racial enlightenment than a way to ward off integration with black Milwaukee school districts.) I made my first close black friend, who became my brother's best friend, who was one of only a handful of black kids who weren't part of ABC. Another sort-of misfit, Joe became my guide to my new white suburban world.

I learned to see the tics, the pretense, the coded contradictions of white liberal racial condescension. Joe mocked the Lilly Pulitzer ensembles as "Lilly White" outfits, so I did, too. I became a race traitor for a while and dismissed entitlement and cluelessness as white. But everyone loved having a black friend; it wasn't just me. They could congratulate themselves on their racial openmindedness, while never missing an opportunity to note, sometimes in front of Joe, that he was "one of the good ones."

When my mother's cancer recurred, I learned a lesson about racial identity that black people learn early in life, but whites don't see up close until later, if at all: your racial identity is sometimes what other people think it is. My mother found a brilliant oncologist, Dr. Roland Pattillo, who happened to be black, except I didn't know that for a while. My parents never mentioned it, and Dr. Pattillo was olive-skinned, like my father. At some point I realized on my own that he was black; maybe it was the way he treated the black patients at County Hospital, where he was working on an experimental cancer-treatment protocol, a new kind of immunology he'd explore for other diseases as well.

Once I got my license, I drove my mother to her cancer treatments at County Hospital. She would go in, while I sat in the waiting room alone, watching a multicultural array of people force themselves to walk into chemotherapy, some hobbling, some still able to pass in the land of the well, except for the telltale wig. I would like to say I talked to these patients or their kin, but we all sat mostly in silence, a nod and a smile telegraphing empathy, afraid we'd hear a story more hopeful than ours or one more hopeless. Dr. Pattillo always made sure to come out and spend a minute with me, to ask me how I was doing with everything going on in my family. I loved him, and so did my mother.

But having a black doctor couldn't stop her political drift to the right. Even in 1968, she had watched the Republican National Convention attentively, but it was only because she wanted to see John Wayne, her father's idol, address his party, or so she told us. By 1972 she was watching the whole GOP convention as part of the team. Not only Jackie Robinson but also Sammy Davis Jr., she informed me, supported Nixon, *proof* that he and the GOP weren't racist. That year, for the first time, she refused to tell me or my father who she voted for. "It's a secret ballot!" she declared solemnly. My father needled her, but we knew that could only mean one thing: she was voting for Nixon.

The safety of midwestern suburbia hadn't calmed my mother's fears that something had gone wrong in our country. Exiled from New York, even if by choice, she still grieved over the continuing decline of her home and worried about the safety of her brothers and cousins. Her mother had died shortly after our move, one more loss of family security. And whether it came from her authoritarian prison-guard father or her anxious, status-conscious mother, my mother deeply believed in authority: the priest, the cop, the boss, the president.

Every time someone disrespected Richard Nixon, her support for him grew stronger. In her world, you didn't have to vote for the president to respect him: Democrat or Republican, he was *our president*. As it became clear that in this new world, people who didn't vote for Nixon didn't respect him, either, she seemed to feel that respecting him required her to vote for him, too.

12

> We are not dealing with sporadic or isolated attacks from a relatively few extremists or even from the minority socialist cadre. Rather, the assault on the enterprise system is broadly based and consistently pursued. It is gaining momentum and converts.
> —Lewis Powell to the US Chamber of Commerce,
> August 1971

Did anyone realize the world as we knew it was going to end in 1973? I didn't, but I was a high school freshman. Just scanning the big happenings of that momentous year, you don't get through January without a dizzying list of epochal events: Nixon is sworn in for a second term, and he signs the Paris peace accords, a first step toward ending the war. Lyndon B. Johnson dies at his Texas ranch. The US Supreme Court legalizes abortion with its *Roe v. Wade* decision. The American Psychiatric Association removes homosexuality from its diagnostic manual, marking the condition's movement from diseased to normal (at least in the eyes of mental health "elites"). A new Middle East crisis triggers the Arab oil embargo, which sends energy costs soaring. The World Trade Center—scene of the Hard Hat Riot in 1970 and the 9/11 attacks twenty-eight years later—opens. All in that first month.

Also, Watergate details began to emerge, first in a drip, then in a flood that would wash away the Nixon presidency and, with it, Kevin Phillips's and Pat Buchanan's dream of a long-term Republican majority to replace the FDR coalition. "We rolled the rock all the way up the hill, only to see it roll right back down

107

on top of us," Buchanan told a reporter. Or so we all thought at the time.

I watched Nixon's resignation speech while visiting Long Island, sitting alone with my mother's twin brother, my Uncle Jack, in his dark below-ground family room. My uncle had lost his leg and with it his job as a firefighter; in addition, he had lost his youngest son, my cousin Bradley, to leukemia. He was also, I learned later, carrying a secret. His and my mother's estranged father had died a few months earlier. Yet although Jack had told my mother their father had had a heart attack, in fact he died in a fire he'd accidentally set himself, smoking in bed, probably intoxicated, in his tiny apartment above a bar in the Bronx. Her brothers didn't want my sick mother to know the truth, that her worst worry had come true, in a way. One of her relatives had been claimed by the chaos she feared in one of our old, crumbling New York neighborhoods—but he'd done it to himself.

Had I been with my friends or even my father, Nixon's resignation would have been a moment of jubilation: ding dong, the witch is dead! But watching it with Uncle Jack, I could see it as sad and a little scary. Nixon's departure was just more evidence that the world was falling apart. As the president climbed the plane's steps and waved his farewell, I knew the chaos and hate of the past few years wouldn't leave with him. Nixon boarded the plane, and my uncle grabbed his crutches and hobbled out of the room.

The mid-1970s are a haze of gas lines and impotent government, best symbolized by "Whip Inflation Now" buttons, which President Gerald Ford hoped might herald the kind of communal crusade we were capable of in wartime, only this time to fight inflation. In fact, the war against inflation had some success, as far as corporate America was concerned: unions became the enemy, lower wages the victory. These were the years when all of the gains the working class had made since the 1930s began to be reversed, with the political acquiescence of much of the white working class.

Union leaders George Meany and Peter Brennan thought cozy-
ing up to Nixon could protect their members from a worsening
economy, as well as from the radicalism, disrespect, and demands
for integration coming from African Americans and women.
They were wrong. With Nixon gone, labor didn't even get the
"cultural recognition" Buchanan and Colson had convinced him
to bestow. Unions became the enemy, just as they'd been the
GOP's enemy before New Deal egalitarianism and postwar prosperity seemed to make class conflict obsolete. In the early 1970s,
Big Business began to wake up to its class interests, even if Big
Labor and the larger working class did not.

The menace of inflation gave corporate America the excuse to
turn on unions under the guise of public interest. Higher prices
hurt everyone, after all. Newly assertive business groups and
publications blamed rising prices on higher wages driven by the
nation's commitment "to full employment and maximum produc-
tion," in the words of *Business Week* in 1974. *Fortune* went further:
"Organized labor has now become a destabilizing and dislocating
force—made more unmanageable by large political influence." In
fact, labor's political influence was waning, but a newly activist
business community decided that unions were the problem—and
convinced a lot of working-class people to go along.

In fact, higher wages weren't the primary reason prices were
climbing; in 1973, the wages of working-class men began to stagnate
(in inflation-adjusted dollars) and then fall. The year 1973 was also
when a brand-new business lobby began to emerge. The Business
Roundtable pulled together corporate CEOs with a broader reach
and grander designs than the stodgy US Chamber of Commerce
(though the Chamber would double its membership in the seventies, too). The advice to the Chamber that became known as
the Powell Memo, after its author, the former Supreme Court
justice Lewis Powell, is widely credited with inspiring a corporate
crusade to push back against unions, taxes, and business regulation.

"The only thing that can save the Republican Party . . . is a
counterintelligentsia," Nixon treasury secretary and stockbroker
William Simon declared in the mid-1970s. So Simon took over a

right-wing foundation and, with a lot of wealthy partners, began to nurture a dense web of writers and social scientists to counter "the dominant socialist-statist-collectivist orthodoxy" that he believed controlled Washington, universities, and the media. The Heritage Foundation and the American Enterprise Institute would do much the same thing. New Right gladiator Paul Weyrich called the counteroffensive "a war of ideology . . . a war of ideas, it's a war about our way of life."

Actually, it was a class war, the haves versus the have-nots, but waged by only one side. Almost no one in the party of FDR seemed to remember he or she had a responsibility to contest the right-wing corporate version of what made a strong economy. Nixon had distracted the white working class with his cultural recognition strategy, his acknowledgment of their alienation and rage. The Democratic Party remained stuck in an identity crisis, partially induced by what became known as identity politics. What began as a split between blacks and the white working class was turning into a battle of everyone against everyone, all for none and none for all. After the McGovern debacle, the fractious left split into caucuses for African Americans, women, Latinos, Asians, and gays and lesbians, with each group convinced that its own history of exclusion demanded its own political remedy and maybe, for a time, political autonomy. Meanwhile, a new generation of pro-business Democrats tried to shed the party's association with labor.

When the Vietnam War ended, the campus left didn't go away; it went inward. Universities became the center of political battle, over the issues of representation for excluded groups in the student body, on the faculty, in curricula. Across the country, campus politics became preoccupied with teaching the histories of traditionally oppressed groups. No one seemed to spend a lot of time thinking about our common future.

The assault on labor during the 1970s was remarkable and unrelenting. In the early 1950s, three thousand workers a year filed complaints with the National Labor Relations Board (NLRB), stating that they were fired for union activity; by 1980, the number was greater than eighteen thousand, and the pace accelerated under Ronald Reagan. In the mid-1970s, under Gerald Ford, the NLRB sided with business 35 percent of the time; by the early 1980s, that jumped to 72 percent. The percentage of workers represented by unions dropped from a high of 35 percent in 1955 to less than 25 percent in the mid-1970s and continued to decline, to only about 12 percent today (and only 7 percent of private sector workers).

Sadly, even as unions were opening up to blacks and women, the industries they represented were shrinking. Those who feared that integration was a zero-sum game, in which white men would lose jobs to blacks and women, turned out to be partly right in some sectors. While the percentage of black steelworkers, for instance, climbed during the seventies, the overall number of black steelworkers actually declined. There was no cause and effect here; it just so happened that just as American industry began to integrate, the economic structure beneath it was starting to disintegrate. Of course, we know that now. Yet at the time, to some of the white working-class men whose jobs disappeared just as their workplaces integrated, it seemed as though their worst fears had come true. It would forever look as if those black guys and the handful of women who showed up on their job sites took their jobs—rather than that corporate decision makers had eliminated jobs for everyone.

Corporate America stepped up its presence in Washington as well. The number of businesses with lobbying (or "public affairs") offices in Washington grew from 100 in 1968 to more than 500 in 1978; the number of corporate PACs jumped from fewer than 300 in 1976 to more than 1,200 in 1980. In the early 1970s, labor PACs outspent business PACs in congressional races; by the mid-1970s, they were about equal; and by 1980, business PACs pulled into the lead, to stay. That year, unions represented less than a quarter of total PAC spending, down from half in 1974, according to Jacob Hacker and Paul Pierson in *Winner Take All Politics*.

Labor's influence with the Democratic Party showed a corresponding decline. Some of it was fallout from the 1972 battle between Meany and "new politics" liberals; McGovern's campaign manager, Gary Hart, would pioneer the idea of "New Democrats"—and later, "Atari Democrats"—who owed no allegiance to labor. When he ran for the Senate in 1974, Hart declared that "labor can't deliver votes anymore" and called for a less intrusive and bureaucratic federal government. That same year, he proclaimed that his new generation of Democrats was not just "a bunch of little Hubert Humphreys," deriding the longtime champion of organized labor and civil rights. Hart won his 1974 race, and so did a lot of other Democrats, thanks to Watergate, but issues of class and economic change were ominously muted in an election year.

They'd stay muted in 1976, when an outsider Southern governor with a decent history of race relations, a scandal-free record, and no strong ties to labor became the Democratic nominee. Jimmy Carter seemed to be just what the Democratic Party needed, a clean, pious Southerner to try to win back the "Solid South." It worked, temporarily: Carter won back all of the Southern states that Nixon had swept in 1972.

My father didn't like him, though, and for the first time in his life, he didn't vote for the Democratic nominee. He distrusted the way Carter wore his evangelical Christianity on his sleeve. My father believed in that whole separation of church and state idea; maybe he chafed at the fact that evangelical Christians had persecuted Irish Catholics decades before he was born. Or both. He turned out to be at least partly right about Carter mixing politics with evangelical Christianity; it marked the beginning of evangelicals turning to politics again, although most of them would drift right from there. Michele Bachmann, an extremist evangelical Christian, got her start working for Carter in 1976; she and her husband Marcus even attended an inaugural ball.

Unbelievably that November, my father voted for his old idol Eugene McCarthy, who was making a cranky, futile comeback, running as an independent. My father did what he'd criticized, what the New Left pulled in 1968 and Big Labor paid back in 1972: he rejected a Democratic nominee because he wasn't good enough. I had planned to do the same, but at the last minute, inside the voting booth for the first time at eighteen, I switched my vote to Carter. I wanted to win, and I believed and still believe that even a weak Democrat is better for the country than a Republican. That's what my father taught me.

I don't know whether my father's odd vote was nostalgia for an earlier era of optimism or anger at what the Democratic Party had become. I don't think he was paying that much attention to politics that year, nor was I. My mother had died earlier that year, in April, after years of defying predictions that she had only a few weeks to live.

Her cancer had recurred in 1973, as I started my sophomore year in high school; that time she was given six weeks to live. Dr. Pattillo's experimental treatment gave her another three years, but he'd run out of miracles. Living with dying changed my mother; she became the loving personality she'd only been able to try out when we had company. We'd become allies, not rivals; maybe my accomplishments became not a rebuke but what she'd see as her legacy.

After she maybe/probably voted for Richard Nixon in 1972, my mother had seemed to mellow about politics. I can't say she became a Democrat again; she loved Jerry Ford for bringing the country together after Nixon's disgrace. Oddly, though, she stopped going to church a few months before she died, after the priest's sermon became a fiery antiabortion harangue, in which he proclaimed that prochoice Catholics weren't Catholic at all and were going straight to hell. The sermon enraged my mother, even though I don't think she considered herself a prochoice Catholic.

She was disturbed by the idea of abortion, but I know from our conversations that she found the issue complex and painful. My mother was too much a realist—and too much a feeling, compassionate follower of Jesus Christ—to blindly insist there could never be a reason, a crisis, a tragedy that caused a woman to make a different choice from one she herself thought was right. Knowing that you're dying and leaving behind three school-age children probably instills empathy and understanding.

I don't entirely know why my mother snapped on that Sunday when she heard the antiabortion sermon. Maybe she worried that the priest was right about her prochoice husband and daughter; the claim that we were headed to hell had to make the idea of heaven less of a comfort. I just know that she was crushed, and she never went back. But she didn't die without the Church. My parents had befriended enough priests over the years that one said Mass at her bedside, gave her communion, and provided her with the last sacrament, the anointing of the sick. He didn't trouble her with talk about abortion.

My isolation from my extended family intensified after my mother died. Some aunts and uncles couldn't see me without getting teary. It was sad and awkward when we connected. I was older, becoming a political radical, a different class, and I was confused; I mixed up my sadness at the world I'd lost with a political critique of that insular world, too small for me. I was a world citizen, I would move on—to college and then to California, as far away from New York as possible. My father set an example of exile I'd follow for a long time.

New York was coming apart as fast as my family. John Lindsay, the patrician liberal mayor my father admired, left behind a crushing deficit when he left office. However well intentioned, however undermined by economic forces far beyond any mayor's control, the Lindsay experiment discredited urban liberalism, perhaps permanently. It left a mess for the next mayor, antipatrician Abe Beame. The son of a Jewish socialist, Beame had spent his life as a loyal New Deal liberal. Now he got to preside over the New Deal's local dismantling, in the city he loved, the city where it had been born.

The July 1977 blackout felt like a low point. New Yorkers remembered the 1965 blackout for neighbor helping neighbor, but this one featured neighbor looting neighbor; small black businesses were among the hardest hit by the mostly black crowd. Those inclined to racism had new excuses for it. An uncle of mine, by marriage—he later left the family through divorce—refused to let my brother come visit when he was traveling with our friend Joe that summer, telling my father, "If he's going to hang out with niggers, he'll have to deal with the consequences." Joe lived with our family the year after my mother died so that he could finish high school when his parents moved away for work. He was family, more so than some of our New York relatives who hadn't been there when we lost my mother. (I should note that the rest of our New York family loved and welcomed Joe.)

Amazingly, things got worse for New York in 1978, and for my extended family. My grandmother's three sisters still lived in the old Bay Ridge three-flat where they'd raised their kids, even though the brothel on one side was now joined by a drug den on the other. Over the Fourth of July weekend, while the three elderly women were away, arsonists killed their German shepherd and torched the house, along with the two alongside it. They got $3,000 for the lot, which represented their life's savings. A few months later, my father watched his old neighborhood go up in flames while the Yankees beat the Los Angeles Dodgers in the World Series. "Ladies and gentlemen, the Bronx is burning," Howard Cosell told the nation, but it felt like he was speaking to my dad.

Back in Shorewood, A Better Chance was losing its funding, as local parents stopped contributing to the private, voluntary deseg-regation effort program. In 1979, it quietly disbanded. It was news enough to make the *New York Times*, in a story headlined "Liberal Whites Turn Cold to Blacks." The *Times* saw the program's demise as evidence that "whites seemed increasingly committed to integration as an ideal . . . but increasingly reluctant to support the mechanisms of integration." One anonymous Shorewood resident told the paper about blacks: "You're sorry for their cause, but after a certain point you think, 'Let's get on with daily life.'"

My father's pessimism about the Carter administration would be validated. A Democratic attempt at labor law reform went down; so did a bid for a new Office of Consumer Representation, after a business lobbying effort that House Speaker Tip O'Neill called the most intense in twenty-five years. With unemployment and inflation running high, the newly emboldened probusiness conservatives found the headlines they needed to press their attack.

A full-employment bill passed, but it was compromised beyond recognition or effectiveness. Carter's chairman of the Federal Reserve, Paul Volcker, gave up on half of his job's dual role: using the money supply to control inflation and unemployment. Volcker focused exclusively but unsuccessfully (until much later) on inflation. Carter's own tax-reform bill, which in its early stages contained an increase in the capital gains tax, wound up *cutting* the rate from 48 to 28 percent, after a lobbying onslaught by business.

It wasn't Carter's fault alone; the sixties were over. A generation had departed the stage with some of its biggest goals accomplished but an economy in trouble. Its inheritors began the process of revising the past, erasing dreams of equality and ending poverty in the name of addressing different political and economic woes. Many on the left began to think that anything approaching equality was impossible, a false promise made by a rapacious ruling-class elite going back to the Founders. From the right, a new kind of probusiness Democrat emerged nationwide, politicians who realized something had to be done to create stability and growth but had no better ideas than to follow conservatives' lead. Jacob Hacker and Paul Pierson wrote, "Both parties were now locked in a determined struggle to show who could shower more benefits on those at the top." Carter's presidency marked the point at which the percentage of white working-class people who identified as Democrats dropped sharply—it would drop 20 points, from 60 percent to 40 percent, between the midseventies and the early nineties, according to the University of Arizona's Lane Kenworthy, and it hasn't recovered since.

After Carter, Ronald Reagan sounded themes of American unity and optimism. Just as Nixon had learned some of his law-and-order, culture-war tactics from Reagan's divisive 1966 campaign, Reagan learned from Nixon's fall. He mostly shed his nasty culture-warrior persona of the sixties to become the man who would awaken us to "Morning in America." Reagan could afford to move to higher ground; Nixon had done the job of dividing us. And Democrats, running away from their own history, had no message to unite us.

PART III

THE LONELINESS OF THE REAGAN-ERA DO-GOODER

13

Government's view of the economy could be summed
up in a few short phrases: If it moves, tax it. If it keeps
moving, regulate it. And if it stops moving, subsidize it.
—Ronald Reagan, August 1986

Ronald Reagan wiped the political slate clean, erasing the
history of American class conflict and the Democratic
Party's legacy of standing with the common man. Reagan made
Republicans the populists, the party that protected the little guy
against a bigger enemy, only this time it was Big Government—
taxing your hard-earned money and giving it to people who
didn't deserve it—not Big Business. Republicans preached
unity, while they let the rich loot the country. And a fractured
Democratic Party let them do it. On its left wing, an identity-
politics identity crisis continued, while its probusiness right wing
gained strength.

Where Nixon gave working class whites "cultural recognition," in Rick Perlstein's words, liberal Democrats bestowed
their cultural recognition, and over time political support, to the
movements that emerged in the seventies for women's, minorities', and gay rights. So many big lefty debates seemed almost
entirely a matter of cultural recognition—fights over college curricula and textbooks, in which advocates for excluded "people of
color" fought faux-defenders of a "common culture" over whose
version of American history would prevail. Although it was, in
some ways, an obvious continuation of the civil rights movement
and personally meaningful for many, it was still marginal to the

daily lives of most Americans, whatever their identity, and rarely touched on the eroding economic status of the working and middle classes. Todd Gitlin later described the conflicts as "marching on the English Department while the right took the White House." No one seemed able to advocate for an inclusive economic vision, except, dishonestly, Reagan, who got to be the tribune of an indivisible America, while the left fought itself.

I learned that Reagan won the election somewhere near Wagon Mound, New Mexico, driving cross-country with a college friend to my first official writing job as a political reporter at a left-wing Santa Barbara newsweekly. When I took the position, I didn't dream I'd be working in the shadow of the new western White House, because I knew Reagan could never be elected. Trying to find early returns on the radio, my friend and I listened over a faint faraway signal to hear Walter Cronkite announce that Jimmy Carter had conceded, at 9:01 Eastern time, 7:01 our time, and 6:01 Pacific time, well before the polls closed in California. It cost Democrats congressional, state, and local races. House Speaker Tip O'Neill, the quintessential liberal Irish pol, told a Carter staffer, "You guys came in like a bunch of pricks, and you're going out the same way."

My friend and I practically skidded off the road at the news of Carter's concession. We found a hotel and then a bar with a television set where we could watch the returns. I was bewildered, even a little scared. Not scared like lefties I knew who claimed they had their passports ready if Reagan was elected. I wasn't Pauline Kael, who famously said she didn't believe Nixon could be elected because she didn't know anyone who voted for him. I knew Reagan voters; they included most of my family. I just didn't believe so many other voters, in other states and other classes and for other reasons, could fall for him. Just as most Democrats did, I had given up on my working-class family; I tuned out their problems and anything they had to say that was legitimate. I was out of touch with the number of people who shared their concerns and blissfully ignorant of what the new Reagan Republicans would impose on the national scene in the coming decades—a full-scaled Republican revolution that used social issues to inflame the people I grew up with, while betraying their economic interests. And the Democrats were so taken up with either selling out their past or catering to the factions inside the party that they conceded the people who had once been a cornerstone of their base to the enemy.

What really scared me was: How could I be a political reporter if I hadn't been able to see Reagan's win coming? How could I be so out of touch? Easy. I certainly wasn't the only one. So self-involved had we Democrats become that few of us saw it coming. I called my father for consolation. He had none. Our liberal Wisconsin senator Gaylord Nelson had lost to Robert Kasten Jr., the underseasoned scion of a wealthy Milwaukee family, who attended Choate, as had Jack Kennedy and Adlai Stevenson.

It was the year of wealthy young winners: A callow Indiana boy with the memorable WASPy name J. Danforth Quayle, beat liberal lion Birch Bayh. Another great liberal, Frank Church, went down in Idaho. And in the country's final insult, George McGovern lost his Senate seat in South Dakota. This wasn't just Reagan's win; it was Richard Nixon's third term. Now McGovern was utterly vanquished. A thrilled Pat Buchanan landed back in the White House, ready to divide and conquer once more.

What an awful time to start a career in the amorphous world of social justice, within which my lefty-founded, collectively run newsweekly, the *Santa Barbara News and Review*, resided. I later realized that Barack Obama shared that experience with me, starting out in community organizing a few years after I became a lefty journalist, and I will tell you that it was politically formative, for me, anyway. Call it the loneliness of the post–civil rights movement, Reagan-era do-gooder. We missed the big party, all the fun, all the meaning, and all the impact.

Those brave civil rights and antiwar activists before us sat down in Woolworth's, marched under blue skies, got beaten by cops, went to jail, and made a difference. We marched down dim corridors of low-rent nonprofits, and rifled through dusty file cabinets; we held meetings in school cafeterias under unforgiving fluorescent lights, trying to figure out what we meant by social change. Committed to consumer lobbying, community organizing, advocacy journalism, we had scant tangible evidence that our work mattered at all. But if it wasn't always rewarding, there was a sense that we could learn from the mistakes of the prior generation—such as riots and cop-killings and bombings—and do things differently, more peacefully and more inclusively, this time around. We were rewriting the sixties, too, in our own way.

At the University of Wisconsin–Madison, I'd tried out political radicalism and worked for the left-wing *Daily Cardinal*, but the leftover campus left spooked me. Long before I got there, the 1970 bombing of the Army-Math Research Center killed a graduate student researcher, Robert Fassnacht (I can still type his name from memory). It blew up the antiwar movement like a crude pipe bomb, its shrapnel taking casualties everywhere. Unbelievably, you could find people still debating the bombing ten years later. I was still too much my father's daughter to accept the amorality and arrogance of the violent faux-revolutionary left, white or black.

A savvy postmovement do-gooder stayed away from that leftover left. At Occidental College, Obama pushed divestment from South Africa (I'd done the same in Madison); at Columbia, he pushed a nuclear freeze (I covered the antinuclear movement). Obama had a brief, frustrating post-Columbia stint at Ralph Nader's New York Public Interest Group (where I once interned, working to encourage recycling by supporting New York's Communist "bottle bill"). Obama went into community organizing, I went into community journalism. Trying to be effective in the Reagan years, we mostly had small dreams.

Republicans under Reagan had the big dreams, especially the dream of a united country whose citizens could move into the future together. You have to admit, their vision was compelling (if you didn't look at the operational details): tame inflation, crush our enemies, and bring prosperity to all. To my left, folks fractured into ever-smaller shards. Then even those caucuses fractured. Fissures of race, class, and sexuality divided the women's movement, so that the influential lesbian feminist theorist and poet Adrienne Rich, whose 1976 *Of Women Born* celebrated newly discovered "forms of primary intensity between and among women," would lament in 1984 that among feminists, "We did not know whom we meant when we said 'we.'"

We still don't.

Reagan put the government firmly on the side of the wealthy, but he gilded his motives with a patina of social conscience. He gave America so many pretty sayings, but when it comes to economic equality, our fortieth president will go down in history for his lyrical lie "The federal government declared a war on poverty, and poverty won."

You didn't have to be grumpy and Nixonian to hate the welfare state anymore; instead, you could project genial optimism and a concern for the poor, as Reagan did. Middle-class folks didn't have to worry that they were indulging resentment, perhaps even racism, by opposing poverty programs; they were doing it because those programs *hurt* poor people; Reagan said so. And if government spending had harmed, not helped, the poor, high tax rates did, too, by discouraging the rich from creating jobs. All could be made right if we just let the wealthy keep their wealth. There may be no more influential bromide than Reagan's lie about the War in Poverty in modern political history.

Of course, Reagan was wrong. Poverty declined sharply after the War on Poverty commenced. According to the Institute for Research on Poverty, in 1959 the individual poverty rate was 22 percent. It hovered there until about 1964, when it began to drop; by 1973, it was 11 percent. There it is again, that magical year, 1973, when everything began to get worse, including poverty; the rate began to climb again, to 15 percent in 1983. Thanks to the economic recovery at the end of Reagan's tenure, it dropped by about a point and then jumped back to 15 percent by the time President Clinton took office. Under Clinton, it fell to 11 percent. Under George W. Bush, it climbed back over 14 percent, and it topped 15 percent under Barack Obama.

It's hard to tease out how much of the drop in poverty in the late sixties was due to government spending and how much was the strong (for a while) economy. Still, the postwar boom only cut the rate by a third, so it seems safe to conclude that the War on Poverty played a role in cutting it in half. We should remember that the Great Society gave the most help to elderly Americans, whose poverty rates dropped even more sharply. For the nonelderly, government assistance helped some but not nearly as much. That's different, however, from saying government programs *hurt* the poor. Mostly, as long as we've measured the poverty rate, it closely tracks the median income and the unemployment rate, except among the elderly. Meaning, "It's the economy, stupid," not, "It's the stupid poverty programs."

The Reagan years saw a boom in flawed research "proving" that welfare itself caused the rise in poor single-female-headed families. Charles Murray's *Losing Ground* marshaled an arsenal of statistics to show that poverty programs, especially what was known as "Aid to Families with Dependent Children," encouraged promiscuity, rewarded the lazy, and destroyed the family—especially the black family. It was the *Moynihan Report* minus the focus on unemployment, the reliable data, and the empathy. Antipoverty scholars fought back, showing that the number of white-female-headed households not on welfare exploded in the same years, making it unlikely that welfare was causing the trend. The share of children born to low-income black single mothers rose sharply at least partly because married black mothers were having many fewer children, not only because single women were having more. Yet thanks to Reagan's sunny claims from his bully presidential pulpit and the right-wing philanthropy spreading Murray's misinformation, the other side prevailed. We fought a war on lies, and lies won.

14

Reagan blindsided us.
　　　　—Dewey Burton, Michigan blue collar "Reagan
　　　　　　Democrat," to author Jefferson Cowie

It's difficult to overstate how much that Reagan-era propaganda about poverty hurt the country. It distorted our understanding of how to help low-income people, as well as our optimism that they could be helped, and it corroded the social contract that had prevailed since the New Deal. Ironically, as Reagan was ranting about the government doing too much for the poor, no one was talking about the real beneficiaries of public largess in those years: the wealthiest Americans. And I'm not just talking about his tax cuts.

Certainly, Reagan's tax cuts did the most damage when it comes to dismantling the machinery of upward mobility. He slashed the top rate from 70 percent to 28 percent, and income inequality has soared ever since. If that top rate of 70 percent sounds high—and it does to those of us who came of age in the 1980s or 1990s—we should remember that at the end of World War II, the top marginal tax rate was 94 percent, and it stayed in the 90s under Republican Dwight Eisenhower. Kennedy slashed it to 70 percent. Those are the tax rates that powered the postwar boom—the expansion of public education and universities, highway construction and home ownership, government-funded research and development—that created what we think of as the American Dream.

Despite his reputation as a tax slasher, Reagan raised taxes three times and tripled the deficit during his eight years in office. Sadly, his working-class "Reagan Democrat" admirers don't seem to remember that he raised payroll taxes for Social Security, Medicare, and disability programs. Those tax hikes hurt poor and middle-class Americans and shielded the wealthy, because people don't have to pay those taxes past a certain upper-middle-class income level. It must be said that Reagan collaborated with Tip O'Neill on those payroll tax hikes in order to strengthen Social Security and Medicare. Even Reagan quickly realized he couldn't touch the pillar of New Deal liberalism, Social Security, or the Great Society's Medicare program, because those universal programs for senior citizens were hugely popular. He could only get away with slashing Great Society programs that benefited the poor.

Reagan began a destructive spiral of concentrating wealth in the hands of fewer people and deregulating business that culminated in the economic crash we're still digging out of today. He even heralded it, by signing the banking deregulation act that waved the "Go" flag on the savings and loan scandal and foreshadowed the repeal of Depression-era Glass-Steagall banking regulations a decade later. Family savings rates began to decline in the Reagan years, while borrowing rates climbed. This is the period when it began to seem as though Big Capital, instead of paying workers higher wages, figured out how to make more money by lending them that cash to stay in the middle class. Under Reagan, income inequality began to grow, household savings dwindled, household debt correspondingly began to rise, and the clout of the financial industry exploded. This trend couldn't continue with anything other than disaster as a result, yet few did anything to stop it.

For all that he helped the rich, Reagan became president with the votes of that working class bloc famously known as "Reagan Democrats": my people. Ground zero for the phenomenon, according to pollsters, wasn't my white ethnic New York homeland but Macomb County, Michigan, a working-class suburb near Detroit that was once known as the most loyal Democratic suburb in the country. Macomb voted 63 percent for JFK in 1960 but went 66 percent for Reagan in 1984.

Pollster Stanley Greenberg made a career out of explaining those Macomb County voters to puzzled Democrats. He concluded that "Reagan Democrats" no longer saw Democrats as champions of the working class. "Blacks constitute the explanation for their vulnerability and for almost everything that has gone wrong in their lives," Greenberg wrote. They saw the government "as a black domain where whites cannot expect reasonable treatment."

In fact, Macomb County had been moving right long before the Reagan landslide. A 1971 forced-busing plan that brought Detroit kids into Macomb provoked a backlash; 66 percent of the county's Democratic voters supported George Wallace in the 1972 primary. Wallace carried the entire state of Michigan that day, the same day he was shot while campaigning in Wisconsin.

We'll never know how much Wallace would have shaped Democratic politics if he'd continued his campaign, by the way. It's a scary thought. The brave Michael Harrington actually talked of uniting a coalition of "the three Georges"—Meany, McGovern, and Wallace—but Harrington was most interested in the populist postshooting Wallace, who renounced his racist past yet still espoused a politics of the economically left behind. That's what it would have taken to put the New Deal coalition back together.

But Harrington was a socialist and a dreamer. No such coalition was possible in his lifetime, and maybe not in mine.

It's possible that Reagan's greatest contribution to income inequality wasn't his high-end tax cuts, but the way he took all of the air out of the labor movement when he fired the striking air traffic controllers in 1981. It's not that the Professional Air Traffic Controllers Organization (PATCO) was an enormous union, but it symbolized a problem for labor that Republicans recognized before Democrats did: as unions lost power in the private sector, their only gains were coming in the public sector, and this divided the working class even more, into labor haves and have-nots. Ironically, PATCO had been one of the few unions to endorse Reagan.

The collapse of the manufacturing sector took a lot of those union jobs. A corporate campaign of union busting and union decertification eroded organized labor's private-sector strength even more. Labor leaders never had been terribly creative about organizing either the service sector or the growing ranks of white-collar workers, who, for a while at least, felt themselves superior to brawny union members, convinced that they were doing brainwork that required flexibility and that they would be rewarded by grateful employers.

The one place organized labor enjoyed continued success was in government. In the sixties and the seventies, the public sector was growing, and so were public sector unions—unions that tended to include more women and minorities, too. Gradually, the rise in public employee unions, combined with the diminishing of private sector unions, made "unions" just another symbol of government, as well as of the rising workforce power of women and minorities. (By 2010, black men were most likely to be represented by unions; 14.8 percent of black male workers were union members, compared with 12.5 percent of white men, 10 percent of Latino men, and 9.4 percent of Asian men.)

Eventually, as private-sector unions shrank, more Americans paid for their own health insurance benefits, and pensions became employee-funded 401(k)s, the dominance of public sector unions would almost seem a form of welfare state redistribution—in which my tax dollars are paying for *your* health insurance and pensions. In busting PATCO, Reagan relied on an early sense that working-class have-nots were coming to resent unionized working-class haves who relied on Big Government.

Yet even as he was posing as a free-market conservative, Reagan's economic policy was anything but free market. Paul Volcker's Fed helped bring on the 1982 recession by choking off the money supply, as a radical cure for inflation. It worked, but unemployment climbed from 7.5 percent to close to 10 percent by the 1982 midterms. After that, Volcker helped ease the recession by loosening the money supply again, and Reagan's hike in defense spending became a hidden form of stimulus. The Reagan boom began. Few Democrats seemed to notice that the right-wing president they denounced for free-market cruelty to the poor and the working class had become a stealth military Keynesian.

I wasn't long for Santa Barbara. After two years, I moved to Chicago (the future president wasn't there yet) to work for the self-described "independent socialist newspaper" *In These Times*. I wasn't sure that made me a socialist, but I admired founder James Weinstein's commitment to tell the truth about his politics and to try to redeem the term. Far from being sectarian, the wry, rumpled, independently wealthy, radical pragmatist looked for signs of left-wing life anywhere there might be a glimmer of it: feminism, gay rights, environmentalism.

Yet deep down, Weinstein believed that unions and the Congressional Black Caucus were the only hopes for the institutional left, though he wasn't terribly romantic about their chances of forming a majority anytime soon. Still, he persevered. I'd landed in a place that reinforced my father's earliest political lessons: that the interests of black people and the working class didn't have to be, and in fact should never be, in conflict. Weinstein also made me realize how unusual my political views were, given my background. At *In These Times*, people were always assuming I was a "red diaper baby" from some left-wing activist family, given my eccentric ideas and passions. No, I'd tell them, my father was a former Christian Brother with no left-wing affiliations, just Catholic values.

My stubborn belief in the possibility and power of a black-labor alliance seemed to be rewarded, right there and then in Chicago, by Harold Washington's unbelievable mayoral campaign in 1983—which was the happiest political experience of my lifetime, at least until Obama's election. Putting a blue Washington button on your coat and persevering through that bitter Chicago winter, you didn't feel the cold. Elegant black women smiled at you on Michigan Avenue. Bus drivers held doors open, rather than pulling away. I didn't venture very far beyond my shabby fringe of Lakeshore liberal territory, so I rarely witnessed the hatred Washington encountered. The Chicago that politically vanquished Dr. King hadn't gone away with Mayor Daley's demise.

When Washington won the primary, a stunning number of white Chicago Democrats, many of them Irish Catholics, abandoned their party to vote for Bernie Epton, who morphed from liberal Republican to George Wallace overnight. Remember those Sarah Palin rallies with people carrying monkeys named Obama and folks yelling "Kill him!" and "Terrorist!"? Epton rallies were like that, only more menacing. Walter Mondale went with Washington to a Catholic church on Easter Sunday, walking through a door spray-painted with the words "Nigger Die," while throngs of protesters chanted "Blacks go home." Mondale and Washington had to leave early for their safety. The vice president said later that it was one of the scariest political experiences of his life. I've never been so ashamed of my people.

Washington won, if way too narrowly in Democratic Chicago, and the Washington coalition—blacks, labor, progressive whites and Latinos, feminists, gay rights groups—seemed to herald the politics that would end Reaganism. It inspired Jesse Jackson's Rainbow Coalition run for president the next year. He won 3.2 million votes—almost 20 percent of the total—and won primaries or caucuses in South Carolina, Virginia, Louisiana, Mississippi, and the District of Columbia.

Jackson's campaign blew up for a while when he was caught referring to New York as "Hymietown," and all of the old angst about black anti-Semitism tainted his candidacy and stunted his potential coalition. Still, his run made history, and he was the star of the 1984 Democratic National Convention in San Francisco, in which he asked forgiveness for errors he'd made with the historic coda "God isn't finished with me yet," summoning a little bit of the moral majesty of the civil rights movement.

It was my first convention, so maybe I can be forgiven for thinking it represented a new start for Democrats, a healing of the wounds of the sixties and the seventies. Along with Jackson, the convention featured two other inspiring leaders, both of them white ethnic New Yorkers, veterans of the racial politics that had turned so many of their community into Reagan Democrats. There was Mario Cuomo of Queens, who'd come out of the ugly battle over low-income housing there. The next night featured the historic Democratic vice presidential nominee Geraldine Ferraro, the first woman on a national ticket. The new vice presidential nominee sounded Cuomo and Jackson's themes of unity in her convention speech: "The daughter of an immigrant from Italy has been chosen to run for vice president in the new land my father came to love."

Walter Mondale didn't pick Ferraro merely for her female credentials alone; being a so-called white ethnic helped her too. She represented the fictional Archie Bunker's district in Queens, that neighborhood nationally known for its bungalows and (to liberals) its backward views about race and the rapidly changing times. Mondale hoped she'd woo back those voters from the "Catholic sidewalks of New York" whom Kevin Phillips had lured to Nixon. The idea that an urban woman could lure back an increasingly suburban male working class seems silly now, but it passed for smart politics at the time.

Each night I stood in a multiracial crowd of activists and union members, some in tears, fervent Democrats thrilling to the words of reunion and redemption from Jackson, Cuomo, and Ferraro. The labor movement energy impressed me. I was there with a friend who was trying to reorganize air traffic controllers in the wake of Reagan crushing their union. It felt as if we were finally putting the Democratic Party back together again after 1968. Of course, Mondale would lose to Reagan more lopsidedly than Carter did, carrying only Minnesota and the District of Columbia. He had assembled the proto-Obama coalition, only about a quarter century too early.

It's not that Mondale didn't try to contest Reagan on economic grounds. He actually talked a lot about the need for a "national

industrial policy," to deal with the very real problems of manufacturing decline and working-class job losses. But it seemed wonky,
bureaucratic, and unnecessary at a time when Reagan's free-
market boom seemed to validate his hands-off approach. Nobody
paid much attention to the fact that Reagan's boom was kicked
off by stealth Keynesianism: Paul Volcker loosened up the money
supply and ended the recession he'd helped induce by tightening
it, and that cheaper money, combined with new defense spending, helped create jobs again. Unemployment fell from 9.5 to 7.2
percent by Election Day. That still wasn't Morning in America
for the unemployed, but it made Mondale's talk about a troubled
economy requiring government support seem like tired old liberalism. Why were Democrats trying to fix something that didn't
seem broken?

I was bewildered by Mondale's crushing loss. What was I still missing about American politics? So I left journalism for a while and
went to work for the California State Assembly Human Services
Committee, the poor people's committee, handling welfare,
child-care, and foster-care legislation under Republican governor
George Deukmejian.

Of course, I was running in the wrong direction, because politics was becoming less about policy and more about culture, but
I learned a lot anyway. I had to grapple with Republicans for
the first time in my life (outside my family). The big issue before
the state legislature was welfare reform. I'll never forget watching an exchange between a GOP assemblyman on my committee and a welfare mom who was testifying about why welfare
reform was bad for families. The Republican used the language
of feminism—women had to work now, his own wife worked,
it was a new world of choice! When the welfare recipient asked,
"Why can't I *choose* to stay home with my kids?" he answered
flatly, "That's one choice you don't have, ma'am."

As a committee consultant, I sometimes attended constituent
meetings in Oakland and Berkeley to hear concerns about welfare

reform and other social policies. It was 1986, but people seemed stuck in the sixties, the bad version of the sixties that I'd missed. In some meetings, men were asked to leave so that women could talk freely. At times, whites would have to exit so that blacks had the space to talk without whites. I didn't always see the point. White men still had most of the power, and if we didn't learn to work with and confront them directly, our separate strength had less meaning. Also, as a feminist, I never understood marginalizing or humiliating male allies to make a separatist point; the men who came to these meetings were trying to make common cause; why shut them out? In at least two different Oakland meetings, heavily attended by welfare-rights groups, the very same African American woman stood up, as if on cue, pointed to me sitting with the decision-makers, and said angrily, "There's only one reason you're sitting there, and I'm standing here." No one needed to spell out the reason: that I was white. I understood her anger, but it felt like theater, not practical politics intended to bring about change. (I also noticed that "minorities" always singled out other "minorities" at such times. Why didn't she suggest an older white male colleague had taken the place that should have been hers?)

Occasionally, doing my work, I ran into the worst nightmares of the Reagan coalition. I remember interviewing a teenage welfare recipient for a magazine article I hoped would show that a new bipartisan wave of welfare reform was bad for mothers and children. The young woman talked openly about getting pregnant with a second child to increase her welfare check and move higher on the waiting list for Section 8 housing. She ignored her adorable toddler son while we talked, except to scream at him when he interrupted us. As we said good-bye, I remember watching her lock that chubby, flailing, adorable little boy into a way-too-small car seat, and the click of the lock reminded me of handcuffs. That girl wasn't the norm, by any means, but it was impossible not to notice that without jobs or capital to start businesses or student grants for college, welfare was one of the few lifelines to cash in her abandoned neighborhood (the other was drugs). It would be stupid not to play the system.

Again, I found myself wondering why we'd ever believed that poor women, especially poor black women, would be supported (however stingily) in raising their children at home, when most mothers were surging to work, because the new economy required an extra paycheck to keep families afloat. I was beginning to believe that "empowering" welfare recipients, the mantra of the constituency groups we heard from, required getting them good jobs, child care, and health care and bringing them out of the economic shadows, where they'd been alone and vulnerable for too long. I wouldn't admit it at the time, but I was starting to agree with Daniel Patrick Moynihan that we were wrong to "pension off" the most vulnerable Americans, that our fight ought to have been for jobs and inclusion. My questions would only get louder.

California Democrats soon joined with Deukmejian in passing landmark welfare reform legislation, which included work requirements for some mothers, nine years before Bill Clinton passed a federal reform law. Ronald Reagan's state was leading again politically, this time with Democrats on board.

I hated Sacramento politics, but I liked my life. I met a kind, smart-aleck liberal lawyer at a political fund-raiser, and within a year we were engaged. He was Jewish, and I wondered whether that would bother my father at all. My father loved Robert. About two months after I told my dad I was getting married, he was diagnosed with late-stage cancer of the esophagus and was given four to six months to live. Robert and I moved up our wedding date to well within the dismal window the doctors gave my father, but he still couldn't travel. So we went to him. We got married in his yard by a local judge, my father in a wheelchair, in front of our siblings, Robert's parents, and my Aunt Peggy. My father's brothers had booked tickets to San Francisco for our planned wedding day to cheer their dying brother, an enormously generous thing to do. Though my father couldn't make it to San Francisco, they came anyway, so we flew back to have the wedding reception we had planned, without my father. Then we returned to honeymoon in my father's hospice-outfitted home.

The last month was hell and then sometimes heaven. Friends and family came from everywhere. Aunt Peggy had moved in to take care of my father when he first got sick. My brother and sister and I stayed full-time; aunts and uncles came and went. Our friend Joe drove from Milwaukee to say good-bye. We listened to Frank Sinatra and Miles Davis and talked constantly. One of us was always up with him. It's still one of my favorite memories and one of the most painful. He had the kind of home base he wanted, if only for a few days. In fact, I did, too.

Before he got too sick to watch television, during the day we'd follow the Iran Contra hearings, which cheered him up a little. John Dean had described the Watergate cover-up as a "cancer on the presidency"; battling the chaos of cancer, my father was soothed by the orderly processes of law: the hearing, the swearing-in, the congressional interrogators rooting out the lawlessness of Oliver North and his enablers. My father believed justice would be done here, if not in his own life, and Reagan would be brought down as Nixon was. He didn't live to find out that Reagan got through it unscathed.

Losing my father, I also lost the political world he created, where his black-Irish fairytale meant you didn't have to choose between the political interests of black people or my Irish working-class family. My father may have been the last person to live on both sides of Nixonland. Certainly, I had come to feel that I needed to choose sides, and I chose to work on issues of racial justice and to put class behind me. On some level, I was in the process of becoming the kind of elite do-gooder my father distrusted, proving my own moral superiority by championing the rights of African Americans and looking down on my "racist" kinfolk. At least for a while.

The fact was, many of my people did, over and over, vote against their class interests to try to go backward, and inward, to take refuge in their culture. A culture in which the sixties never happened: divorce rates didn't rise, abortion stayed illegal, drugs remained in bohemia, kids obeyed their parents—and nobody got something for nothing. The result was, nobody got nothing, to use the working-class vernacular of my childhood, except the very rich. Nixon's strategy of "cultural recognition" continued: Republicans such as Reagan pitched themselves as working-class heroes, even as they shook down the working class to redistribute wealth to the wealthiest.

The blue-collar pride of the white working class had itself become an empty form of identity politics, all about symbolism, relying on an imagined cohesion, ignoring the way a new corporate elite, not blacks or liberals or feminists, was grinding them down and obliterating their way of life. But if the Republicans manipulated them, the Democrats mostly ignored them. The party of the New Deal was in the process of becoming the party of Wall Street. We'd all be the poorer for it.

15

If you convince them I don't have any conviction, that's
fine, but it's a damn lie. It's a lie.
—President Bill Clinton to *Rolling Stone*'s
William Greider, November 1993

Losing my father, I lost my liberal optimism for a while. I
wound up internalizing Reaganism, at least a little, asking, What if we were wrong? What if our side helped trigger the
Reagan backlash—not just the left's violent dead-enders, but also
good liberals, with our zeal for government programs and our
inattention to their unintended consequences? If poverty programs hadn't made poverty worse, in many communities, especially isolated urban neighborhoods, they hadn't made things
all that much better. In fact, parts of inner-city America looked
worse than in the 1960s, a result not of poverty programs but of
the profound changes transforming the economy and politics that
the left hardly talked about.

Unionized jobs for people with a high school diploma or less
were disappearing. Wages had flattened for all but the highest
earners. Families made do by sending a second earner into the
workforce, but they were running out of folks to send to work.
Now they had begun the process of borrowing the money they
would have been earning, had wages continued to rise the way
they did from 1947 to 1972. That rising household debt, encouraged by the way government kept interest rates low and bank regulations flimsy, would culminate in the financial sector meltdown
of 2008. Yet very few of us were paying attention back then.

Two things saved me from political nihilism: a new generation of civil rights activists working pragmatically but passionately on urban poverty and, later, the presidency of Bill Clinton. A scrappy kid from Hope, Arkansas, who had never known his father, Clinton was a kind of working-class hero. Although he, too, would cozy up to Wall Street and court business, Clinton tilted the balance of power at least a little bit back toward the besieged middle and working classes. He determined to use government to make people's lives better—if he could do it in stealthy ways, people wouldn't recognize it as a Big Government move, so he could get away with it. Yet even the pragmatic centrist met a new kind of radical Republican opposition determined to protect what they'd accomplished on behalf of plutocracy in the seventies and the eighties.

If Reagan's "We fought a war on poverty and poverty won" formulation was the single most influential Republican lie of the 1980s, the work of scholar William Julius Wilson provided the most effective and influential pushback. The University of Chicago labor-market expert catalyzed a new wave of activism with a series of books showing how the decline of work in black communities—particularly, decent-paying jobs for those with only a high school education—was the real reason poverty was winning again.

Wilson's first book, *The Declining Significance of Race*, made the provocative case that the troubles of the black urban poor deepened after integration opened new doors for the black middle class. He called Daniel Patrick Moynihan's work on the Negro family "important and prophetic"; he even used the term *pathology* that got Moynihan in so much trouble. Trying to bring a class focus back to discussions about race and poverty, he labeled the black urban poor an "underclass." Those rhetorical decisions would get Wilson thrown in with the "blaming the victim" crowd for a while.

Some leading black academics attacked the book, partly because Wilson seemed to suggest that those achievers had won their battle against racism—of course, they hadn't—without helping the black poor. Part of Wilson's argument was that black middle-class success—his own success; Wilson's family had relied on welfare—unintentionally *hurt* the poor, because when middle-class African Americans left the inner city, they took a lot of social, political, and economic capital with them. He wasn't attacking those professionals for moving up; that was the American way. He was calling attention to the world they left behind, which was many times more isolated and disabled by the effects of poverty than when Moynihan sounded the alarm in 1965. The Association of Black Sociologists tried to block Wilson from receiving the American Sociological Association's top honor because of the book's "misrepresentation of the black experience."

Wilson put his analysis more carefully in his 1987 book *The Truly Disadvantaged*, and backed it up with meticulous research on the disappearance of work in the inner city; it was transformational. The scholar also came out of the closet as a social Democrat, calling for new investment in job training and public works programs, which he hadn't been willing to do when *The Declining Significance of Race* came out. Blurbs on the back of *The Truly Disadvantaged* included those of socialist Michael Harrington, as well as Moynihan, two influential Irish Americans whose call for jobs programs for the urban poor had been ignored by Lyndon Johnson and Sargent Shriver more than twenty years earlier.

The Truly Disadvantaged used data to move the debate back to larger structural changes in the economy, particularly the loss of manufacturing jobs for workers who didn't go to college, a trend that was also hurting the white working class. He exposed the way a decline in black male employment tracked with rising rates of single parenthood, teen pregnancy, youth unemployment, and violent crime, with a particular focus on his city of Chicago, which had coincidentally just become Barack Obama's hometown. He didn't win everyone over with his new work; Obama's own pastor, Rev. Jeremiah Wright, would call Wilson another of those "miseducated black brothers" who blamed the victim and let whites off the hook for their racism.

Despite the carping of critics such as Wright, Wilson's work inspired a new generation of African American activists and advocates, from Savannah, Georgia, to Oakland, California, to tackle the cluster of problems that contributed to persistent poverty—single parenthood, high dropout rates, chronic health troubles, and problems that started even earlier, such as babies born at low birth weight. They traced it not to culture or character, but to an economy that had left people behind. I joined a visionary group in Oakland, the Urban Strategies Council, which introduced the city to Wilson's analysis with data showing that the disappearance of manufacturing jobs and the skyrocketing rates of poverty and sin-gle-headed households tracked closely in Oakland, too.

There was a strong personal appeal to Wilson's work for this new generation of community builders, and for me, too. Many black middle-class reformers welcomed his message as a catalyst to get reinvolved in the neighborhoods that success had allowed them to leave behind. An analysis developed around Wilson's work, that along with jobs and investment, neighborhoods of chronic poverty lacked "social capital." I knew that a web of churches, community groups, small businesses, and unions had helped my family climb from poverty to the working middle class in their little Irish village of Highbridge in the Bronx; a com-parable network of teachers, entrepreneurs, artists, and unions helped produce a growing black middle class within segregated communities. But when successful white and black families left those neighborhoods, they took many of those advantages with them. This was my father's old message, in a way. The work put black urban poverty on a continuum of economic disadvantage that connected it to white urban poverty, which we'd made great strides in reducing.

So I loved working with this new band of community build-ers, on the issue of African American poverty, the issue I'd always cared most about. I had an unusual gig "documenting" this work for foundations, scholars, and other activists. I got to interview both new and old local civil rights leaders—the heroes who'd kept working in poor black communities, even after the nation's atten-tion wandered away, as well as people who'd left and come back. I met teachers, youth workers, nurses, shop owners, academics, and activists whose faith hadn't wavered despite years of social neglect and local despair. I made a close group of friends, too, most of them black.

In those years after my father died, I figured out what had always resonated with me about African American culture. Most black people seemed to know a truth that I'd had to learn on my own after losing my parents: life is heartbreakingly unfair—and it's not our fault. A long history of suffering and oppression helped African Americans develop a cosmology that makes sense of injustice and misfortune and offers the strength to persevere. White people in trouble can find themselves alone, stuck with an individualist American culture in which bad fortune may seem not only deserved but also contagious. Every black person knows that life is deeply unjust, while a remarkable number of white people seemed to me to skate through huge portions of their lives unscathed, unmarked, unaware of the stacked hand they've been dealt.

I'd lost my mother in my teens, my father as I got married, and now I had a baby girl who would never know her amazing grandparents. I'd developed a dangerous self-pity streak; I needed a kick out of the world I'd locked myself into, where everything was about me. The Prayer of St. Francis had hung on the wall of my home while I was growing up, and both of my parents emphasized the words *"it is in giving that we receive."* I'd been taught that God made us a perfect world, with one sad flaw: it's unfair and indifferent to suffering. So justice, along with art, is our job; it's what we're here for. I felt as if I were doing the work I was born to do.

The national picture looked brighter, too. Along came Bill Clinton. I didn't much like the political movement he came from, the Democratic Leadership Council (DLC), founded in the wake of the Mondale debacle as part of the Democratic effort to look more Republican or, at least, less like themselves. DLC leaders believed that being "the party of government" had hurt the Democrats, and it was time to acknowledge that government programs weren't always the answer and that government made mistakes. No one could argue with that.

Yet the DLC made a couple of other sly maneuvers. Trying to get beyond the party infighting of the previous two decades, they simply declared themselves the winners. The group took a tough line on problems of crime, welfare dependency, and single motherhood, largely to lure back working- and middle-class Reagan Democrats. But they paid little or no attention to the chronic unemployment or the intergenerational poverty that created those "pathologies." They wanted white working-class voters to know that they were no longer, as pollster Stanley Greenberg had put it, the "black" party. Yet in trying to address the legitimate concerns of those voters—that the economy was getting worse, and government was not only not helping, but might be contributing to the decline—they essentially conceded the economic fairness argument to the Republican Party. The DLC didn't respond to white working- and middle-class voters' well-founded fears that they were losing their hold on security by proposing a new government role in growing the economy; they just reassured them that unworthy people wouldn't keep getting help, while co-opting the GOP's procorporate agenda.

Those post-Reagan reformers were also trying to make the party competitive in the South again. Most early leaders—from Louisiana's John Breaux to Tennessee's Al Gore to Arkansas governor Bill Clinton—were Southerners. That strategy didn't work, however; Democrats continued to lose ground in the South. Where the DLC succeeded was in making Democrats a probusiness party. The group played a huge role in helping Democrats catch up with Republicans in corporate fund-raising. The DLC offered "retreats" with its powerful elected officials, where corporate leaders could mingle with the party's rising stars. They pushed tax cuts and deficit reduction and framed "entitlements," those great Democratic legacy programs such as Social Security and Medicare, as a looming problem.

The DLC got one thing right: its leaders wanted to contest Republicans to be the party that made the economy run better. In the words of DLC founder Al From, "Its centerpiece was economic growth, not redistribution." The problem was, they too often pushed the same old Republican solutions. And the growing power of the DLC created a "fundamental, revealing asymmetry between the parties," as political science professors Jacob Hacker and Paul Pierson observed. Democrats suddenly had a probusiness force pulling the party right. It wasn't as though they were proposing innovative economic ideas and collecting corporate dollars on the basis of their bold new approach. They were borrowing ideas from corporate America and its right-wing think tanks and tailoring their platform to attract corporate dollars, in order to take them away from Republicans. The GOP had no comparable ideologically moderating force; in fact, it was skidding even farther right. So the center of American economic debate lurched to the right, where it remains today.

The DLC's preaching about "sacrifice" and "responsibility" and its castor-oil approach to politics and citizenship would never have put together a winning national coalition without Bill Clinton. His working-class Arkansas background, his roots in the civil rights and antiwar movements, his formative experiences in George McGovern's sad, brave campaign: all of those things let Clinton appeal to African Americans and to the Democratic left, while reassuring the DLC wing that he could rein in the party's too-liberal base and restrain its zeal for government activism. Speechwriter Michael Waldman called him "a one-man coalition."

We laugh at Clinton's "I feel your pain" politics, but an enormous part of his draw was that he believably empathized with both African Americans and the white working class, the estranged partners in that once-great New Deal political marriage. He had cultural affinity with both. He tried to offer the "cultural recognition" that Nixon pioneered but to both groups, not merely to the white working class, as well as race-neutral programs for economic opportunity that might arguably help black people more because they had the highest poverty rates.

The April 1992 Los Angeles riots offered Clinton a platform on which to demonstrate his DLC-with-a-heart approach. It didn't go entirely smoothly. Like so many other urban uprisings before it, the LA violence was triggered by police brutality—in that case, the acquittal of four white cops whose savage beating of a black man named Rodney King was caught on videotape. Also, like so many riots before it, the LA conflict engulfed mainly black neighborhoods—but it also featured scenes of violence by African Americans against whites, Latinos, and Asians. At the end of the four days, fifty-three people were dead, thousands more wounded.

Clinton headed to Los Angeles to tour the scenes of destruction with Representative Maxine Waters, who represented the area in Congress. Whereas President Bush denounced the "anarchy" as "purely criminal" and never bothered to visit, Clinton blamed the Reagan-Bush administrations for "more than a decade of urban decay," intensified by federal spending cuts. After Bush press secretary Marlin Fitzwater blamed the unrest on "the Great Society," Clinton shot back, "Republicans have had the White House for twenty of the last twenty-four years, and they have to go all the way back to the sixties to find somebody to blame. I want to do something about the problems." No white Democrat had talked back to the race-baiting right that way in a long time.

Yet the LA riots also provided the backdrop to one of the most controversial racial moves of Clinton's campaign, one that seemed straight out of the DLC playbook, when he attacked rapper Sister Souljah for the disturbing antiwhite remarks she made to the *Washington Post*. She called the LA violence a "war," a "rebellion," and "revenge." And when the *Post* reporter asked her about the black-on-white violence, she famously answered, "If Black people kill Black people every day, why not have a week and kill white people?" Could black people ever be condemned for violence in the name of "revenge"? the reporter asked. She said no. "I don't think that anything we can do to white people could ever even equal up to what they've done to us. I really don't."

Her interviewer, *Post* writer David Mills, was disturbed by Souljah's comments. Her empathy for the rioters, he wrote, reached a "chilling extreme." I am not sure many people noted at the time that Mills himself was black. The hugely gifted Mills later became a writer for David Simon's black urban chronicles, including *Homicide*, *The Corner*, *The Wire*, and *Treme*. He won two Emmys before he died of an aneurism at forty-eight in 2010.

A month after Sister Souljah horrified David Mills, she and Bill Clinton addressed Jesse Jackson's Rainbow Coalition, a day apart. Clinton used the opportunity to rebuke the rapper in what became known as his famous Sister Souljah moment. "If you took the words 'white' and 'black,' and you reversed them," he said about her comments to Mills, "you might think David Duke was giving that speech." Souljah's remarks, he told the Rainbow Coalition, "are filled with a hatred you do not honor."

It's hard to find anything wrong with what Clinton said, but his remarks touched off the worst racial conflict of the campaign. The *New York Times* liberal columnist Anthony Lewis laid bare the racial divide, even among liberals, over Clinton's statement. Lewis applauded it; rhetoric such as Souljah's should be attacked by all of us, he believed. But then Lewis talked to writer and civil rights activist Roger Wilkins, who was furious—at the slight to Jesse Jackson, not to Sister Souljah. In fact, Wilkins told Lewis, Jackson had himself challenged Souljah's remarks when she spoke to the Rainbow Coalition a night earlier. "In that context Clinton's speech was arrogant, and it was cheap," Wilkins charged. "He came there to show suburban whites that he can stand up to blacks. It was contrived." Harlem representative Charlie Rangel compared it to the GOP's using Willie Horton against Michael Dukakis.

A seething Jesse Jackson said Clinton's remarks "again exposed a character flaw." Jackson insisted that the Arkansas governor decided to "stage a very well-planned sneak attack, without the courage to confront but with a calculation to embarrass" him— and threatened to support H. Ross Perot. Howard University political analyst Ron Walters urged blacks to vote in November but to boycott the top of the ticket, over Clinton's courting of white voters at the expense of blacks.

To this day, it's not clear whether white working-class voters even noticed Clinton's rebuke of Sister Souljah or Jesse Jackson. His campaign's famous motto "It's the economy, stupid" had much more demonstrable sway. It signaled his understanding that Democrats got in trouble when they ceded economic competence to the Republicans and got mired instead in battles over race and culture. And while yes, Clinton spoke that DLC language of "responsibility," he won the election by promising to build "a bridge to the twenty-first century" with government investments in education, job training, child care, and, most famously and futilely, health care.

In 1992, Clinton didn't quite succeed in luring the white working class back to Democrats, even though he'd hired Stan Greenberg; he lost Macomb County, along with that bloc nationally. Yet he did better with that group than Mondale or Dukakis had (and by 1996, he won Macomb County). Clinton seemed to have put most of the old New Deal coalition back together. The perception that he had courted white voters at the expense of blacks may have hurt him with black voters, however; he got a solid 83 percent of the black vote in 1992, but that was a drop from the 90 percent-plus support won by Jimmy Carter, Walter Mondale, and Michael Dukakis. That old tension would come back to haunt Clinton's wife in 2008.

Personally, I loved Bill Clinton, except when I didn't. I thought a lot of his trouble with the political and media establishment had to do with his working-class "Bubba" background—but he gave his enemies a lot to work with, thanks to a lack of self-discipline, or maybe it was flat-out self-destruction. I've seen that a lot in working-class people who rise.

People can argue that Clinton sold the party's soul to corporate America and Wall Street; I've thought that way myself. He gave an enormous gift to the banking industry with the repeal of Depression-era Glass-Steagall regulations, which separated investment from commercial banking and kept in check the kind of risk-taking and corruption that brought down the economy in 2008. It may well have been the worst domestic move of his presidency; Clinton says he regrets it himself. The party became more dependent on Wall Street campaign cash on his watch. His early missteps on health-care reform and gays in the military have been widely cataloged.

Yet he also faced an immediate and debilitating right-wing backlash from congressional Republicans. Clinton disappointed much of his liberal base when, after his election, he took the DLC line on the budget deficit, listening to his treasury secretary (and future Citibank head), Robert Rubin. Cutting the deficit, not investing in the "bridge to the twenty-first century" infrastructure he had promised, became his first priority. But even Clinton's bipartisan, DLC-crafted, deficit-cutting policies couldn't placate Republicans. Faced with a sluggish economy, he tried to push a small stimulus bill during his first months in office, and he was blocked by Republicans—as well as by conservative Democrats, foreshadowing President Obama's wrangle with "Blue Dogs" in his party sixteen years later. Balancing the budget with program cuts and tax hikes the next year, he got zero Republican votes for tax increases. His display of political courage was rewarded by seeing Democrats lose control of Congress in the next election.

Maybe more important, Clinton faced a ferocious political assault from what his wife called "a vast right-wing conspiracy," abetted by the mainstream media. It's hard to say which was more damaging to Clinton's presidency, though—his famous far-right antagonists or their media enablers. Banking scion Richard Mellon Scaife and Christian Right leader Jerry Falwell, among others, peddled a scurrilous string of lies—that Clinton was involved in drug running, murder, and even the death of his close friend Vince Foster, all of which was hugely influential on the right. Yet the right wing's attempted Clinton takedowns didn't have the influence of the mainstream media's relentless focus on nonscandals such as Whitewater, the firing of travel-office employees, or allegedly unethical Chinese fund-raising. The *New York Times* and the *Washington Post* treated the Clintons as ethics-challenged yahoos from the beginning. Looking back, the hyper-critical, allegedly liberal *New York Times* editorial pages editor Howell Raines may have hurt the president as much as the vengeful Republican independent counsel Kenneth Starr did.

There was such a clear class bias in the way the elite treated the president: many Washington mandarins saw Clinton as trailer trash. He hadn't learned to control his appetites, whether for cheeseburgers or women, or to at least have the manners to hide them. Later, the *Washington Post*'s Sally Quinn wrote a stunning obituary for the Clinton years in which she revealed that a resentful "Washington Establishment" spent the eight Clinton years feeling that "their town has been turned upside down" by the Rude First Couple. "He came in here and he trashed the place," said the late *Washington Post* columnist David Broder, "and it's not his place."

"It's not his place." If there's ever been a better example of the Washington Establishment's class bias, I can't think of one. The great blogger Digby used Quinn's piece to label clueless Beltway mandarins "the Villagers." The Villagers' obsession with Clinton bordered on madness. For some, it was a way to prove their own fitness for fine Washington society. Sally Quinn, for instance, married the *Washington Post*'s Ben Bradlee after they'd had an affair, and she was widely, perhaps unfairly, blamed for wrecking his marriage. So she became the spokesperson for all that was right and proper in the Village. Howell Raines of the *New York Times* was a Southerner like Clinton, but he came from a wealthy elite family (he would win a Pulitzer Prize for telling the story of what his family's black maid taught him, "a pampered white boy," about race). There seemed to be class friction between Raines and Clinton.

From all sides, there was a sense that this hillbilly interloper didn't know his place; that he was disgracing himself and Washington with his bad manners. What was worse, he seemed to enjoy himself, without shame. So they would shame him.

No organized left rose to defend Clinton, even though he retained his popularity with the American people, right through impeachment; in fact, his popularity only climbed.

16

In the metaphor wars of the post-Reagan years, Democrats could not agree on a common story. They did not march onward together toward an extension of rights or a rally of the whole people; they did not march on together, period.
—Todd Gitlin, *Twilight of Common Dreams*, 1995

I didn't pay close attention to Clinton's travails early in his presidency; I was busy creating a new multicultural world for myself and creating a family, too. Like a lot of people, I found myself preoccupied by the transition from child to parent. I developed a new political identity on a local scale, trying to make sense of the multiracial Bay Area, as a writer but also as a parent, trying to understand local institutions such as schools and child-care centers, putting together the building blocks of adult life. I was still busy with community-building work, but increasingly I was looking inward, trying to square my life as I was living it with my values. They didn't always line up neatly.

We had named our daughter Nora, after searching for a name with both Irish and Jewish roots—thank you, Nora Ephron! I realized how thoroughly I'd transformed myself one Friday afternoon, sitting on a tiny chair at a tiny table at my daughter's preschool, eating challah the kids had baked themselves, drinking grape juice, and singing Shabbat songs. I realized I was as observant a Jew as I was a Catholic. Nora attended a wonderful Jewish Community Center preschool, and I never missed Shabbat. I held on to what my father told me: Heaven isn't a country club. God is where you find him. Or her. God made a point of attending

Friday Shabbat at the JCC. And so did I. Here I was, the Irish Catholic girl, celebrating Shabbat more often than I went to Mass.

At the JCC preschool Nora had a rainbow of friends, about half of them Jewish. Some of their silly Shabbat songs had been written by Nora's Chinese American teacher, George. I saw it there: Jews know how to do community. They know how to do inclusion, of everybody. They're the mixers. They've been forced to be, by history; outbreaks of religious or ethnic chauvinism and purity don't usually turn out well for the Jews. I know about Jewish tribalism, but it's less common than Jewish generosity. Sure, that's stereotyping, but I had a Jewish best friend, a Jewish husband, and that's the world I lived in.

I was mostly happy—except when I felt lost. My life in the public world hadn't done anything to prepare me for my private world. After I got married and had a daughter, the feminism I'd grown up with had no lessons for me. I knew how to be separate, not engaged. I was great at independence, yet motherhood makes you dependent on a partner or on someone, at least for a while. Feminism had lots of advice for thinking about me, but none for thinking about "we," the bewildering realm of family, husband, and children—except not to think about it at all. All of those years we'd fought for the choice not to have children, we hadn't done much to help women when they did. I'm glad we have abortion rights; I wish we had more help with child care, too.

I found myself in my early thirties with a baby I loved to distraction, a career I treasured almost as much (yes, I said almost), and a marriage coming undone at least partly due to my bewilderment and resentment at being unable to manage both gracefully. I wanted to be home, I wanted to be working, and nothing in my feminist reading or debates had prepared me for the pull in both directions. Not working made me feel like my mother; working too much, I missed my daughter.

My discomfort with identity politics began to emerge around the same time, and there's probably a connection: I was having my own identity crisis. I wasn't sure I wanted to foist my own black-and-white, good-and-evil narrative on my innocent, half-Jewish baby girl. And our historic civil rights model didn't entirely make sense anymore in a world where Latinos and Asians were the fastest-growing minorities.

My parents were gone, and what I knew of their early years together—my father's coming out of Christian Brothers exile, their early adjustment troubles, his alcoholism, her anger—didn't help either. Would I have been better prepared to navigate those early years with better models? The fact is, few of us have better models. But I learned particularly early how to be on my own, and so that's what I did. My marriage ended and I moved on, with my amazing daughter in tow.

My questions about the way the multiculturalist world looked at race got too loud to ignore. Working in Oakland, I watched the city's school board get sidetracked in a dead-end battle over American history textbooks. A new series cowritten by a respected historian who'd worked on Angela Davis's defense committee, designed to cover historical wrongs—slavery, Indian eradication, and Japanese internment, for instance—got rejected as "Eurocentric pap: slanted, racist, and wrong." The new series had flaws, but years later, some students in the poverty-scarred district still didn't have textbooks, thanks to the conflict.

I became a regular contributor to *San Francisco* magazine, where my work experience made me a natural for the race and education beat. I covered Stanford's controversial decision to multiculturalize its Western Civilization curriculum, and I wound up finding it hard to worry about the problems of privileged Stanford students, whatever their race. My passion was low-income kids, locked away in awful schools as grim as prisons or in actual prisons once those schools failed. Yet a narrow focus on race didn't always help there, either, as I learned when I set out to do an admiring profile of an embattled local black juvenile probation officer as he shifted resources to community-based programs over the objection of white officers I assumed were racist.

And some were. Yet visiting the community programs that clamored for funding, I found a patchwork of rickety institutions unready for a wave of needy, troubled offenders. Some did great work, nonetheless; others were a white racist probation officer's worst caricature. I saw programs where teenage violent offenders just dropped in, signed their names, and left, without talking to an adult, let alone seeing a counselor or engaging in any kind of educational or social activity.

Having staff and leadership who were the matching color too often became a proxy for being effective, and they were not. Of the three most inspiring youth workers I met, one was African American, one was white, and one was Filipino American. What made the difference, I learned, was love; the best youth workers provided the kind of love and protection most of us get from an attentive parent, and whatever their race, most of the kids I was talking to just didn't have enough of it. I believed, and I still believe, that we should invest in great black and Latino youth workers. Not only do they do good work, but also they become role models, job-holding community pillars, able to support their own families. But racial matching didn't guarantee success.

I'm embarrassed to admit that some of my pique was personal. I'd picked one of the only careers where being white occasionally felt like a disadvantage. Rarely, but occasionally. In my consulting on poverty issues, I was sometimes, apologetically, excluded from certain kinds of "community" meetings because my presence alone would make whatever group I represented appear to be a front for imagined white puppetmasters. I understood that; it was true. It also occasionally came to bother me.

Then there were the meetings I was allowed to attend, but where I would find myself singled out and hectored because I was white. Unbelievably, the very same woman who used to tweak me at welfare reform meetings when I worked in the state Assembly confronted me again two years later as I sat taking notes in a meeting about Oakland education reform. She made her racial charge one more time: "There's only one reason you're sitting there, and I'm standing here." No one said anything, and I began to wonder why it was acceptable to shame white allies. I was also beginning to wonder if anyone had the courage to tell the woman there might be more to my career success than being white. Who was being helped by that assertion? Those were heretical thoughts, and I tried to suppress them.

As the lone white person in a group, I was often privy to unintended insults, and I developed a little bit of a chip on my shoulder. "White" was an epithet: you could deride "white teachers" or "white social workers" or "white foundation executives" with no other modifier, because *white* was a universally understood shorthand for clueless, culturally incompetent, and, as often as not, racist. I remembered my old friend Joe, the rare black kid in a white world, complaining about being told he was "one of the good ones." I got tired of being one of the few good ones.

It surprised me that people didn't know the version of Irish history or labor history that I did. A close black friend once asked about the ancient Irish independence struggle, "So, who were the good guys, the Irish or the English?" I was happy he'd asked— that's the kind of question we don't ask in our multicultural world, out of fear of seeming unforgiveably ignorant. Yet I was shocked that someone who worked on social justice, a good person, an educated person, someone I loved, didn't have that historic conflict in his database of righteous struggle.

I had learned to accept, against my integrationist instincts, that black self-segregation was natural, even developmentally important in a community constantly measured against white people and found wanting. Black kids setting up their own houses in universities, proverbially sitting at their own tables in the cafeteria, were protecting themselves, pulling away for a while from a majority white culture that defined black as deficient, developing, and relying on their own power. I understood it; I still understand it. But when the Supreme Court ruled that universities could still use "diversity" as a goal and a value in assembling students but not race, I asked this question: If diversity is a valid reason for affirmative action, because we all benefit from diversity, how does self-segregation advance that goal? A good friend, someone who loves me despite my annoying questions, snapped at me, "We didn't fight the civil rights movement so white kids could have black friends." I know she wasn't talking about me, except, of course, she was.

Some slights were even more personal and utterly unintended as slights. After I got divorced, a black female work colleague persistently tried to nudge me toward the only other single Irish Catholic in our world; he was as romantically uninterested in me as I was in him. I belatedly realized that the old chestnut about black people being fine, but you wouldn't want your daughter to marry one, had a black correlate. Still, I fell in love with someone I met in my do-gooder world, who eventually had to break the news to me that we could never be together long term because I'm white and he wanted a career in politics. He was shocked that I was shocked; he thought I knew that. I did not. Finally I got to be a victim, too.

Some of my pain came from needing to find a new family, having lost my own, and feeling as if the new family I'd found ultimately didn't want me. Which really wasn't true, but I wouldn't figure that out until later. Was I a racial cliché, a wounded misfit looking for comfort among society's proverbial outsiders? Maybe a little. Certainly I had inherited my father's passion for belonging to a wider world, as well as his talent for exile, hurt, and then self-exile.

Beyond my own issues, I had a young daughter, and I couldn't help but experience the world differently. In California, white kids were about to be a "minority"; in San Francisco schools, they already were. And our traditional black-white model of race relations wasn't making a whole lot of sense. San Francisco public schools had been governed by a consent decree that settled an NAACP lawsuit back when the district was largely black and white. There was no denying that black kids were clustered in terrible schools.

Now, though, we lived in a polyglot city where the largest group of students was Chinese. Chinese parents chafed at the consent decree's caps on ethnic enrollment; no school could have more than 40 percent of any one racial group, which kept their kids from attending neighborhood schools in heavily Asian neighborhoods. The biggest problem with the consent decree, though, was the fact that it hadn't worked. African American students still had an average that hovered around D. The original schools in black neighborhoods that had been "reconstituted" by the decree—their staffs were dispersed and new teachers hired—improved little, if at all. Parents with resources, of every race, were fleeing for private schools or the suburbs. Chinese parents sued the district, and the lawsuit eventually ended the consent decree. Today 75 percent of the students at the district's prestigious Lowell High School are Asian.

Race was becoming increasingly divisive in the University of California system, too. More students were fighting over roughly the same number of places in the state's elite public universities, as state funding stagnated. In the early 1980s, the University of California–Berkeley admitted roughly half of its applicants; in 2011, it admitted fewer than 20 percent. By the time my daughter was born, Asian students were the largest group at the university; today they make up more than half, and whites are less than a third. I did a story about the first classes of white students to become a "minority," and I expected to find that the disgruntled were small-minded racists. Most weren't; they were just college kids looking for a way to belong and facing the discomfort of being "outnumbered" for the first time in their lives—as well as outperformed academically. So why could Asian students form an Asian Business Students Association that excluded white kids? I didn't have a convincing answer.

White-Asian relationships were particularly fascinating. The fastest-growing romantic pairing was white men with Asian women, for a mind-blowing array of contradictory reasons: the Asian women I met complained that Asian men were sexist and patriarchal; white women imperiously and defensively insisted that white guys wanted Asian women because they were subservient. Scholars of intermarriage said "marrying out" let Asian Americans "marry up," but some noted that marrying Asians could represent "marrying up" for white people, too. People of every race wondered whether the pairing was driven by a desire to create a new, white-Asian master race, a fusion of the two groups in California with the most social, political, and financial capital.

"Now we know how black women feel," a rejected white friend said to me, only half joking. Of course, it was silly to compare the plight of dateless white college students to the pernicious historical forces that have limited the romantic choices of black women. But I talked to white kids who found themselves on the wrong end of unfamiliar and demeaning stereotypes. Some Asian parents, even some Asian kids, believed white kids were lazy, not too smart, and sexually kind of . . . promiscuous. As in, white people were okay, but you wouldn't want your child to date or marry one. It was kind of funny; it was also a little bit sad. And when blacks and Latinos clashed, as groups consigned to the bottom of society always do—and which those two groups were doing with greater frequency—which side was I on? Instinctively, I took the African American side, but that wasn't always the side of justice. In fact, some African American complaints about Latinos in Oakland—they were taking over their neighborhoods; they were taking jobs; they were getting forms of help, such as English as a second language classes, that took resources away from black peple—sounded like those of my Irish family a few decades earlier.

It was in this multicultural maelstrom that I got fed up with the term *people of color*. I challenged a friend who put together a "people of color" caucus in a professional group that had very few white people; what was the point? He answered, "Well, they've excluded us for so long, they should know how it feels." (Yes, I noticed the "they"; I wasn't really white anymore, I was one of the good ones.)

The "people of color" alliance sometimes seemed less about inclusion than retribution for past misdeeds, real or imagined or committed hundreds of years before you were born. It also seemed silly. When San Francisco's African American superintendent told me in an interview that the Chinese parents who scuttled the desegregation plan didn't understand American civil rights history, she was attacked as a racist after my article appeared, which made her head spin. "People of color" sure didn't agree on education issues. None of us was served by the way we talked about this stuff anymore.

I came to hate the term *white privilege*, even as I believed it still existed, as colorless and odorless (to white people) as oxygen. White privilege was embedded in that superstructure of government help that white families got to rise that African American families didn't get. It's the assumption that your experience is the norm, your culture the dominant one. Yet culturally in California, even economically, things were rapidly changing. Try explaining white privilege, as I once did, to a poor Oakland teenager who's been beaten up by Latino kids, mocked by blacks, ignored by the Chinese, and become close friends with a self-described "Blaxican," with one black parent and one Mexican. "White means you're . . . nothing, really. You have no culture. You don't belong anywhere," he told me.

Sometimes I felt the same way.

Luckily, my daughter didn't feel that way, but her early experiences didn't fit into any of my boxes, either. At four, Nora decided she wanted to be Los Angeles Lakers star Shaquille O'Neal for Halloween. I worried about how we'd do that—how could a little white girl with long, blond ringlets look like a bald, bearded, seven-foot, two-inch black man? Simple: she just wanted to wear his jersey. So I bought her a men's extra-small, which hung down to her knees, and she carried a basketball along with her trick-or-treat bag, and as far as she was concerned, she was Shaq. Neighbors seemed bewildered but amused.

Nora attended one of the best public schools in the city, where no racial group made up a majority, though the largest single group was white. A rambunctious tomboy, she mostly hung out with boys in the early grades, including black boys—and she spent a lot of time on the time-out bench with them in kindergarten and first grade. A black friend suggested that she was being punished for befriending black kids, but I couldn't see it that way. My girl was a handful. She wound up the only white kid in a special Kwanzaa study group that doubled as a small-group session on impulse control.

The dad of one of the black boys in her group told me his son was there because he was just wired differently, being black. He couldn't sit still, and he shouldn't have to. Of course, white parents don't think that about their fidgety kids: once it was believed they just needed discipline; now they all apparently needed Ritalin. Either way, I was again struck by my friend not noticing that my daughter had some of the same issues his son did.

No matter; she thrived. In first grade, she came home during the season of winter holidays and told me she wasn't Catholic, she wasn't Jewish. "I'm everything, Mom!" she told me; she was Christmas, Hanukkah, Kwanzaa, and Dr. King Day! She was living the life I'd envisioned growing up, with friends of all races, a whole lot of biracial kids, the children of Dr. King's dream. She was my father's granddaughter, updating his lesson about the black Irish for the twenty-first century.

We hadn't conquered racism; far from it. But I was seeing the limits of the worldview I'd designed for myself. I still counted the kids at Nora's birthday parties, careful not to overdo it on white kids, but I was beginning to look for ways to measure good and bad that didn't always correspond to color.

17

I just want to know one thing. How come there's no
table for *Salon* magazine?
                    —President Bill Clinton, White House
                          correspondents' dinner, April 1998

I have Bill Clinton to thank for pulling me back into full-time
journalism. Watching the working-class Clinton face down
his elite Beltway enemies inspired me and made me realize that
the Democratic Party I'd revered in my youth could use my
help. It wasn't perfect, it sold out its history; now it was run by
too many Wall Street–connected con men and -women. And yet
it was all that stood between us and plutocracy. Under Clinton, the
economy soared, unemployment ticked down, and the pace of economic inequality slowed. A man who should have been judged an
uncommonly successful president was instead being hectored and
humiliated, shamed for his private sins, when his real sin was having moderately liberal values—and the temerity to think a rube
like him could run the country.

I watched Clinton as he was demonized by conservative media,
savaged by mainstream media, derided by liberal media, abandoned by the party's left, yet defended, significantly, by African
Americans—fighting so many battles with so little help. Most
of the Democratic left abandoned him after his welfare reform
"betrayal"; many paid little attention even before that. While
I'd been focused on my daughter, my family, and my city, the
Republicans were using sex to do what they failed to do at the ballot box in 1996: topple the Democratic president.

So when I got a job offer to be news editor at *Salon*, I grabbed it. I admired its work standing up to the right-wing anti-Clinton jihad. *Salon* was notorious for publishing the story of an extramarital affair conducted by Henry Hyde, the House Judiciary Committee chair who was overseeing Clinton's impeachment. More important, its reporters investigated the Starr investigation, a $70 million political dirty trick that uncovered none of the scandals it was set up to examine but shamed a president for sexual behavior that many in Congress got away with. *Salon* also exposed the mainstream media reporters who'd served as Starr's stenographers, hyping his "findings" in credulous news stories that damned Clinton.

Right then, journalism felt like the most important way for me to make a difference and, particularly, to cast my lot with a Democratic Party that, while imperfect, still remained the best vehicle to right the wrongs of the country. Certainly, the GOP backlash against Clinton made me realize Republicans were determined to undo even his halting efforts to pull the country back to the center. Their paymasters were angry at higher tax rates. They didn't like the language of corporate responsibility he increasingly preached. I felt as if *Salon* let me try to wake people up to the attempted coup in Washington, DC.

Thwarted by the GOP, persecuted by the media, and constrained by his own attempts to be a new kind of postsixties Democrat, Clinton still made a huge difference in reversing the worst trends of the Reagan era. Yet on the left, he was never forgiven for his 1996 welfare reform bill. Poverty advisr Peter Edelman quit the administration; the Robert Kennedy staffer and husband of Marion Wright Edelman—who'd brought MLK into the Poor People's Campaign, then founded the Children's Defense Fund—called it "a war on the poor of the United States" and "the worst thing" Clinton had ever done. At the time, I was ambivalent about welfare reform; I'd developed my own doubts about AFDC and I saw why it made political sense, necessary, and, too. Still, I worried that it was another Sister Souljah moment, at once commonsensical and cynical. I hoped Clinton was gambling that he could use the political capital the move gave him to finish building the social infrastructure that would keep low-wage workers afloat, extending them subsidized child care and health insurance in particular.

Although he never did complete that agenda, Clinton's economic boom, combined with some of his stealthy redistributive policies, actually let the country undo some the ravages of the Reagan era. The galloping pace of social inequality, for the first time in twenty-five years, began to slow. Between 1993 and 2000, real wages went up 6.5 percent; they'd gone down 4.3 percent during the Reagan-Bush years. The country enjoyed the longest economic expansion in US history, with roughly 4 percent annual growth since 1993. Wages increased in every income bracket for the first time since the 1960s, as did family incomes. The poverty rate hit a twenty-year low. Unemployment dropped to 4 percent.

The Clinton boom created 22 million jobs and lifted 4.1 million children out of poverty; in Reagan's eight years, by comparison, only 50,000 kids left the ranks of the poor. Not only had the president raised taxes on the very wealthy, he had stealthily redistributed income by doubling the earned income tax credit. Clinton's college tuition tax credit, underheralded even though it was ultimately bigger than the GI Bill, helped increase college attendance.

Conditions improved dramatically for African Americans, even without a specific race-based policy thrust. The black unemployment rate dropped by almost half, from 14.2 in 1992 to 7.6 in 2000. (It was 16.7 percent in 2011.) In 1999 alone, the median income of African American families jumped 7.7 percent, the largest annual jump ever recorded. The black poverty rate fell and the African American child poverty rate dropped by almost 30 percent. Rates of teen pregnancy and infant mortality, two scourges in the black community, fell dramatically.

Under Clinton's administration, Congress finally passed the Family and Medical Leave Act and the Child Health Insurance Program, a first step toward a national health insurance system that still seems distant. In 1996, it raised the minimum wage for the first time since 1990 (and only the second time since 1981). Clinton also built up some Great Society programs; Head Start funding jumped 90 percent.

Yet Clinton accomplished some of his most dramatic improvements in the lives of the poor, the working class, and the middle class through the tax code, making the help he provided stealthy, if not invisible. Maybe that's what let him do it. Once Republicans figured out that the EITC actually gave money to poor families, they crusaded to cut it. Clinton's stealth had the unintended consequence of contributing to the philosophy that we need less, not more, government.

For a while, I thought his compromise on welfare reform, placing time limits on how long women could receive assistance and conditioning it on work or training, might help end the GOP-led demonization of poor people. And as former welfare recipients streamed into the labor market, I thought Clinton's compromise might point the way toward a bipartisan agenda to support the low-wage, no-benefits jobs our economy increasingly created, even in those boom years.

That was a crazy notion. If anything, Clinton's compromises emboldened the right, a dynamic we'd see again under Barack Obama.

People like to say that you can judge a nation by how it rises to a crisis. I also think you can judge it by what it does in peacetime and prosperity. By that standard, our nation shamed itself at the turn of the twenty-first century. Instead of turning to the problem of persistent and corrosive economic inequality, even in a booming economy, or the slow-motion apocalypse of climate change, or the growing threat of al-Qaida, Republicans impeached a president over a blow job, Democrats ran scared, and the media reached new lows covering the tawdry circus while global troubles festered.

I admire Al Gore, but he learned all of the wrong lessons from the 1990s. During the 2000 presidential campaign, he tried to downplay the environmental vision that helped make him famous, running against the callow governor of Texas whose father once mocked Gore as "Ozone Man." Clinton's sex scandal pushed Gore into the embrace of sanctimonious Holy Joe Lieberman, who famously denounced the cheating president on the Senate floor. Nothing proves you're an impotent Democrat better than embracing your enemy. Gore ran away from the terrific Clinton economy by running away from Clinton.

While trying to stay true to his DLC roots, Gore abandoned the most useful tenet of DLC politics: that Democrats had to declare themselves the best stewards of economic growth and show that smart government keeps the economy expanding. Before Clinton, that was mostly a leap of faith; in 2000, it was demonstrably true. Gore let Americans take the good economy for granted, a tragic mistake.

There's no better symbol of the Gore campaign's—and the party's—confusion than its top campaign team: Jesse Jackson's 1984 campaign chief, Donna Brazile, was manager, and tobacco lobbyist and corporate lawyer Carter Eskew was the "top strategist." Gore was trying to use Brazile to turn out the party's loyal African American and progressive base and use Eskew to reassure big Democratic donors he was still the business-friendly DLC leader they knew and loved. This was the worst of both worlds; it acknowledged that the interests of corporate bigwigs and average Americans were different. Yet if that were true, how could Gore pledge to serve both?

Gore wasn't responsible for all of his troubles. The shallow media did him in. They mocked his wooden campaign presence, they accused him of lies about preposterous things. A lion of liberal journalism, *New York Times* columnist Frank Rich, trashed Gore frequently. The regularly savage Maureen Dowd, who didn't like Clinton's philandering, questioned Gore's manhood. Everybody liked the Texas governor, the "compassionate conservative"; he was the regular guy, the one reporters wanted to have a beer with, even though George W. Bush, a nasty drunk by his own admission, gave up drinking after too many debauched nights, including an arrest for drunk driving.

And yet even with all of those problems, Gore won the popular vote, and by most accounts, he would have won the electoral vote and the presidency had the votes of swing-state Florida been counted properly. Most famously, Pat Buchanan—there he is again!—running for president on the Reform Party ticket, got his largest share of votes in heavily liberal, Jewish, Democratic Palm Beach, because of the bizarre butterfly ballot. It was a debacle. In the end, though, Republicans can accurately say that the recount Gore requested wouldn't have made him president, because Democrats asked for a manual recount in only four trouble-plagued counties. Only a statewide manual recount would have found enough votes to make him the winner—yet Gore didn't fight for the most thorough but politically controversial method of counting. Eighteen counties never bothered to conduct even a recount; no one from the Gore campaign complained, because no one even knew it.

The episode made vivid what I'd long known: Democrats just don't fight as passionately or as viciously as Republicans, about anything. Republicans turned out a mob of angry preppy white guys to protest the recount in Miami, in what was called "the Brooks Brothers riot." No one on our side did anything of the kind. Looking back, I don't know why liberals weren't out in the streets demanding that the recount continue. Donna Brazile sent *Salon* an e-mail at the height of the recount battle, thanking us for depicting it as a civil rights issue, which it most certainly was. A media consortium would later reveal that African Americans were four times more likely than whites to have their votes disqualified.

Finally, Antonin Scalia, a Supreme Court justice handpicked by Bush's father, stopped the recount, which was overseen by Bush's brother Jeb, and made George W. Bush president. A founder of the right-wing Federalist Society, one of those seventies-era groups that was established to push back on liberals (in this case, among lawyers), Scalia was a passionate partisan brawler. The network of probusiness interest groups established to turn back the 1960s had reached all the way to the Supreme Court, and it was about to make George W. Bush president.

To settle an election scarred by race, Scalia relied on the Fourteenth Amendment, the one that guaranteed freed slaves their rights—but he used it to protect the rights of Bush, not of disenfranchised black voters. Then he declared that his ruling didn't set a precedent; it applied only to the Bush case. After he left office, President Clinton called it the worst Supreme Court decision since the deeply racist *Dred Scott* ruling, which the Fourteenth Amendment effectively reversed.

Weak Democrats and street-fighting Republicans helped make Bush president, but so did the ideologically rigid left. Proclaiming no difference between Bush and Gore, prominent lefties from Michael Moore to Susan Sarandon, Barbara Ehrenreich to Cornel West campaigned for Ralph Nader in 2000. Even without a hand recount, Gore would have won Florida if he'd gotten one one-hundredth of Nader's ninety-five thousand votes there.

The out-of-touch American left helped elect Richard Nixon in 1968 and George W. Bush in 2000. My father would have been screaming. Yes, DLC Democrats took over the party, but the left barely bothered to fight for it. A multiracial elite battled for control of universities, liberal foundations, and a handful of jobs at the pinnacle of corporate America. Unions continued to decline. There was no countervailing force to the Republican reformation. The gains of the Clinton years, on economic equality and a fairer tax code, were quickly reversed. It was as though they'd never happened.

I know a lot of good people voted for Bush. Most of my extended family did. And I was seeing a lot more of them. Just as Nora pulled me into a new multiracial world, she also pulled me back to my family. I wasn't estranged, exactly; after my father died, I tried to reach out more, because he would have wanted me to, and because I needed family—but distance persisted.

Yet my daughter loved the idea of cousins, and I have dozens of cousins, which means so does she. My daughter particularly loved one of my favorite cousins, a New York police detective, just like his father, my mom's oldest brother—an artist and a Grateful Dead fan who had moved as far to the right as any of my uncles. We rarely saw each other, but he now had a wife I adored and a daughter just a few years younger than Nora. The two girls looked like sisters. We reconnected and just made sure not to talk politics.

As I saw more of my extended family, even though so many of them were Republicans, they accepted me as one of them again. I wasn't just that liberal know-it-all they saw when they switched over from Fox to MSNBC. At a time of growing political polarization, it felt right to engage and love my family and know they loved me. I'm not saying I changed a single mind or a single vote, by visiting more regularly—showing up at weddings and wakes and making the occasional impromptu appearance. Except, maybe, my own mind. No, I wasn't thinking about voting Republican; I was thinking about the intolerance that led me to flee much of my family. Now they saw that I was a good mother, with a great daughter, even though living in godless San Francisco. Democrats could be good people, too, even if we had bad ideas, and vice versa.

Being closer to my family, I got a little tribal, for the first time in my life, after September 11, knowing that so many cops and firefighters like my uncles and cousins died in those buildings, a lot of Irish and Italian guys, the boys I'd grown up with in Oceanside. They were brave and loyal and hardworking, and they died that way, trying to save lives. My police-detective cousin hadn't been there at the time of the attack, but he immediately headed over, and he worked "the pile," looking first for survivors, then for remains, for weeks.

In *Salon*, a hipster writer mocked the 9/11 benefit concert where cops and firefighters got maudlin and rowdy and booed Democratic senator Hillary Clinton, and one declared "Osama bin Laden can kiss my royal Irish ass!" I wrote a counter to the nasty, condescending review. It had come to seem to me that the left is never happier than when it can sneer at white working-class people. I mean, really, who did we think died in those buildings,

Alice Walker and the Dalai Lama? Who went into the inferno trying to save lives, knowing they were risking their own? Why couldn't we let those men, those families, have their grief without mocking or judging?

My cousin took me into ground zero a little more than two months after it happened, with his brother-in-law. He was there every day, so he drove right in; nobody asked about his passengers, but in case anyone was looking, he made me take off my fuchsia cashmere shawl and stuff it in the backseat. "That's not a cop scarf," he growled. Even with the sound of machinery in the background, it was eerie and still, hushed by an enormous grief, gray on gray. We stood in a canyon surrounded by mountains of rubble. A horrible sooty mud clung to everything. He took us to see the famous cross, the twenty-foot-high mangled steel beams left standing in the perfect shape of that Christian symbol, where rescue workers left notes of prayer. My cousin's brother-in-law took pictures of what he believed was a holy site. I wasn't sure what I believed.

Security was tighter getting out of ground zero than getting in. We had to stop at a station where they washed the mud off everyone and everything before we headed back out onto the city streets. Officials already knew there was something toxic in that silt; cops and firefighters would later die from breathing the lethal air in the cleanup, and the GOP would block funding for their illnesses. A black cop solemnly hosed down our car's tires and our boots before we left and said good-bye. Later, there was a conflict over whether to allow the cross we'd seen within the World Trade Center memorial. It would become one of those faux controversies that make me ashamed to be a liberal. Couldn't they just have their freaking cross? Actually, the Jewish Anti-Defamation League agreed with me, and the cross stands within the memorial today.

18

Take your families and enjoy life, the way we want it to be enjoyed. Get down to Disney World in Florida.
—George W. Bush, September 27, 2001

Coming after a genuine working-class guy, Bill Clinton, George W. Bush was a confectionary cowboy, a Texan rancher by way of Andover, Yale, and Harvard. He was the culmination of Pat Buchanan's strategy to make Republicans seem like the working-class party. The Texas good ol' boy stepped up the fleecing of the working class, to levels Ronald Reagan hadn't dared approach.

After an impossibly close election decided by a Republican-dominated Supreme Court, you might have expected Bush to govern as a moderate, to heal the divided country after an election many considered suspicious. Instead, he came in with a surprisingly aggressive agenda and took the country into a ditch.

Bush did something else: he squandered the sense of national unity and purpose we had after 9/11. It's the kind of trauma that often propels the country forward, more united. People wanted to volunteer, to give blood, to do something to help out. Bush told us to go about our daily lives and asked for our "continued participation and confidence in our economy." No, he didn't actually tell us to "go shopping," as many people remember. Karl Rove rightly complains about that. Instead Rove's boss told us to go to Disney World.

No, he really did. On September 27, Bush told the country, "One of the great goals of this nation's war is to restore public confidence in the airline industry. It's to tell the traveling public: get on board.

Do your business around the country. Fly and enjoy America's great destination spots. Get down to Disney World in Florida. Take your families and enjoy life, the way we want it to be enjoyed."

I can't think of a better coda to the Bush years. After the awful attacks, he went ahead with his tax cuts and looked away while his advisers concocted a case for the Iraq War. He will be judged as one of the worst presidents in American history.

Yet I also remember the help Bush got from Democrats, particularly going to war. An astonishing twenty-nine out of fifty Democratic senators voted to authorize the use of military force against Saddam Hussein in October 2002, including, fatefully, Hillary Clinton. They were still trying to recover from their association with Vietnam, the antiwar left, and the sixties. Some were willing to risk the lives of American soldiers to silence accusations of weakness and pacifism. The notorious DLC centrist senator Evan Bayh actually made the political calculus explicit, summing up the case for the war on the eve of the 2002 midterm elections. "The majority of the American people tend to trust the Republican Party more on issues involving national security and defense than they do the Democratic Party," the Blue Dog Indiana senator told Fox News back then. "We need to work to improve our image on that score by taking a more aggressive posture with regard to Iraq, empowering the president."

I'm sure some Democrats voted to authorize the war because they genuinely believed it was the right thing to do. A few apologized later, when they learned the case for war had been fabricated. But to defend your vote by saying "We need to work to improve our image" on national security is indefensible. It defines the deficit of values and courage that has plagued too many Democrats since the sixties. Bayh, like a lot of conservative Democrats, also came to support Bush's tax cuts for the rich. He then left the Senate in 2010, deploring its excessive partisanship, and went to work as a hedge-fund adviser, a Chamber of Commerce lobbyist, and, of course, a Fox News analyst. He remains the perfect symbol of a Democratic Party that had lost its political and moral moorings.

. . .

I owe my presence on television and in the wider media to the Iraq War, however. As it spiraled out of control, former Republican congressman Joe Scarborough started having me as a guest on MSNBC's *Scarborough Country*. Like a lot of Republicans, he was turning against Bush's war, too. The way I connected with Scarborough, though, made me see the extent to which conservatives can forget liberals are people. Scarborough and I met on his radio show, talking about Dan Rather's retirement. The right wanted to make the CBS anchor's departure all about some forged documents he had unwittingly used two years earlier, in a story about Bush's missing National Guard years. I was on to defend Rather, but I did two things that disarmed Scarborough. I agreed that it was a bad thing that CBS used documents that turned out to be fake. Then I talked about my family.

As we reminisced about the glory days of Walter Cronkite, I recalled watching the evening news with my parents, though we were an NBC, Huntley-Brinkley family. Scarborough warmed up, as if maybe he was surprised I had a family, as if liberals were raised on communes reading *Pravda* or something. He asked me to come defend Rather on his TV show that night, and I spent the next year or so with him, criticizing George Bush's Iraq War and hailing the comeback of the Democrats, often sparring with my boy Pat Buchanan. I learned to play the normal American card, even the working-class Irish Catholic card, when Buchanan tried to dismiss me as a San Francisco liberal, and it started to work.

But if I started out playing my working-class Irish Catholic identity as a card, I realized it was less a persona than the person I'd actually become. As I watched the economic carnage of the Bush years, I recovered a working-class spirit I should have held on to all along. Nobody was speaking up for the people who'd lost so much ground in the past thirty years, even if they'd done some of the damage to themselves by voting Republican. The Democrats had one success under Bush: they beat back his brazen effort to destroy the signature Democratic Party success story

Social Security by privatizing our retirement accounts; in short, handing us over to Wall Street. I saw the political power that came from standing up for one of the few recognizable New Deal programs, as well as opposing the greed and corruption that led the GOP to believe it could deliver that well-funded program to its corporate masters. What would happen if Democrats stood up to efforts to shower riches on Wall Street and corporate America a little bit more often?

I also felt more comfortable with my working-class Irish Catholic persona at least partly because of Nora. Unbelievably, after nine years in a great public elementary school, she wound up in a Catholic high school. We looked at dozens of schools, but early in the process she picked one as her favorite, Sacred Heart Cathedral Preparatory. It happened to be a Christian Brothers school.

She didn't know her grandfather had been a Christian Brother. She didn't know who Christian Brothers were. She just loved the warm communal atmosphere of the big school, known for its sports teams and a strong scholarship program that powered its comparative racial and economic diversity. It wasn't a Catholic thing for me or Nora; Sacred Heart was on all of our friends' lists of good private schools, in a city with only a couple of decent public high schools left. We met other Jewish families on the tours. Nora's father bonded with another Jewish dad on the Saturday we visited, as we sat below looming crosses in almost every classroom.

On the other hand, I hadn't picked Sacred Heart; Nora had. Nora sat me down one day to explain her choice.

"Mom, you have to understand something. I'm more normal than you and Daddy."

You know, she was. I didn't know how that happened.

"I want to go to a school that has school spirit! I want to go to football and basketball games. I belong in that school."

We didn't let her make big decisions by herself, but in the end, we said she'd go to the best school she got into, and it was the best school. Her father was a good sport about it.

How did Nora wind up with the Christian Brothers? I have no idea. Actually, there were only a couple of Brothers there, because the order has dwindled to only a few hundred in the United States. But for four years, she started her day the way my father did at Barrytown, with the same simple prayer. The prayer leader begins, "Let us remember," and the students answer, "That we are in the holy presence of God."

As I carved out a role for myself as the working-class Irish Catholic liberal Democrat on TV, I got to watch the resurrection of the Democratic Party during the Bush years up close.

We had George Bush to thank. He did what a generation of Democrats failed to do: he pulled the old New Deal coalition together all by himself. The lying that led to the Iraq War, along with pro war media cheerleading, inspired a new wave of online organizing and blogging, and the so-called netroots, a combination of progressive journalism and online organizing, formed a cornerstone for a liberal revival. The shame of Hurricane Katrina, when the federal government left poor black people stranded and then exiled, woke us up again, at least a little, to the shame of racial exclusion and the government's indifference to it. When Kanye West interrupted a Katrina benefit to say, "George Bush doesn't care about black people," he exposed a widely-shared anger about the role of race and poverty in the calamitous lack of government urgency about the hurricane.

The disastrous economy, meanwhile, gave labor greater political and moral clout, even if it wasn't inspiring a new wave of workplace organizing. Young people began voting in higher numbers in 2004, though it wasn't enough to elect John Kerry. But by 2006, Democrats took back the House and the Senate for the first time since they'd lost them in 1994.

I saw something else, though, that a lot of progressives didn't always seem to see. The Democratic revival depended on two things that thwarted progressive politics, rather than advanced it: recruiting conservative "Blue Dog" Democrats in borderline conservative districts, and raising a ton of cash, a lot of it from Wall Street. The so-called FIRE sector—finance, insurance, and real estate, the one that got out of control and torched the economy in 2008—had become central to Democratic fund-raising. The business wing of the party had almost totally reinvented it. Even as netroots leaders recruited progressive candidates and raised money for them, they were outmuscled by the official Democratic Party recruiting team: Senator Chuck Schumer, who headed the Democratic Senatorial Campaign Committee (DSCC), and Representative Rahm Emanuel, who ran the House counterpart.

Nothing illustrates the influence of Wall Street money more than the career of Schumer, the middle-class Queens kid who represented Geraldine Ferraro's district and then beat Long Island Republican Al D'Amato to take his Senate seat. Schumer is a solid liberal, a reliable voice for the needy—and for needy investment bankers, too. For years, Schumer defended what eventually became a tax scandal: the practice of allowing hedge fund operators and other investment bankers to pay taxes on their earnings at the much lower capital-gains level. It's what let megamillionaire Republican Mitt Romney pay a lower tax rate than most middle-class workers. And Schumer was rewarded with campaign cash. Schumer raised a record $240 million for his DSCC and upped contributions from Wall Street by 50 percent, according to Jacob Hacker and Paul Pierson. I like what Robert Reich says about campaign donations: they don't buy your vote, they buy a share of your mind. Politicians get to know these friendly donors, the hardworking men of Wall Street, over meals and drinks. They're good guys. They grow the economy. They have kids, too.

In 2006, Schumer and Emanuel brought in a new crop of moderate and conservative probusiness Democrats. Netroots groups such as MoveOn, ActBlue, and Howard Dean's Democracy for America couldn't compete. They helped elect some great progressives, such as Maryland representative Donna Edwards, but Schumer and Emanuel brought in Blue Dogs faster.

That's the Democratic congressional majority that would be in charge when the Wall Street pyramid of greed collapsed and took down the economy in 2008.

As Michael Moore and the rest of the purist-left learned the hard way, there turned out to be an enormous difference between Bush and Gore.

Thanks to the Bush tax cuts, the country endured a bigger experiment in supply side economics than Ronald Reagan had sponsored, and it was a flop, especially for the working and middle classes. It turned out that the tough cowboy, the one voters and journalists wanted to have a beer with, ran off with their beer money and gave it to his wealthy friends. Thirty years of Republican policies, sometimes abetted by Democrats, had reached their intended culmination. The result was an economy run on debt, in which banks made money off people's need, not just on consumers' supposed greed, until it all came tumbling down.

In eight years, under the Bush supply side experiment, the United States saw a series of historic economic lows and, overall, the slowest overall rate of economic growth since World War II. Although wages for certain groups, such as working-class men, had declined since the seventies, household income had mostly held steady, mainly because women surged into the workplace, and most "households" now had two earners. Under Bush, household income declined, too, for the first time since the Census Bureau tracked that data in 1967.

Labor force participation had reached an all-time high in 2000 but dropped steadily under Bush; relatedly, the economy created fewer jobs than at any time since World War II. Unemployment jumped from 3.9 percent when Clinton left office to 7.2 percent at the end of 2008. Clinton left Bush a $236 billion budget surplus; Bush would leave his successor saddled with a $1.2 trillion deficit. Dick Cheney, of course, famously declared that "Reagan showed deficits don't matter" (although he should have added, "unless there's a Democrat in the White House"). Yet it was incredible hubris to slash taxes, start two wars, and also add an expensive "entitlement"—the Medicare prescription drug benefit—and not expect economic consequences. The Bush-Cheney team believed the economy would take care of itself, and it did, as long as people could keep themselves afloat on rising home equity and cheap, easy credit.

It turned out that beggaring the working and middle classes created problems for everyone. The economic crisis that emerged in 2008 was a crisis of economic demand: fewer people could afford to live on their wages anymore, and when the financial bubble collapsed, they couldn't keep borrowing, either. Republicans like to call the rich the "job creators." In fact, consumers are the real job creators and, with less money to spend, they stopped playing that vital role.

Unemployment rose, tax receipts declined, and the formerly employed, who once contributed to the nation's coffers, were now draining them, as unemployment claims and food stamp recipiency climbed to record levels. Because fewer people had money to spend, the economy couldn't recover. Employers wouldn't hire new workers to make products that no one had the money to purchase. These were the problems that FDR had addressed with government spending, which established the conditions for the postwar boom. It looked as if a Democrat would have the challenge and the opportunity to repair the economy that way again.

As the 2008 election approached, polls showed that many independents and even Republican voters, as well as working-class whites, were ready to give the Democrats a new chance, thanks to the economic catastrophe that occurred on Bush's watch. Bush set the stage for Democrats to take the White House in 2008, galvanizing a new coalition and a country ready for change. I saw no way for the party to lose in 2008. Unless it defeated itself.

PART IV

SOME OF MY BEST PRESIDENTS ARE BLACK

19

I am a Rorschach test. Even if people find me disappointing ultimately, they might gain something.
                                                                    —Barack Obama, June 2008

I thought the 2008 election would be all about the economy, and that the Democratic primary campaign would sort out the candidate with the best solutions to the worsening economic crisis, as well as the strongest pitch to worried voters. Finally, we'd have a contest in which Democrats embraced their traditional egalitarian economic values, in which the fissures of race and ethnicity, the understandable but divisive anger of identity politics and the nation's culture war obsessions, would be sidelined. People seemed ready to come together to solve the problems that were throwing millions of Americans out of their homes and millions more out of their jobs.

I was wrong, at least for a while.

Choosing between the nation's first prominent black and female presidential contenders touched off wrangling over race and gender, with class just a murky undercurrent, that rivaled anything we had seen in earlier Democratic primary battles. It reignited conflicts over whose problems and whose advancement deserved to be our national priority. For a time, the bitterness threatened to scare away the working-class voters who seemed ready to take a new look at the Democrats. It even started to alienate me.

If Barack Obama's election grew out of the multiracial Mondale coalition I'd seen in San Francisco in 1984, as some people would later observe, it didn't feel that way at first. I saw the same forces, even some of the very same people, who had been central to Mondale's black-labor-feminist alliance, working the 2008 campaign. But they squared off from different camps, divided between Hillary Clinton and Obama.

At a Las Vegas, Nevada, Democratic caucus site in January 2008, I saw, in person, the cracked-mirror image of 1984 convention-floor harmony as Clinton and Obama supporters nearly came to blows in a ballroom at the kitschy Paris Casino. It was made spookier by the fact that I ran into the friend and labor organizer who'd been my companion at the 1984 San Francisco convention. Back then, we stood on the convention floor teary-eyed at the eloquence of Jesse Jackson, Mario Cuomo, and Geraldine Ferraro, but more than that, at the fired-up delegates, of every race and class, uniting to close the rifts of the sixties and the seventies. In 2008, my friend was supporting Obama; I was leaning toward Clinton, but we huddled together in that casino ballroom, watching as our party seemed to unravel again: union member vs. union member, men against women, blacks against Latinos and whites.

The caucus started off fine, though we were surprised to see the national president of the powerful government workers' union American Federation of State, County, and Municipal Employees (AFSCME) working the small room, ushering voters to the Clinton corner. "I think she's gonna upset [Obama] here," Gerald McEntee told me with a smile. But the locally influential Culinary Workers Union endorsed Obama, and its members refused to let McEntee anoint Clinton the labor candidate. "Hillary Clinton has never walked a picket line in her life!" an African American Bally's pantry worker shouted at a female AFSCME leader, and she bellowed back, "*I've* walked picket lines with Hillary Clinton!"

A Paris Casino cocktail waitress, still in a tiny skirt and spike heels from her shift, jumped in the middle to defuse the tension. "All the candidates are good," she told the pair. She wore a Clinton T-shirt, she said, "because she's the woman for the job."

Waitress diplomacy didn't help. Obama supporters began yelling insults about Bill Clinton and Monica Lewinsky, while the Clinton caucus, which was mostly Latino, tried to shout them down with chants of "Hillary!" AFSCME's McEntee, then a wiry seventy-three, almost got in a fistfight with a heavyset young Obama supporter who was chanting "Lewinsky! Lewinsky!" Clinton won the Paris caucus 2–1 and most of the votes in Nevada, although Obama would ultimately get more delegates because of the way the state apportioned them. My Obama-supporting friend and I were in shock. "Have you ever seen anything like this?" he asked me with some alarm. I had to tell him no. We'd witnessed a bizarro-world version of San Francisco 1984: hatred, not harmony; all of the grievances of race, class, and gender on display, the "rainbow coalition" seemingly in shards on a casino ballroom floor.

What happened in Vegas mostly stayed in Vegas; I never saw such naked, nearly physical hostility between Clinton and Obama supporters again. But the ugliness didn't go away. The 2008 primary showed that Democratic politics could still be shattered by race and gender, with class and economic issues tangential, even during an economic crisis worse than anything since the Great Depression.

All during the primary season, Clinton assembled the same coalition she had in Nevada: white women, Latinos, older voters, and the white working class. Obama's backers were younger, wealthier, and better educated; he attracted independents and, as the campaign wore on, more than 90 percent of African Americans. There were actually issues, not merely identity politics, driving the coalitions gathered behind the two candidates, but policy differences were mostly lost in charges of racism and sexism, while Republicans cheered from the sidelines.

Forty years after the Democratic Party divided in Chicago, we would see an election year in which the aspirations of African Americans once again wound up pitted against the worries of the white working class—and no one, it seemed, had an investment in trying to lessen the tension rather than stoke it.

• • •

It started off a great year. The field of Democratic candidates had never been so liberal or so diverse: an African American, a woman, a Latino (Bill Richardson); the son of working-class Irish Catholics (Joe Biden), the son of a Croatian truck driver (Dennis Kucinich), and the self-described "son of a mill hand" (John Edwards). Only Chris Dodd, the son of a senator, was a white guy born into the elite. All but Kucinich, however, had participated in their party's fevered courting of corporate America. Yet in a time of economic anxiety, all jostled to be populists. Like a lot of antipoverty advocates, I began the season leaning toward John Edwards because he made American poverty a top issue. Yet soon I was torn between the front-runners, Obama and Clinton.

I'd admired Obama ever since his 2004 convention speech, which I'd watched on the Boston convention floor. I'd always been ambivalent about Hillary Clinton, but as New York senator, Clinton won my respect with hard work and a progressive economic record, although I distrusted her hawkishness on Iraq and Iran. When the choice came down to Obama vs. Clinton, and the economy worsened, I came to see Clinton as the more progressive of the pair, at least on economic issues. As millions of Americans lost their homes, she came out for a freeze on mortgage foreclosures and interest-rate hikes; Obama opposed both measures. In the Senate, Clinton had supported legislation to cap credit-card interest rates; Obama voted against the bill. Her health insurance plan was more inclusive and contained an "individual mandate" that everyone buy insurance; Obama opposed the mandate and proposed a phased-in plan that would still leave at least fifteen million Americans uninsured.

The Illinois senator made me nervous when he echoed Republican talking points to insist that Social Security needed "fixing"; it didn't. He praised Ronald Reagan in an early interview, lauding the Republican hero for returning "optimism," "entrepreneurialism," and "accountability" to government. And with regular assurances that "I come from a new generation of Americans; I'm not interested in the battles of the sixties," he tried to separate himself from the roiling politics that divided the nation in his youth but in a manner that minimized the gravity of the clash. In his second book, *The Audacity of Hope*, he had confided that "in the back and forth between [President] Clinton and [GOP House Speaker Newt] Gingrich, and in the elections of 2000 and 2004, I sometimes felt as if I were watching the psychodrama of the baby boom generation—a tale rooted in old grudges and revenge plots hatched on a handful of college campuses long ago—played out on the national stage."

Really? That's what the vicious, take-no-prisoners GOP crusade against Clinton seemed like—a campus grudge? Newt Gingrich had proposed putting the children of welfare recipients in orphanages, and Obama likened his clash with Clinton to the rumbling of rival frat boys? I saw a disturbing naïveté and a dangerous indulgence of Republican ideas about the role of government in Obama's words. Most of all, even though I admired the newcomer's faith in his own power to break the gridlock that had paralyzed Washington—at least when Democrats had the White House; George W. Bush got the wars and the tax cuts he wanted, with some Democratic support—I didn't share it. I thought Clinton's experience fighting the vast right-wing conspiracy would make her the stronger president.

I knew reasonable people could disagree about all of that, particularly my last wager. Some of my friends argued that President Hillary Clinton would wage the Clinton wars all over again, taking the country backward, not forward. Certainly, Obama's campaign drew some of the most innovative and progressive organizers from Howard Dean's 2004 insurgency. Maybe it could launch a movement, not just a presidency. Obama said so himself. "Even if we don't win," he told one Dean veteran, "how we do it, by getting people involved and building a grassroots movement, will leave the political process and the party better for having done it that way."

Marshall Ganz, a veteran of 1964's Mississippi Freedom Summer, early United Farm Workers organizing, and the Bobby

Kennedy campaign, saw the old spirit in a new form and signed on. Ganz set up the famous "Camp Obama" network of training camps, which weren't about policies or nuts-and-bolts vote tracking and turnout; they were about teaching people to reach voters with Obama's personal story and their own; in fact, volunteers were taught to avoid policy debates. "The first thing we taught was story," Ganz explained. "It was tapping into that moral resource and coupling it with strategy and leadership."

Ganz was on to something. Republicans pushing social wedge issues such as gay marriage and abortion demonized Democrats as amoral; not just bad leaders but also bad people, as I was learning in my forays on television, where my GOP sparring partners often tried to marginalize me as a godless San Francisco liberal. One forlorn Democratic organizer in North Carolina told the *Nation*'s Ari Berman, "We've got to do a better job of letting people know that we're good people." That personal approach made staff and volunteers not only supporters but also evangelizers; the Obama campaign took on the look of a great moral crusade. But a crusade to achieve what, besides a campaign victory? It wasn't clear.

The Clinton campaign's cavalcade of political miscalculation became obvious in the very first contest, the Iowa caucuses, as I saw when I landed in Des Moines two days before the vote. Obama volunteers boasted about all of the new young voters they'd added to the process, while the Clinton folks bragged that they'd stocked up on snow shovels to get their elderly supporters out of their homes and to the caucus sites. Clinton, the supposed front-runner, knew who came to Iowa's caucuses and went after them avidly. Obama's team counted on expanding the number of caucusgoers, which Clintonistas knew was starry-eyed silliness.

It didn't snow on Election Day; the shiny new Clinton shovels stayed in the garage. But the shiny new voters electrified by the Obama campaign came out, for real. The caucus site I covered at Drake University more than doubled its 2004 turnout. You could argue that the 2008 race was over, then and there. The Obama team had already moved its Iowa operatives into the next round of states, such as South Carolina. They were gearing up for later caucuses where Clinton was unready to compete. That first win unleashed a cascade of new supporters, who suddenly believed the skinny black guy with the funny name might have a chance to win this thing.

Most important, it inspired black voters, many of whom had stuck with Clinton only partly because of her long civil rights loyalty. Some worried that the country would never elect a black president in their lifetimes, while others, fearful of violence, "want to protect him from the bad people, and in order to protect him, they won't support him," an Obama supporter in South Carolina told the *New York Times*. In the end, the courage that let people face down Jim Crow terror in the South and rock-throwing racists in the North inspired many to join the Obama crusade, despite those fears. It took on the fervor of a new civil rights movement. Electing our first black president had become possible, and once it was possible, trying to defer the dream seemed an act of racism.

Not surprisingly, race entered the race in new and unsettling ways in the days to come, as Clinton shocked Democrats by winning the New Hampshire primary.

Clinton owed her come-from-behind victory at least partly to female empathy stirred by the candidate's choking up with emotion at a New Hampshire campaign stop after a woman asked her sympathetically how she kept herself going, day after day, given the obstacles she faced. "It's not easy," she said, as she seemed to fight off tears. The day after Clinton's win, Representative Jesse Jackson Jr. questioned that emotional moment with a sharp racial barb. "Those tears also have to be . . . looked at very, very carefully in light of Katrina, in light of other things that Mrs. Clinton did not cry for, particularly as we head to South Carolina, where 45 percent of African Americans will participate in the Democratic contest," the Obama campaign cochair told a reporter. Given that Kanye West had made indifference to Katrina code for not caring about black people, Jackson's were fighting words.

His race-baiting shocked me. Yet no one paid much attention to it, because Clinton and her husband were suddenly fighting charges that they had made insensitive racial remarks of their own. Fox News asked Clinton to respond to Obama's claim that her jibes against his hope-powered campaign derided the hope inspired by leaders such as Martin Luther King Jr. Unforgettably, she replied: "I would point to the fact that Dr. King's dream began to be realized when President Johnson passed the Civil Rights Act of 1964, when he was able to get through Congress something that President Kennedy was hopeful to do, the president before had not even tried, but it took a president to get it done. That dream became a reality, the power of that dream became real in people's lives because we had a president who said we are going to do it, and actually got it accomplished."

We can debate Clinton's version of history, but major media outlets distorted it beyond recognition. In most news stories, her comment was truncated to say: "Dr. King's dream began to be realized when President Johnson passed the Civil Rights Act. It took a president to get it done." A white president, in fact. It sounded as if Hillary had handed over the accomplishments of the civil rights movement to a Caucasian—which would have been shocking, had she said it. Most reports also left out the fact that she'd been asked to reply to something Obama charged about King. That made her King-Obama association seem gratuitously racial.

The same day, an angry President Clinton derided Obama's claim to political bravery in opposing the Iraq War, calling it "a fairy tale," because he did it from the safety of his state Senate seat. The comment was widely reported as a knock on Obama's entire candidacy, though in context it clearly referred to his Iraq claims. And since fairy tales are told to children, soon it was as if Clinton had called the black politician a "boy." Donna Brazile, a former Clinton adviser, as well as the chair of Al Gore's and Jesse Jackson's campaigns, told Wolf Blitzer on CNN, "I tell you, as an African American, I find his words and his tone to be very depressing."

The charges of racism enraged Bill Clinton, and the ex-president dug in deeper. When he seemed to dismiss Obama's victory in the South Carolina primary by noting that Jesse Jackson had won the state, too, ABC's Jake Tapper (who'd expressed skepticism about the racism charges until then) immediately quipped on his blog: "Boy, I can't understand why anyone would think the Clintons are running a race-baiting campaign to paint Obama as 'the black candidate.'"

Whether it was racism or frustration, Clinton's comments made him look particularly small in the wake of Obama's inspiring South Carolina victory, where he even won the votes of whites under thirty. That was the first time even I cringed at the possible racial subtext to a controversial Clinton remark. It was certainly tone deaf, if it wasn't racist. Even to admirers, the former president's inability to be magnanimous seemed to mean one thing: he knew his wife's candidacy was over.

20

Sen. Obama's support among working, hard-working Americans, white Americans, is weakening again, and [whites] who had not completed college were supporting me. There's a pattern emerging here.
—Hillary Clinton to *USA Today*, May 2008

Except it wasn't. In early February, Hillary Clinton wound up edging Obama narrowly in the colossus of contests known as Super Tuesday, designed as a national primary day that could stop a scrappy but untested insurgent from toppling the party's strongest candidate. I agonized until the last possible moment about whether to vote for Clinton or Obama in the seemingly crucial California primary. How could I be on the wrong side of history, not supporting the man who could become our first black president? But I went for Clinton, who won the state. For the first time, I sympathized with my mother for refusing to tell us whether she had voted for Nixon in 1972. It was *so* not cool, on the left, to support Clinton, I was tempted to remind people, as my mother did, that we have the right to a secret ballot.

Super Tuesday was the day Clinton's overconfident campaign had expected to clinch the nomination. Instead, though she won more contests that night, she still trailed Obama in the overall delegate count, and her campaign's spectacularly bad planning, along with Obama's surge, led to her trouncing in the rest of February's contests, mostly in purple and red states that weren't supposed to matter. Clinton recovered in March, too late to win the nomination, but just in time for the campaign's undercurrents of race vs. class to surface and make the primary season even uglier for a while.

The debate ignited after Clinton won the March 4 Ohio primary, in that crucial swing state where John Kerry bet his entire candidacy in 2004 and lost. Exit polls showed that the New York senator was the overwhelming favorite of Ohio voters who made less than $100,000; of people who said the economy and health care were the most important issues (those who said Iraq went for Obama), as well as those who said the nation's economy was either not so good or poor. In fact, in almost every state Clinton did better among lower-income and less-educated Democrats and people who rated the economy as "poor"; also among union members, Catholics, Latinos, older voters, and white women. Obama did best among those making more than $100,000 and those with advanced college degrees and with independents, Republicans, and younger voters—as well as with the vast majority of African American voters, across lines of class and age.

Obama supporters began to blame Clinton's Rust Belt victories on the racism of the white working class, and there certainly was some of that. Yet to me, that wasn't the whole story. Clinton ran on a specific, populist program touting a foreclosure moratorium, universal health care, repealing tax cuts for the wealthy, and providing more government help with college. She wasn't as gifted as her husband, but she'd learned from his success at feeling our pain. Her campaign pitch was populist and rat-tat-tat specific: create jobs, stop foreclosures, solve the health-care crisis. Her specificity contrasted with Obama's stirring but vague appeals to hope and change and postpartisanship.

On television and in *Salon*, I argued that Clinton's working-class wins exposed a weakness in Obama's movement that he'd have to address to succeed in November; Clinton's critics accused anyone who noticed that weakness of exploiting it and trying to make it worse, in order to help the white Democrat. After her Ohio win, a close black friend, someone I love, "praised" my stalwart defense of Clinton by marveling that apart from me, her campaign seemed to be "the last refuge of white people who won't vote for a black man." A black historian charged that Clinton was playing on white racial fears, making a vote for Clinton "a vote for whiteness." To me, it looked like she was able to articulate the basis for white working-class fears, that the economy was leaving them behind, and no one in power cared, in a way that wooed them.

In just two days, a pair of racial controversies made the 2008 campaign seem like a referendum on race that nobody could win.

On March 11, former vice presidential candidate Geraldine Ferraro complained to a reporter, "If Obama was a white man, he would not be in this position. And if he was a woman of color, he would not be in this position. He happens to be very lucky to be who he is." Declaring a black man "lucky to be who he is" was ludicrous, given the persistence of racism. The former Democratic hero became a racist goat; she resigned as a Clinton campaign finance cochair. In *Slate*, Ta-Nehisi Coates called Ferraro's comments "racist" and complained that her self-defense only made things worse, because she seemed to feel that being called a racist was worse than actually being one. Coates didn't mention that Ferraro also referenced Obama's gender, not merely his race; he saw only race driving her resentment. A mortified Ferraro told my colleague Rebecca Traister in 2009 that the controversy was something "I probably will go to my grave with." And she did. Ferraro died in January 2011.

The day after Ferraro's remarks came out, ABC News broadcast old videos of Obama's pastor, Rev. Jeremiah Wright, blaming American foreign policy for the 9/11 attacks as "the chickens coming home to roost" and accusing the government of "inventing the AIDS virus as a means of genocide against people of color." One Wright sermon closed with a fiery and memorable crescendo: "The government then wants us to sing 'God Bless America.' No, no, no, not God Bless America. God damn America!" In a later NAACP speech, Wright preached specious science about learning differences between (creative, right-brained) black children and (logical, left-brained) white children. He mocked the way white people talk, dance, clap, worship, and sing. He pointed to the way the Irish had once been denigrated:

"People thought that the Irish had a disease, when the Irish came here." Then he referenced Fox's Bill O'Reilly, and added, "Well, they might have been right."

The Wright and Ferraro controversies exposed a racial empathy gulf, and I surprised myself, again, by being on the wrong side. I thought Ferraro's remarks were deplorable, but I heard the pain behind them—the pain of women who had dreamed of a female president and now knew they were unlikely to live to see it. My seventy-two-year-old aunt, a passionate Hillary supporter, grieved for her lost presidency. (The dumbest thing I did during the whole campaign, though, was suggest that people try to empathize with an unhinged Clinton supporter named Harriet Christian, who became a YouTube sensation with a teary speech lamenting Clinton's loss to "an unqualified black man." Yuck. I apologize.)

Wright's invective bothered me because, in years of working on education and community development, I've seen personally how that divisive bluster and specious black-difference rhetoric can be an impediment to social change. I didn't want to believe that Obama looked away as Wright preached the unredeemable evil of the United States (and most white people), along with self-defeating theories of black difference and downright lies about genocide. Yet a lot of black people empathized with Wright, even if they disagreed with what he said. Black men of the pre–civil rights era, such as Wright, had plenty to be angry about.

Predictably, Fox News spent weeks on the controversy, just as it spent months hyping every silly allegation it could find about Obama and "reverse racism" against whites. That accounted for the outrage, among some Obama supporters, at any liberal who insisted that Wright mattered, even a little. In a world where Fox, Rush Limbaugh, and a blogsophere of dittoheads did nothing but fan white fears that Obama himself was just a younger, paler Jeremiah Wright, a liberal expressing concern about Wright seemed traitorous. And indeed, MSNBC's Joe Scarborough got me in trouble by noting on the air one morning that even the well-known liberal *Joan Walsh* was uncomfortable with Wright's remarks.

The only person who seemed able to feel empathy for both Ferraro and Wright, two older people bitter about sexism and racism, was Obama himself. In his remarkable March 2008 speech on race, he described the "zero-sum game" of racial politics that has divided Democrats for two generations. The country tried to improve the lot of black Americans, the candidate noted, with social and educational programs and affirmative action, just as the living standards of the white working class began to erode. Most working- and middle-class whites "worked hard all their lives, many times only to see their jobs shipped overseas or their pension dumped after a lifetime of labor." But the anger of both blacks and whites is "counterproductive," he argued, distracting attention "from the real culprits of the middle-class squeeze": corporate "greed" and "economic policies that favor the few over the many."

He didn't stop there. "[T]o wish away the resentments of white Americans, to label them as misguided or even racist, without recognizing they are grounded in legitimate concerns," Obama argued, "this too widens the racial divide, and blocks the path to understanding." While saying that both Wright and Ferraro were wrong in their remarks, he refused to damn them to political hell. That's the Obama I ultimately supported.

Yet that kind of empathy was in short supply on the campaign trail. A month later, Obama stumbled at a tony San Francisco fund-raiser and talked about "bitter" working-class white voters in Pennsylvania who "cling" to their guns and religion. I said at the time I didn't think his words should be an issue, but I understood why they became one. They seemed to prove he was an out-of-touch elitist, insulting working-class voters for the entertainment of San Francisco snobs. If you read his full remarks, there's not much for any Democrat to disagree with, but Clinton's campaign depicted Obama's words in the most negative way possible.

The Obama camp got payback when Clinton, under pressure to drop out of the race, mentioned Robert Kennedy's June 1968 assassination, to make the point that other primary seasons had continued down to their last contest. Obama supporters charged that she had mentioned Kennedy's murder in order to play on fears that Obama might be assassinated, a last ghoulish attempt to convince Democrats she was the better candidate, if only because she was more likely to stay alive. An Obama spokesman shot Clinton's comments out to thousands of campaign reporters via e-mail, saying the remark "was unfortunate and has no place in this campaign." In an outraged "Special Comment," once reserved for the depredations of Dick Cheney and Donald Rumsfeld, Keith Olbermann declared that Clinton's remark "shows something not merely troubling, but frightening" about her "soul." I couldn't believe we were debating whether Clinton had raised the terror of Obama's assassination deliberately, for political gain, and I went on *Hardball* to defend her. Clinton apologized, but it didn't help.

Behind the two campaigns' cheap-shotting, I saw ancient American political tensions in the Obama/Clinton fight. Drinking shots and beers in working-class taverns, Clinton appeared to be going after the retro, often racist, hard-hat vote that was so hostile to the legitimate ongoing effort to fight racial discrimination. Yet Obama could at times look like the candidate of those old New England Protestant Evangelical do-gooders and wealthy elites. That's part of why I thought working-class voters, new immigrants, and Catholic ethnics, so often attacked or at best neglected by that elite reformer coalition throughout history, backed Clinton. Especially in the left-behind enclaves of "bitter" voters in Pennsylvania, which had been the scene of anti-Irish nativist violence and bloody Molly Maguire coal riots, the Obama campaign might well seem like the latest crusade of wealthy moral "reformers" who sometimes cared about black people but never gave a damn about poor white workers, particularly the Irish. It was Kevin Phillips's "Toryhood of change" all over again.

The anti-Clinton race-baiting on the white left grew intolerable. Sometimes bullying, sometimes guilt-tripping, always high on self-righteousness, the lefty evangelical crusade to pronounce Obama the only progressive in the race sent me around the bend.

It seemed a rerun of that faction's clueless indifference to issues of labor and class in the 1960s and the 1970s.

Forty years after he wrote the Port Huron Statement, Students for a Democratic Society (SDS) founder Tom Hayden composed another manifesto in 2008, cosigned by Barbara Ehrenreich, actor Danny Glover, and labor leader Bill Fletcher. It began with a totalitarian lilt: "All American progressives must support Barack Obama." It went on to state, "We believe that Barack Obama's very biography reflects the positive potential of the globalization process. . . . By its very existence, the Obama campaign will stimulate a vision of globalization from below." His *very biography*? Really? His campaign's *very existence*? Hayden had the gall to channel the young Hillary Rodham, who'd worked on the McGovern campaign, and to inform her that she, too, would be supporting Obama, not herself, were she an activist in 2008.

The young lefty blogger Chris Bowers went to similar lengths in 2008, praising the Obama coalition as an epochal "cultural shift" in which "the southern Dems and Liebercrat elite will be largely replaced by rising creative class types." He went on: "Obama has all the markers of a creative class background, from his community organizing . . . to being an academic, to living in Hyde Park, to shopping at Whole Foods and drinking PBR. These will be the type of people running the Democratic Party now, and it will be a big cultural shift from the white working class focus of earlier decades."

What Old New Left and New New Left Obama supporters had in common was a desire for a political formula that left out the troublesome white working class. Whatever the formula, white college-educated cultural elites always wind up on top in their dreamy lefty scenarios. And if their standard-bearer doesn't carry the day, it's the fault of racist, benighted working class whites rejecting what they should know is best for them.

Both sides of the Democratic coalition seemed ready to insult the other into political oblivion. Obama campaign chief David Axelrod shrugged off Clinton's strength with white workers by arguing that "the white working class has gone to the Republican nominee for many elections going back even to the Clinton years" and noting that Obama would "attract independent voters . . . younger voters" and "expand the Democratic base."

Likewise, the normally inclusive Donna Brazile appeared to validate the Hayden/Bowers vision when she told CNN mid-primary season, "A new Democratic coalition is younger. It is more urban, as well as suburban, and we don't have to just rely on white blue-collar voters and Hispanics. We need to look at the Democratic Party, expand the party, expand the base, and not throw out the baby with the bathwater." Fellow Democrat and Clinton supporter Paul Begala didn't do any better when he replied to Brazile by calling Obama the candidate of "eggheads and African Americans."

Black Clinton supporters came in for the worst abuse. It didn't seem to matter that Clinton's campaign had come to be run by a troika of longtime African American Hillary loyalists—campaign manager Maggie Williams, lawyer Cheryl Mills, and fixer Minyon Moore—or that some Congressional Black Caucus members stayed at her side, even after many bolted for Obama. At the fervently pro-Obama website Jack and Jill Politics, which bills itself as "a black bourgeoisie perspective on politics," bloggers called Clinton congressional stalwarts such as representatives Emanuel Cleaver and Stephanie Tubbs Jones "handkerchief-headed Negroes" for supporting the white candidate. The slur seemed all the more cruel when the feisty populist Tubbs Jones died of an aneurism just before the 2008 Democratic convention, at fifty-eight.

Jack and Jill Politics didn't like me either. The same blogger known for attacking black Clinton supporters as "handkerchief-headed Negroes" called me a "snake" for defending Clinton from claims of racism. Now I was a racist, too.

21

The country that we carry in our hearts is waiting.
                    —Bruce Springsteen, October 2004
                                    (four years too soon)

Tangled in a web of charges and countercharges, sorting through real and imagined Clinton campaign wrongdoing in the surreal, sped-up world of the Internet and television news, I couldn't see in the middle of 2008 what is so clear to me now: that the steady accretion of what defenders such as I termed "slips of the tongue" or "inartfully worded" remarks or "missteps" on the part of the Clinton campaign betrayed a sense of racial superiority and entitlement, if not racism, to Obama supporters. Later I could understand how even fair-minded people, inclined to believe the best about the former First Couple, finally ran out of patience. At the very least, both Clintons seemed insulated from, and unprepared for, a new world of high-speed multicultural campaigning—as though they didn't understand why they had to worry about any of it, after all they'd done on the civil rights front.

Yet at the time, I keenly felt Bill and Hillary Clinton's pain. Too keenly. They were rarely given the benefit of the doubt when it came to racially questionable campaign missteps; their long career of work for racial justice meant little or nothing. I'd felt that pain, too. There seemed to be little recognition that despite "white privilege," white people who worked for equal rights have sacrificed for our racial views. We've often found ourselves outcasts at that big, fun 24/7 party and networking event, also known as mainstream America. We can wind up outcasts in our own families. We ruin Christmas and Thanksgiving and family reunions by objecting to racial jokes and racist commentary. And then, if, after a lifetime of decency, a white person stumbles, she or he is no longer sister or brother but racist? That was no kind of beloved community.

On the other hand, if white liberals were gob-smacked by being treated unfairly on a racial issue, that in itself proved we've been sheltered. Black people can find themselves treated unfairly, without the benefit of the doubt, every day on racial issues. Maybe it was just our turn.

I also took in the fact that my "black Irish" fairy tales aside, I could at best understand the black community's pride and protectiveness of Obama; the fear and the pain that his rise was impossible; and then, that once it seemed possible, it might be met by violence. I could *understand* all of that, but I couldn't fully *feel* it. To question the backlash against the Clintons' misdeeds, to lecture black people on what was and wasn't actually racism against Obama, seemed the very definition of "white privilege."

So for a while, I think, I became part of the problem. Passionate about wanting Democrats to return to issues of economic disadvantage, I didn't entirely see the transcendent racial appeal of the Obama campaign. And my personal experience, wanting to belong but feeling like an outsider, made me oversensitive to charges of racism that seemed to me unfair and politically inspired, undersensitive to the pain driving those charges, and sometimes unable to see racism itself.

I also realized later that I found the flickering and sometimes awkward spotlight on Obama's white family a little sad— and I still do. During his terrific race speech, Obama made one off-putting move, comparing Jeremiah Wright's prejudice to that of his white grandmother, "a woman who helped raise me, a woman who sacrificed again and again for me, a woman who loves me as much as she loves anything in this world, but a woman who once confessed her fear of black men who passed by her on the street, and who on more than one occasion has uttered racial or ethnic stereotypes that made me cringe." He then described his grandmother as "a typical white person" in a follow-up radio interview.

In fact, Obama's grandmother, who at the time lay sick in Honolulu, was a woman who accepted her daughter's marrying a black man in the early sixties and who loved and raised her black grandson. Would that she were "typical." Obama's mother, Ann Dunham, remained a muted presence compared with Obama's father, even though both had died young. She was a specter, a young white face in ads and news segments, hugging her adorable black son. No one knew much about the brave anthropologist researching Javanese craftsmen in Indonesia. Yet clearly, Dunham's liberal, multicultural views had at least as much to do with the person Barack Obama grew up to be as the fact that he had a black father.

What made things worse was that on the right, some tried to promote the story of Ann Dunham but got it all wrong. Conservative Shelby Steele, who is also biracial, chided Obama for neglecting his white mother's role in his life by choosing "blackness," and he argued that for Obama, "liberalism *is* blackness." That's ridiculous. For Obama, liberalism is the legacy of being raised by Ann Dunham and her parents in Hawaii and Indonesia. He grew up to live his mother's values: curiosity about the world, egalitarianism, concern with social and racial justice. You might say that for Obama, liberalism is whiteness, because he got his liberal American politics from the white side of his family. Both are silly claims.

Obama himself admitted that he wished he'd paid more attention to his mother's loving, formative role in his life in *Dreams from My Father*. Yet the book showed Obama's rare and noteworthy understanding of race mixers such as his mother and her parents, who were, let's be honest, not at all "typical" as the fifties made way for the sixties. I loved the way he connected his grandparents' acceptance of their daughter's marrying a black man to their own willingness to leave their native Kansas for ever more different environs: Texas, Seattle, and finally Hawaii. He notes the curiosity and openness to change and difference that often mark the white race mixer, as well as a tendency to be a misfit and an exile in the buttoned-down white world of achievement and conformity.

Obviously, I could relate.

Yet focusing on Obama's mixed background during the campaign was suspect: were you trying to claim the president as biracial, not black? Half white? I thought it was possible to respect Obama's blackness while acknowledging his unique background—and that the *whole* story is important to understand as we look at how we elected our first black president.

James Baldwin wrote that one secret to Martin Luther King Jr.'s success was King's "intimate knowledge of the people he is addressing, be they black or white, and the forthrightness with which he speaks of those things which hurt or baffle them." King's "intimate knowledge" of white people, his sensitivity to the things that "hurt or baffle them,"—us—was extraordinary for his time, and given the abuse he suffered, saintlike. Obama's skills at reaching white voters were unrivaled in a black politician, and they come from a place of ease and intimacy that I think has to do with being raised by his mother's family. He gave white people the benefit of the doubt until they proved themselves racists, when so often it worked the other way (as it worked the other way with so many of his supporters, during the campaign and afterward).

What if Obama's empathy with white people let white people, in turn, empathize with him? That seemed like interesting political information in a multiracial society, but discussing the psychological crosscurrents of race in the campaign was dangerous on the left —unless you were diagnosing the racism of the white working class.

On the other hand, my comparing Obama to Dr. King showed that I was probably subjecting our first black presidential nominee to outsize expectations, scrutinizing his every move, not only for political efficacy but also for its moral, political, and racial justice. It was too big a burden. Obama represented an advance beyond King in terms of our foreordained roles for African Americans. We want our black leaders to be the country's conscience, to make us better than we are. It was hard to just let Obama be an extraordinary American politician but a politician nonetheless, a skilled transactional Chicago leader, one who would disappoint me and make mistakes just like the rest, as he had every right to do.

Barack Obama accepted the Democratic nomination on the forty-fifth anniversary of Martin Luther King Jr.'s "I have a dream" speech at the 1963 March on Washington. (That really happened; it's not just an association I made up out of my racial yearning.) In that huge crowd at Denver's Invesco Field, I never had a moment of doubt that he could bring the country back together.

Nora came to the Democratic National Convention with me and left from there to start college. She had graduated from high school that May, winning the highest honor for student volunteerism, known as the "Christian Love" award. Her Jewish father was very proud. She made a surprising college choice: she wanted to go to Fordham University, the Jesuit school in the Bronx. Yes, the Bronx, about a mile away from Highbridge. The Walshes were back in the Bronx. Her father's father had grown up there, too, but in a Jewish enclave, of course. The fact that she had so much family in New York, on both sides, was part of her choice. My NYPD cousin, now retired, and his wife gave Nora a Tiffany key ring for graduation; it held the key to their Long Island home. My cousin's wife, who by that time had been battling breast cancer for four years, told her to come out anytime. "You'll always have a home with us," she said to Nora, but she was also talking to me. It made it easier to send my only child three thousand miles away.

At Fordham, she immediately joined the college Democrats and spent her weekends in Pennsylvania campaigning for Obama. They sent the white kids in their Fordham gear into Irish Catholic neighborhoods to talk to working-class voters. Most of the people she canvassed, she told me excitedly, were voting for the black Democrat. So were my Democratic relatives, even the passionate Hillary supporters. To my knowledge, there were no "Obamacans" in my family; all of the Republicans were sticking with Senator John McCain.

In fact, McCain was sending his running mate into some of the same white working-class areas where Nora was fighting for Obama. McCain picked the little-known female governor of Alaska, Sarah Palin, hoping to take advantage of Hillary Clinton's run, but it didn't work. Women didn't flock to the McCain-Palin team, despite the presence of a lady on the ticket. So Palin went after another potentially disgruntled Clinton constituency: working-class voters who might have reservations about voting for a black man.

Those late-stage Palin rallies were proto–Tea Party events. Down in the polls, Palin did everything she could to play up doubts about Obama—from his religion to his patriotism to his ability to keep the country safe. She famously accused him of "pallin' around with terrorists," making up a story that he began his political career in the living room of former Weather Underground leader Bill Ayers, whom he knew in passing. It seemed so fitting and yet so disturbing that to revive their Nixonian divide-and-conquer strategy, the GOP went all the way back to Nixon's era to find a sufficiently scary radical to use against Obama. At a Florida stop, as Palin used her red-meat "pallin' around with terrorists" line, a man shouted, "Kill him!"

The VP nominee simply turned up the heat. "I am just so fearful that this is not a man who sees America the way you and I see America," Palin told crowd after crowd. And her crowds agreed. Voters at Palin events routinely called Obama a terrorist. "He's got the bloodlines," a woman said. One Palin fan held up a Curious George stuffed monkey with an Obama sticker on its forehead. McCain got in on the act, calling Obama a "socialist" in a speech attacking Obama's support for that socialistic earned income tax credit invented by Milton Friedman, signed into law by Gerald Ford, and expanded by Bill Clinton. McCain took to casting Obama as a shadowy "other," too, asking crowds, "Who is the real Barack Obama?" During at least one rally someone yelled back, "A terrorist!"

Palin exposed the undercurrents of fear and hate that would surface in the fringe of the Tea Party, but could her shrill shtick work with working-class Democrats? *New Yorker* writer George Packer went to Ohio, where Clinton had won the Democratic primary, to see. In midfall, many Ohio voters told Packer they hadn't yet warmed up to Obama. A few admitted that race was part of their problem, but many complained that his ethereal campaign approach wasn't talking to their issues. Mostly, they showed the extent to which Democrats generally, long before Obama, had left the working class behind. "I can remember the hard times, I can remember the things the Democrats have done for the working people," one Hillary Clinton primary supporter told Packer. "I don't think anybody cares what we think. I just wish our party would pay more attention to people down here in the grass roots."

Labor unions worked hard to convince skeptical working-class voters to support the black Democrat, in Ohio and nation-wide. One of my favorite moments came when AFL-CIO leader Richard Trumka confronted the racism that was making some white union members, even lifelong Democrats, reluctant to vote for Obama. The son and the grandson of coal miners from Nemacolin, Pennsylvania, Trumka described challenging an old family friend who confided she wouldn't vote for Obama because he was black. He told her,

> "Look around. Nemacolin's a dying town. There're no jobs here. Kids are moving away because there's no future here. And here's a man, Barack Obama, who's going to fight for people like us and you won't vote for him because of the color of his skin." Brothers and sisters, we can't tap dance around the fact that there are a lot of folks out there just like that woman.
>
> . . . I don't think we should be out there pointing fingers in people's faces and calling them racist; instead we need to educate them that if they care about holding on to their jobs, their health care, their pensions, and their homes—if they care about creating good jobs with clean energy, child care, pay equity for women

workers—there's only going to be one candidate on the ballot this fall who's on their side . . . and his name is Barack Obama!

Trumka's argument won. Obama carried Ohio 52–47 percent, and although McCain got a majority of the white vote, Obama won a majority of the state's white voters who made less than $50,000 a year, and he did better among whites in Ohio than he did nationwide. He was the overwhelming choice of those who said the economy was the nation's most pressing problem. He won those white Hillary Clinton supporters and then some; Ohio's wealthy went with McCain.

Nationwide, Obama won a higher percentage of white votes than John Kerry, 43 percent to Kerry's 41, and more than Al Gore in 2000 or Bill Clinton in 1992. He narrowed Kerry's deficit with the white working class to 18 percent from 24. He took 52 percent of independents. According to CNN exit polls, just under 70 percent of first-time voters, 96 percent of African Americans, 67 percent of Latinos, 62 percent of Asians, and 60 percent of union members went for Obama. He'd reassembled most of the old New Deal coalition (minus the South, of course), as well as a twenty-first-century bloc of young people, Latinos, Asians, and the unaligned; people who didn't remember the New Deal or didn't think it had anything to do with them.

When the networks finally called it for Obama—fittingly, after he won Pennsylvania, home of those "bitter" voters who'd resisted him during primary season—CNN and MSNBC did something magical. The talking heads stopped talking, and the cameras made their way from one celebration to another: at King's Ebenezer Baptist Church in Atlanta to Harlem to Times Square to historically black Spelman College. They settled on Grant Park, the scene of the bloody destructive 1968 convention where "the whole world was watching," and we watched a very different scene: the Democratic Party coming back together again.

On Inauguration Day itself, a bright, freezing morning, Nora and I walked five miles through city streets and Capitol corridors and security checkpoints to get to the ceremony. The day is a bright blur to me now. The Obama girls, Malia dressed in royal blue and Sasha in peach, were unbearably adorable; my face hurt from smiling. At an Inauguration concert, we saw Bruce Springsteen and Pete Seeger sing the left-wing national anthem, "This Land Is Your Land," its radical verses about "hungry people" and "private property" and all. I remembered what Springsteen said on the campaign trail in 2004, working his heart out for John Kerry: "The country that we carry in our hearts is waiting." It felt as if it had finally arrived.

22

I think there are going to be a fair number of Republicans
who are going to want to cooperate, because they're not
going to be on the wrong side of the debate.
                    —David Axelrod, just after Election Day 2008

On that sunny Inauguration Day, President Obama stood at
the mountaintop of American approval. Between Election
Day and January 20, much of the nation swooned over the
president-elect, including a lot of people who didn't vote for him.
Though he got only 53 percent of the votes, he took office with
a 69 percent approval rating. White people gave Obama 43 percent of their votes on Election Day; by mid-January, his approval
rating among white voters hit 63 percent in Gallup tracking
polls. Maybe we approved of ourselves for electing our first black
president.

Yet only three months after I attended the joyous multiracial
Inauguration party, I found myself surrounded by angry white
folks wearing dried-up brown tea bags in a grim gray federal
plaza in San Francisco, as I covered the local version of the first
national Tea Party rallies on April 15, Tax Day. It drew a respect-
able 250 people in liberal San Francisco, mostly from the tony and
more conservative suburbs that ring the city. Like all of the Tea
Party events that day, mine was sponsored by a right-wing talk
radio station, KSFO, the local home of Rush Limbaugh and Fox
host Sean Hannity—a sign of the role Limbaugh and Fox News
broadcasters would play in creating the anti-Obama movement.

I covered that first local Tea Party meeting because I wanted to understand the new dissent. Even though Pat Buchanan would later chide me for calling them names, I set out that morning wondering whether there might be any left-right common ground. The early protests focused mainly on the stimulus—which I considered too small, but which many on the right considered socialism—yet there was also anger about the few-strings bank bailout, anger that I shared. Although the TARP program had passed under President Bush, the Obama team made the first key decisions, and on virtually every one, the team sided with the banks. I wondered how much a populist anti–Wall Street animus motivated the new protests.

The answer was, not much at all. At the San Francisco Tea Party, I met my first real-live "birther," the forlorn souls who insisted Obama wasn't born here and was thus ineligible to be president (a group that would come to include the ridiculous Donald Trump). My first birther carried an "Obama=Imposter" sign and handed me a flyer demanding that Nancy Pelosi begin impeachment proceedings because Obama, he told me, "is not a natural-born citizen." I saw signs denouncing Obama's stimulus bill as socialism and lots of hammers and sickles from the old Soviet flag. A man wearing a coonskin cap carried a big sign adorned by a picture of a gun. It read "Reload for the Revolution." Out of several dozen speakers, one attacked Wall Street giant JPMorgan Chase, but everyone else focused on Obama's radical programs and his deficit spending, which, of course, had begun under Bush.

I marched to City Hall next to an amiable balding guy who carried a makeshift brown cardboard placard: "I can't afford a better sign because Obama raised my taxes." Did Obama really raise your taxes? I asked him. He assured me Obama had. Working in the "private security business," he made about $50,000 a year, he said. "I think Obama lowered your taxes," I told him (the stimulus bill passed in February cut taxes for all but the top earners). He told me I was wrong.

At City Hall the crowd chanted, "Nobama! Nobama!" and riot-ready police officers guarded the doors, but the Tea Party dispersed peacefully. An African American neighborhood regular, clutching his black hoodie against a cold April wind, shook his head as he watched them walk away. "Eight years of Bush and y'all out here *now*?" Dirty tea bags and placards littered the steps, and city workers moved in to clean up the mess.

Not even three months into his presidency, Obama faced a shrill national backlash that fed off a right-wing minority's lingering racism. The postelection blowback had two almost contradictory effects: It made the primary-season accusations of "racism" against the Clintons and their supporters look silly and specious, by contrast. And yet it validated the political fear that motivated many Obama supporters' vigilance against anything that looked remotely like racism. During the next three years, I'd find myself suffering political whiplash, one day calling out the racism of the president's worst critics, the next day being accused of racial bias by Obama's defenders if I criticized his disturbingly centrist political maneuvering.

There is no denying that racism drove some of the right's abuse of Obama: there were just too many racist protest placards, offensive viral e-mails, and disgusting simian imagery in Photoshop caricatures. All of those could be, and usually were, dismissed as the work of bad actors at the Republican fringe. Yet mainstream Republicans rarely rejected the racially tinged Obama hatred; some even encouraged it. Certainly they abetted the birther movement, right up through the 2012 GOP primaries. House Speaker John Boehner refused to chide birthers in his caucus or the GOP base, insisting, "It's not my job to tell the American people what to think" about whether Obama was born here.

Then the ludicrous Donald Trump took up the bullying, pretending he was mulling a run for president, and Obama finally had to tell the state of Hawaii to release his long-form birth certificate, a sad ritual of humiliation for the most powerful man in the world, having to show his papers to GOP bullies. Even after that, Texas governor Rick Perry played the birther card when his presidential run began to stumble, and primary finalist Rick Santorum, an ultraright former Pennsylvania senator, took the Boehner line when a Florida voter told him Obama was a Muslim who is ineligible to be president. "I don't feel it's my obligation every time someone says something I don't agree with to contradict them, and the President's a big boy," he told CNN.

The disrespect was astonishing. When backbencher representative Joe Wilson of South Carolina, the capital of secession, screamed out, "You lie!" during a presidential address to a joint session of Congress, no one could remember anything like that happening to a president in modern history. Newt Gingrich criticized Obama's "Kenyan anticolonialist mind-set," even though the all-American Obama hadn't known his Kenyan father, Gingrich later called him "the food stamp president," updating Reagan's famous food stamp slur about "strapping young bucks" buying "T-bone steaks" on the government's dime. Even Obama's self-described GOP "friend," Oklahoma senator Tom Coburn, tried to defend the president in August 2011 with bizarre and condescending racial stereotyping. "His intent isn't to destroy," Coburn told a constituent at a Tulsa town hall meeting. "It's to create dependency because it worked so well for him. I don't say that critically. As an African American male, coming through the progress of everything he experienced, he got tremendous benefit through a lot of these programs." The racism and the racial idiocy were dizzying.

It was also well organized. Hillary Clinton exaggerated a little when she talked about "a vast right-wing conspiracy" against her husband in 1998. Yet ten years later, an intimidating nationwide apparatus of overt and covert right-wing character assassins, fearmongers, and race baiters made the anti-Clinton Arkansas Project look like a friendly fund-raising group for his presidential library.

Rush Limbaugh had the loudest single voice within the anti-Obama media movement. He set the tone for the leaderless Republican Party when he announced on the eve of Obama's Inauguration, "I hope he fails." Limbaugh went on, "We have to bend over, grab the ankles, bend over forward, backward, whichever, because his father was black, because this is the first black president," a glimpse of right-wing psychosexual anxiety I'd rather not have seen.

I saw more of it on *Hardball*, debating Limbaugh's attacks on Obama with former House leader Dick Armey, who dismissed my Limbaugh criticism as "political malarkey." Then Armey let loose a sexist tirade for the ages, telling me, "I'm so damn glad that you can never be my wife, because I surely wouldn't have to listen to that prattle from you every day." Stunned, I said simply, "That makes two of us, sir." A lot of people marveled at my composure, but Catholic school trains you to be able to say things like that while thinking much worse. The exchange upset my aunt, the Hillary supporter. A lifelong feminist, she came from an era when the worst thing you could do to a woman was to publicly impugn her marriaglability. I didn't feel it the way she did, but it was more evidence that reactionary sludge had been stirred by almost electing a woman president and actually electing a black man.

Later I'd chalk up Armey's outburst to overwork, not only sexism. A few days after our *Hardball* exchange, he'd be announced as the head of the Tea Party Astroturf group FreedomWorks, which funneled corporate money and support to the "new," supposedly grassroots right-wing movement. Armey had been very, very busy since Inauguration Day; no wonder he snapped at me when I tried to get him to criticize Limbaugh, his party's leader.

At that point, Obama had been president for eight days.

If Limbaugh held the largest megaphone of the anti-Obama movement, Fox News ran its headquarters, and Richard Nixon's media adviser, Fox chief Roger Ailes, was its chairman. More than thirty years after Nixon left office, the GOP imagemaker ran the nation's largest cable news channel, and his 2009 programming showed that Fox had a fifty-state Southern strategy to scare its white, older viewers about Obama and the Democrats. The network featured one black bogeyman after another—the minuscule New Black Panther Party, Jeremiah Wright, Obama "green jobs" czar Van Jones, the mild-mannered Harvard professor Henry Louis Gates. I thought about that long-ago *Life* magazine headline from my childhood: "Plot to Get Whitey: Red-Hot Young Negroes Plan Ghetto

War." That's the narrative Ailes used to drive Fox News programming during Obama's presidential campaign and presidency.

No one bashed Obama harder or crazier than Fox's Glenn
Beck. Ominously, he launched his Fox show on January 19,
Inauguration Eve. It went on at 5:00 P.M. Eastern time, a strange
slot to make a big splash, but as Will Bunch would explain in his
Tea Party book *The Backlash*, Beck had a captive and rapt audience: retirees and the unemployed. By March, Beck was hosting
National Rifle Association president Wayne LaPierre to warn that
Obama had a plot to take away people's guns. But Beck also reassured his viewers that even though they lived under a totalitarian
left-wing government, "You are not alone," adding, "The truth
is, they don't surround us, we surround them." In March, Beck
launched what he called his "We surround them" movement, a
threatening rejoinder to the Obama movement's self-congratula-
tory "We are the ones we've been waiting for."

Against that backdrop of racism, along with rhetoric that was
occasionally not merely abusive but also intimidating, it can sometimes feel ridiculous to blame the president for his troubles, even
a little. But I do. Obama and his team failed to capitalize on the
goodwill he'd earned by Inauguration Day with a vivid explanation for our economic troubles and a bold agenda to respond.
Chief of staff Rahm Emanuel would be attacked by the right for
telling a conference of Wall Street executives in early 2009, "You
never want a crisis to go to waste." Yet that's exactly what they did.

In a decade bracketed by the 9/11 terror attacks and the economic meltdown of 2008, Obama had a rare chance to move the
country toward a new vision of American purpose and identity.
"I hope this is going to be a Rooseveltian moment, when the president stepped up and took the action that was needed," Christina
Romer told the *Wall Street Journal* during the debate over the
stimulus bill. "And I think it will be."

It was not. A disappointed Marshall Ganz would later put it:
"We listened in vain for an economic version of the race speech."
It never came.

Now, to this day Obama's defenders deride his progressive critics for a childish view of politics in which a president can change the country with an inspiring speech or two. That's not the case I'm making. From the stimulus bill onward, Obama failed to give voters a vision of the kind of government role that would be required to fix the economy, even if he had to compromise and settle for less. And let's be clear. He did have to settle for less: because the Senate barely passed the $787 billion stimulus bill, even though 40 percent of it went to tax cuts, it's hard to imagine the president getting more than that.

Yet what if the president had laid out bigger, bolder plans for the stimulus, even if he later had to compromise with centrists and conservatives? Some might argue that would have been futile grandstanding, out of character for the pragmatic "no drama" Obama. Really? That's exactly what he did when he tried to sell his proposed "grand bargain" to settle the 2011 debt-ceiling stalemate, even though, in the end, the GOP didn't bite. That let the president tell voters he was the one who really wanted to cut the deficit, but Republicans wouldn't let him. In the process, he accepted the GOP premise that deficit reduction was more important than job creation, a hallmark of the Democratic Leadership Council "third way" politics he'd supposedly rejected. But even critics had to admit it was a bold move.

Imagine if the new president had told a comparably bold story about the 2008 recession: that he was the one who knew how to use government to fix the economy—but Republicans and Blue Dog Democrats wouldn't let him do all that was needed, so he compromised to do what was possible. Then, when the stimulus worked as well as it did—and it did work, keeping the country out of a depression, according to McCain's economic advisor Mark Zandi, and reversing the steep trend of job losses that began under Bush—but its effects trailed off, he'd have been in a much stronger position to push Congress to do more. Yet Obama never made that case.

Maybe most important, he missed the opportunity the 2008 crash provided to tell a bigger Democratic story, about the way thirty years of tax cuts for the wealthy, finance-sector deregulation, declining unions, and depressed wages created this long-term and long-coming crisis. The entire machinery of government, under Democrats and Republicans, had been rigged to privilege the financial sector over any other business sector for the past three decades. Essentially the economy had come to rely on the financial sector's genius in finding ways to profit by lending Americans the money they haven't received from their employers in wage increases since income began to stagnate in the 1970s. Unfortunately, Obama was the preferred candidate of the powerful financial insurance and real estate (FIRE) sector, hauling in 40 percent more in donations than John McCain. Obama's number-one contributor was Goldman Sachs, and most of his top financial advisers had either spent time in investment banking, or, like Treasury secretary Tim Geithner, spent their career making that sector stronger.

The 2008 crisis gave Obama the chance to frame a new Democratic response to the long-term problem of wage stagnation as well as to the short-term crisis. He had a chance to identify the debt machine that destroyed the economy and to begin to dismantle it, and he didn't take it.

Instead, Obama's opponents filled the vacuum with a very different explanation for our troubles.

23

Stop talking, Ms. Walsh.
                                    —Bill O'Reilly, June 2009

As much as I believe a bold, twenty-first-century Keynesian strategy to restore the economy would have helped Obama politically, even if Republicans and conservative Democrats opposed it, the president had political opponents who couldn't be soothed by inspiring Rooseveltian rhetoric. Sometimes I tried to write off the madness of Rush Limbaugh, Glenn Beck, and the Tea Party as mere right-wing ranting, therapeutic identity politics for aging white people. Yet there was something more disturbing going on. At the same time that the Tea Party emerged, to "take our country back" from a president they insisted was illegitimate, several high-profile murders by right-wing crazies made it feel as if the increasingly extreme political rhetoric might be driving the unhinged to violence.

In April 2009, an unemployed Beck fan named Rich Poplawski, who'd been stockpiling weapons, shot and killed three Pittsburgh police officers. "Rich, like myself, loved Glenn Beck," his best friend told reporters. Poplawski feared "the Obama gun ban that's on the way," his friend said—the fictional gun ban that had been conjured up by Beck and his NRA friends. The next month an antiabortion zealot walked into a Lutheran church and murdered Dr. George Tiller, a local abortion provider, as Tiller served as an usher during Sunday services.

Tiller had been the object of an organized smear campaign on the right; he'd been shot before, and his clinic had been firebombed.

213

Fox's Bill O'Reilly in particular had crusaded against the man he called "Tiller the Baby Killer," with twenty-eight segments on the Kansas doctor in four years. He depicted Tiller as a Nazi who had "blood on his hands"—and he insisted that Kansas governor Kathleen Sebelius and anyone else who didn't "stop" Tiller had "blood on their hands," too. The fanatical Scott Roeder stopped Tiller, all right, with a bullet through the eye at close range.

A few days after Tiller's murder, an elderly white supremacist who was also an anti-Obama "birther," James Von Brunn, walked into the United States Holocaust Memorial Museum and murdered an African American security guard before he was arrested. It was getting a little scary. On *Hardball*, Chris Matthews announced, "This is a political action today by a far-right extremist, and I just wonder what's in the water."

> I fatefully replied, "I want to be very careful here, Chris. The only people responsible are the people who pulled the triggers. . . . However, I don't think you can deny that there is a rising climate of right-wing hate, a lot of it directed at Obama. . . . He's a secret Muslim. He hates America. He wasn't born here. This guy, Von Brunn, he was one of the birthers. . . . I don't blame mainstream Republicans, by any means, for this. But they could help in ratcheting down some of the rhetoric. When Bill O'Reilly goes on TV every night and calls Dr. Tiller a baby-killer and a Nazi and a Mengele and shows where he works . . . demonizing a private citizen for doing a lawful job. Why is that acceptable? I would like to see a debate about that."

I got my debate. The next day, O'Reilly invited me onto his Fox show to discuss my charges.

Preparing for the *O'Reilly Factor*, I foolishly rehearsed a rational argument for why the right's violent talk about liberals might be contributing to the climate of violence, especially in the months since we'd elected our first black president. I had examples of times O'Reilly himself had attacked folks on the left for their inflammatory rhetoric (though none of it ever led to murder). Yet O'Reilly made the debate all about the evil of Dr. Tiller and late-term abortion—and turned me into Tiller's accomplice.

"Do you feel that late-term fetuses deserve any protections at all, Ms. Walsh?" he asked to open the segment and he badgered me with the same question at least three more times. Having been raised Catholic, I'm prochoice but still ambivalent about abortion, especially late-term. I told O'Reilly I considered it a tragedy and accepted current law limiting it to saving the life of the mother.

O'Reilly was an angry bully, telling me once, "Stop talking, Ms. Walsh," and berating me for accusing him "of being a vile accomplice to murder."

I corrected him.

"I said you were vile. I did not accuse you of being an accomplice to murder."

He kept it up. "You know who has blood on their hands? You . . . you have blood on your hands because you portray this man as a hero when he killed late-term babies for casual reasons."

It was traumatic. I got a lot of praise from liberals for standing up to O'Reilly. I also got several thousands of e-mails and letters to *Salon*, many of them calling me a murderer and telling me that they wished my mother had aborted me or that my daughter had been forcibly aborted, in vivid, disturbing detail. Such good Christians. I didn't receive any actual death threats; a more experienced journalist friend explained it's not a death threat if someone merely wishes you were dead, only if they specifically threaten to kill you themselves. I guess that was reassuring.

The hate mail rattled me. Yet the worst thing was, I knew a lot of my uncles and cousins had standing dates with O'Reilly every night at 8:00 P.M. sharp on Long Island. It was one thing to defend Obama; now I was defending abortion, of all things, an issue we had stopped discussing in my extended family back in the early 1970s. In the hours between when the show taped and when it aired, I thought of my retired-cop cousin, who loved me despite my politics but loved O'Reilly, too. He would almost certainly be watching, along with his wife, whose cancer had returned and whom I knew wasn't doing very well.

The minute the awful segment ended, my cell phone rang. It was my cousin's wife. "I'm very proud of you," she told me in a voice so soft I could barely hear it. "And I love you." I thought of my mother's grief after a priest condemned prochoice Catholics to hell, just before she died. I felt a kind of grace coming from my mother, through my cousin's brave wife. I didn't know whether my mother or my cousin's wife was personally prochoice; they were just good Catholics who knew the issue wasn't as simple, morally, as bullies such as O'Reilly tried to make it seem.

She died three weeks later. At her funeral, my cousin told me it was the last phone call she had made. Other than that, no one in my family mentioned the O'Reilly segment at all.

The political bullying continued. By August, the Tea Party movement exploded into congressional town halls, where raging protesters shouted down Democrats and Republicans alike, demanding that they block "Obamacare." Hundreds descended on a Tampa Democrat's meeting, and a local newspaper described the event as "more like a wrestling cage match than a panel discussion on national policy." Maryland representative Frank Kratovil was hung in effigy, Long Island representative Tim Bishop needed a police escort from an angry town hall to his car, and North Carolina representative Brad Miller reported death threats.

In New Hampshire, a government-hating activist sported a gun in a leg holster outside an Obama speech while carrying a sign proclaiming, "It's time to water the tree of liberty," a disturbing reference to Thomas Jefferson's "The tree of liberty must be refreshed from time to time with the blood of patriots and tyrants." Ominously, a protester dropped a gun at a raucous Safeway "Meet and Greet" sponsored by Tuscon's Gabrielle Giffords.

Sarah Palin turned up the heat with her fateful claim that Obama wanted to establish "death panels" to decide who deserved life-saving treatment and who didn't. Instead of denying Palin's lie, formerly centrist GOP senator Chuck Grassley amplified it, charging that the president wanted "to pull the plug on Grandma." (Even after that vicious charge, Democrats would still spend weeks seeking Grassley's support for a bill before giving up.)

Violent talk got louder as the health-care vote approached the next March. A Christian libertarian with militia ties called for "Days of Rage" to block the bill, writing on his blog: "If you wish to send a message that Pelosi and her party cannot fail to hear, break their windows. . . . Break them with rocks. Break them with slingshots. Break them with baseball bats. But BREAK THEM."

The weekend after that blog post, a brick reading "No Obamycare" sailed through the window of the Wichita, Kansas, Democratic Party headquarters; another brick smashed the window of the party's Rochester, New York, office, this time adorned with Barry Goldwater's old message "Extremism in the defense of liberty is no vice." Someone shot out the front door of Gabrielle Giffords's Tucson office, and another Arizona Democrat, Raul Grijalva, reported death threats. The Senate's sergeant at arms reported that threats against Congress members rose 300 percent in the early months of 2010.

Gabby Giffords complained about the violence in an interview a few days later, telling MSNBC that she'd been targeted for defeat in 2010 by Sarah Palin's PAC with gun imagery. "We're on Sarah Palin's targeted list, but the thing is that the way that she has it depicted has the crosshairs of a gun sight over our district," she told Chuck Todd. "And when people do that, they've gotta realize there are consequences to that action."

Nine months later, Giffords was struggling to survive an assassination attempt, the first against a member of Congress since 1954. An unemployed community college dropout, Jared Lee Loughner, shot eighteen people and killed six, including a nine-year-old girl, at one of Giffords's "Congress on your Corner" gatherings, the same event where a protester had dropped a gun during the Tucson Democrat's tense August 2009 town hall appearance. It wasn't far from Giffords's district office, where someone had shattered the glass front door the night the health-care reform bill passed. Although it turned out that Loughner had no known right-wing ties, it's easy to understand why Giffords's father, when asked whether his daughter had enemies, told the *New York Post* tearfully, "Yeah, the whole Tea Party."

Yet again, as after the Tiller murder, the mere suggestion that we examine the increasingly violent rhetoric of politics was itself derided as politically inflammatory in the days after the Giffords shooting. Of all of the overheated rhetoric that came in for scrutiny, Sarah Palin's poster putting Giffords in crosshairs got the most discussion, especially because of the eerie March interview where Giffords herself suggested that such violent imagery could have "consequences."

In the days after Giffords's shooting, Palin self-destructed in a mess of rage, narcissism, and revenge over complaints about her rhetoric, making herself out to be the victim in a tragedy where six people had died. In an interview with Sean Hannity, she made it clear that she would not let her enemies stop her. "We should not use an event like that in Arizona to stifle debate," Palin told the admiring Hannity. "They can't make us sit down and shut up. And if they succeeded in doing that, our Republic would be destroyed."

After her Giffords meltdown, I wrote in *Salon*, "Sarah Palin will never be president." Yet the strategy of bullying and dehumanizing and intimidating Democrats that she pioneered in 2008 didn't go away.

With some of the media's blessing, conservatives smeared liberals who questioned intimidating right-wing rhetoric as the real intimidators. They did the same thing when it came to race. Liberals who complained about racism in the right's treatment of President Obama found themselves derided as *the real racists*, seeing slurs where none existed and tossing the term *racist* at innocent whites with intent to harm.

I was caught in a particularly dizzying hall of mirrors, where one day I'd be denouncing anti-Obama racism on the right, and the next day I might be denounced by Obama supporters for my own supposed racial bias if I criticized the president's decisions.

My role as one of Obama's white-liberal defenders intensified during two racial controversies in the summer of 2009: Obama's nomination of the first Latina, Sonia Sotomayor, to the Supreme Court, and the flap over Harvard professor Henry Louis Gates's arrest by a white police officer when he appeared to be breaking into his own home. They exposed what a minefield 21st century racial politics had become, for all of us, whatever our color or our politics.

Republicans immediately denounced Sotomayor as a "racist" because she had suggested, during a speech encouraging nonwhite students to pursue legal careers, that the life experiences of "a wise Latina" might make her rulings "better than" a white judge's. (At her hearings, she backed away from the remarks, which I thought was the right move; the point is equality, not replacing white men with Latinas as the "better" group) Sotomayor had also sided with an appeals-court majority in backing the city of New Haven's fire department's affirmative action plan, which had been challenged by a white firefighter denied promotion. I got dragged into that mess in a *Hardball* debate that was shocking for its tribalism.

It was Chris Matthews, Pat Buchanan, and I, three Irish Catholics, with the two men yelling at me for suggesting (with plenty of evidence) that fire departments had worked hard to keep their ranks white. In New York, a city that's majority black and Latino, the fire department was at the time 91 percent white. In San Francisco, the position of fire chief had been handed down from one Irishman to another, a roster of Sullivans and Kellys and Murrays and Murphys and a Walsh (no relation). When the string was broken by former mayor Willie Brown's pick, the veteran African American chief Bob Demmons, the heavily Irish union went into near-mutiny. Matthews, normally my ally, lost it a little when I described how hard fire departments fought to exclude blacks.

He yelled at me, "Damn it, Joan, the guys that got killed on 9/11, a lot of them were Irish and they chose to be firefighters, because it's a family tradition going back to the nineteenth century . . ."

And I yelled back. "Don't race-bait me, Chris. There are firefighters in my family. God bless them . . ."

"Then why are you accusing them of bigotry?"

"Because the fact of the matter is that they have protected those jobs for their brothers, for their sons, and they're public sector jobs. This isn't the family business, Chris. Bravery comes in all colors."

Of course, the real issue was that good jobs for working-class kids, of every race, had all but disappeared, and the only way to create opportunities for African Americans in cities such as New Haven was to take them away from whites. So, who won my debate with Matthews? Pat Buchanan, without saying a word.

Right after the Sotomayor storm passed, Harvard's African American studies chair Henry Louis Gates returned from a trip without his house keys and got arrested for trying to break into his own Cambridge home after a verbal scuffle with a local cop. Asked about the Gates arrest, Obama first said he didn't know all of the facts about the case of "my friend Skip Gates"—and then waded into the controversy anyway, opining that the Cambridge police had "acted stupidly." The minor squabble became national news because it fit an unfortunate narrative: race trumping class for a Democratic president. Race aside, the class optics of the Gates dispute weren't great for Obama: an Ivy League president sides with his Ivy League buddy, "Skip," against a working-class Irish American cop named Crowley.

It's not hard to see how partisans interpreted this event with two diametrically opposed mind-sets. On the race-obsessed right, it showed that no matter how high privileged black people climbed—to the top of the Ivy League, even to the White House—they'd still play the race card against a working-class cop just doing his job. On the left, it was proof that a black man, no matter how accomplished, would always be guilty in the eyes of a cop. In the end, blowback forced the president to "recalibrate" his remark about the cops behaving "stupidly" and invite Gates and Crowley to the White House for a "beer summit."

Fox had its magic moment in the Gates affair. After the president weighed in on Gates, Glenn Beck called our half-white president a "racist" with a "deep-seated hatred for white people." Rush Limbaugh loudly agreed. When I called that notion ridiculous on *Hardball*, Limbaugh named me the "Magic Honky"—and said I was "the real racist."

That long summer of strife—the town hells, the Sotomayor debate, Gates-gate—took a toll on Obama's standing, especially with white voters. His approval rating among whites had stayed above 60 percent in Gallup's tracking poll well into May 2009, when he nominated Sotomayor. Then it began to drop, and it dropped sharply the week the Gates flap dominated the news. It continued to drop, down into the 30s by September, where it would stay persistently through mid-2012.

Yet nothing summed up the degraded state of racial discourse in the age of Obama more than the saga of Shirley Sherrod, a black woman smeared by the president's right-wing enemies and too quickly abandoned by the Obama administration itself, whose message held the key to reconciling the too often conflicting claims of race and class—except no one bothered to listen to her.

Sherrod owed her awful fifteen minutes of racial infamy to the late right-wing provocateur Andrew Breitbart. A Web self-promoter who'd worked with Arianna Huffington and Matt Drudge, Breitbart launched his own network of right-wing sites and declared his intent to "take down the institutional left." By the end of Sherrod's ordeal, media critics were debating whether Sherrod, not Breitbart, was the racist. There I was again, on television decrying racism, a piñata for the right. Yet this time, the Obama administration and some of its allies wound up on the wrong side, for a while.

The mess began with the historic health-care reform vote, when thousands of Tea Party supporters converged on Washington,

D.C., to protest the bill. Some Tea Partiers harassed black legislators as they walked to cast their votes. One spat on Representative Emanuel Cleaver of Kentucky, on camera; another called civil rights hero Representative John Lewis "nigger," Lewis told reporters. That triggered a renewed debate over how much the anti-Obama movement was powered by racism. Andrew Breitbart denied that the racial insults even happened. He offered a reward to anyone who could prove that John Lewis, the firebrand of the 1963 March on Washington, who'd been brutally beaten in the 1965 Selma march, was actually called the N-word.

When the National Association for the Advancement of Colored People (NAACP) asked the Tea Party to "repudiate" its racist fringe after the attacks on Lewis and Cleaver, Breitbart took revenge. He released video that appeared to show Sherrod, a U.S. Department of Agriculture official, boasting about her own racism against a white farmer, to the laughter and applause of her NAACP audience. He headlined his story "Video Proof: The NAACP Awards Racism—2010." Sherrod and the NAACP's "racism," he wrote, is "a perfect rationalization for why the Tea Party needs to exist."

The right wing finally found its black racist—and she worked for the Obama administration. But not for long. The USDA quickly fired Sherrod, and NAACP president Benjamin Jealous denounced her.

As the world now knows, the video was deceptively edited. Sherrod had told the opposite of a racist tale; she shared the moment she realized that poverty, not race, was the main factor keeping Southern farmers down and decided to help a white farmer on the verge of losing his land. "Working with him made me see that it's really about those who have, versus those who don't," she told the NAACP, to applause. "They could be black, and they could be white, they could be Hispanic. It made me realize that I needed to work to help poor people."

Sherrod's father had been murdered by local whites who were never brought to justice, but her mother, she said, taught her that "if we had tried to live with hate in our hearts, we'd probably be dead now." Sherrod tracked the root of the problem all the way back to the country's beginnings. She told a story we rarely hear, and I heard in it echoes of my father's black-Irish fairytale:

> You know, back in the late seventeenth and eighteenth century . . . there were black indentured servants and white indentured servants, and they all would work for seven years and get their freedom. . . . They married each other. They lived together. And they started look-ing at what was happening to them and decided "We need to do something about it" . . . Well, the people with money, the elite, decided, "Hey, we need to do some-thing here to divide them."
>
> So that's when they made black people servants for life. That's when they put laws in place forbidding them to marry each other. That's when they created the racism that we know of today. They did it to keep us divided. . . . Over four hundred years later, and it's still working. What we have to do is get that out of our heads. There is no difference between us.

Within hours of Breitbart's smear, the truth about Shirley Sherrod came out. The wife of the farmer in the story, Elise Spooner, contacted CNN, and soon the Spooners were on TV praising Sherrod for helping them keep their farm. Civil rights historians recognized Sherrod as a veteran of Georgia's storied Albany Movement; her husband, Charles, had been its leader; he went on to serve as an Albany city councilmember. I tracked down King biographer Taylor Branch, who told me that when he heard the news, "I said, 'Oh, my God, it's Shirley Sherrod?' She is such a gem. We should be listening to what she has to say."

Yet few people listened to what she had to say. Representative Jim Clyburn told the *New York Times* that the Obama adminis-tration's ignorance about Sherrod's past showed that the president "needs some black people around him." Really? Why go there? If our black president didn't know enough civil rights history to recognize the Sherrods, clearly being black didn't guarantee that knowledge. Maybe the president needed more people around him who know civil rights history, regardless of their race. Clyburn didn't get Shirley Sherrod's message, either. Here was a black woman standing up for poor people of every color, talking about class, not just race. Predictably, the right distorted her message and made her into a racist villain—that's what they do. But liberals also found ways to make her story all about race and ignore her message about class.

When Sherrod complained about Breitbart's racism and sued him, mainstream television news shows began debating whether her complaints about racism were "fair." I defended Sherrod on MSNBC and CNN. In one segment, conservative Matt Lewis harrumphed that Sherrod had gone too far in calling Breitbart racist. I disagreed, noting that her father had been murdered by a white farmer, with witnesses, but the murderer never went to jail, adding, "She's entitled to talk about race any way she wants to."

Lewis shot back, "So, if you've had a bad experience in your background, you can say just anything you want?"

I got a little apoplectic. "'*A bad experience in your background?*' I'm talking about murder. Murder, Matt. . . . The idea that she shouldn't be able to say Breitbart is racist is preposterous. She gets to say that because it's true, and because from her vantage point it's especially true."

I couldn't move the focus from Sherrod's justifiably angry reaction to the right-wing assault on her character. Instead, the story remained Sherrod's "smearing" of her smearers, and I was widely attacked on the right for defending Sherrod's "racism."

Yet soon I'd be facing down charges that *I* was the racist—not from Rush Limbaugh this time, but from Obama supporters.

24

What I think I was able to recognize was that, at this juncture, the country will feel better about itself . . . if they see Democrats and Republicans agreeing on anything.
—Barack Obama, December 2010,
after extending the Bush tax cuts

Even with all of the anti-Obama racism I saw, I didn't believe his administration's mounting troubles were all about race. The health-care reform bill, though a triumph, went badly. The White House frustrated progressives by cutting deals with big health-care corporate interests to gain their support. The pharmaceutical lobby kicked in an estimated $95 billion in drug subsidies in exchange for the administration agreeing to keep Medicare from negotiating discounts or re importing lower-cost drugs from other countries. The administration promised a public option for government-provided insurance as part of the bill but never pushed for it.

Rahm Emanuel was unapologetic about the White House nods to the health-care industry, pointing to the way those forces had blocked health-care reform going back to Harry Truman. "The lesson is, you gotta get the constituency groups to participate in the reform process," he said. Teddy Roosevelt might have called the health-care titans "malefactors of great wealth"; FDR liked to denounce "economic royalists" who stood in the way of his plans; Emanuel called them a "constituency group." That was one difference between the Obama administration and FDR's.

Battling over the health-care bill opened a rift between the administration and the left that never healed. When progressives told Emanuel they wanted to run ads in the district of Blue Dog Democrats to urge them to back the administration's bill, Emanuel famously exploded, calling the idea "fucking retarded." After a union-funded Democratic primary challenge to Blue Dog senator Blanche Lincoln of Arkansas failed, a White House official anonymously trashed the AFL-CIO. "Organized labor just flushed $10 million of their members' money down the toilet on a pointless exercise," the official told *Politico*. Lincoln went down to defeat in November and joined a conservative business lobby to fight new EPA clean-air rules, cashing in as her fellow Blue Dog Evan Bayh had. Still, progressives hadn't proved, for all of their effort, that any Democrat to the left of Blanche Lincoln could be elected in Arkansas, either.

As the midterm debacle looked certain, progressive critics began to squawk, including some who had worked hard to elect Obama. "I am one of the millions of frustrated Americans who want to see Washington do more than it's doing right now," Steve Hildebrand, a former Obama field campaign director, told a reporter. Hildebrand had objected when the White House folded the organizing juggernaut Obama for America into the DNC, neutralizing it as an independent force for change. "We face a possible loss for both the House and Senate Democratic majorities, and I really believe it comes down to whether or not you chose to lead. And, I don't think they chose to lead. I think they ran scared from day one." Economist Robert Reich, the Clinton labor secretary who backed Obama early, warned that "an enthusiasm gap," due to the administration's halfway measures on the economy, could keep Democrats home.

Yet some in the White House blamed the enthusiasm gap on the carping of lefty critics such as Reich and Hildebrand. Obama spokesperson Robert Gibbs blasted what he termed "the professional left" as "crazy," caricaturing progressives in terms Richard Nixon might have used: "They will be satisfied when we have Canadian health care and we've eliminated the Pentagon," and suggesting they ought to be "drug tested." Great. A Democrat associated the party's liberal base with socialized medicine, a naive antimilitary stance, and drug use, all of those stereotypes from the sixties. Nice work, Mr. Gibbs! The next month Vice President Joe Biden told progressives to "stop whining" and appreciate the administration's many achievements in brutally hard economic and political times.

I took the vice president to task for his left-bashing on *Hardball*, while noting that I loved the Irish Catholic pol "like an uncle." A half-hour later, Biden called me from *Air Force 2*. He admitted his words had been intemperate, maybe even counterproductive, but he said they reflected the administration's genuine fear that dampened Democratic turnout was going to mean big losses in November. (Being Joe Biden, he told me he loved me, too. And I believed him.)

Biden was right about disappointing Democratic turnout. The GOP took back the House, picking up sixty seats, with twenty-eight of the winners official Tea Party candidates. The Democrats kept the Senate, after several Tea Party candidates ran disastrous campaigns and lost badly, squandering a solid chance for the GOP to take back the Senate. Yet the Democratic circular firing squad was just assembling.

Beyond the electoral carnage, I saw bad news for Democrats buried in the same voter turnout data and exit polls that had revealed such transformative good news just two years earlier. Key members of the Obama coalition stayed home. Only 12 percent of 2010 voters were eighteen to twenty-nine years of age, compared with 18 percent in 2008. Likewise, minority-voter turnout dropped from 26 percent of the total to 23 percent in 2010—and that was the first minority-voter drop recorded since 1992. The share of voters who were union members went down.

Two other data points jumped out at me. In 2008, voters who thought the economy was in bad shape voted overwhelmingly for Obama, according to CNN exit polls. This time, they voted

Republican. Maybe more disturbing, those who said Wall Street was the primary culprit in the country's economic woes overwhelmingly backed GOP candidates in 2010. The Democrats' biggest loss of support came among white working-class voters: congressional Democrats lost this group by 10 points in 2008 but by a whopping 30 points two years later.

Was the problem that white working-class racism returned after 2008? Or was it that Democrats once again stood with big business and failed to help working people, at a time when unemployment topped 10 percent? The banks we'd bailed out with tax dollars were doing better than ever. Most of corporate America had recovered. The average CEO got a 23 percent raise in 2010. Corporate profits had climbed 22 percent since 2007. Yet those profits represented 88 percent of economic growth since the recession had ended; wages and salaries accounted for 1 percent. That was the lowest share of growth going to employee income in any recovery during the past thirty years.

Obama sided with the wealthy again right after the election, when he agreed to extend the Bush tax cuts for the rich, which were set to expire at the end of the year, breaking a campaign promise. In his defense, Obama didn't have the votes at that point to repeal the high-end tax cuts—although many wondered why he hadn't pushed congressional Democrats to schedule the vote sooner—and in exchange for his "compromise," he got extended unemployment insurance that helped some of the jobless and a payroll-tax cut that juiced the economy a little. The midterm disaster, plus the tax-cut deal, sent some of Obama's lefty critics around the bend. In the *Huffington Post*, Robert Kuttner raised the idea of a Democrat challenging Obama in the 2012 primaries, but in the very same piece, he rejected it as "premature and far-fetched." The mere mention was all the *New York Times* needed to write, "Talk on the left of a primary challenge to Obama." The *Times* found only tepid interest from Kuttner and a couple of other bloggers, including one who quickly recanted the idea. *Politico* followed with a story speculating that "some angry liberals *may* want to see President Obama face a primary from his left in 2012"—yet even in that very hedged first sentence, quickly added, "but they have no answer to a basic question: Who?" Just as in the *Times* story, every single progressive leader *Politico* quoted shot down the idea of a primary challenge to the president. And every possible challenger mentioned, including Howard Dean, Russ Feingold, and Dennis Kucinich, immediately rejected the notion.

I said repeatedly, in *Salon* and on television, that a primary challenge to Obama was a waste of time; I still think Ted Kennedy's 1980 primary challenge to Jimmy Carter, which I supported, helped elect Ronald Reagan. If we want a more progressive president, I argued, we need to work to elect a more progressive Congress.

Yet the empty speculation touched off an unsettling new round of racial sparring. Two older-generation African American writers penned angry screeds attacking the white left for its Obama criticism. In "Memo to the Left: Hands Off Obama," veteran *Washington Post* columnist Colbert King warned Democrats, "Sabotage the nation's first black president and the Democratic Party might as well bid farewell to its most loyal base of supporters: African Americans." He added, "That's a promise, not a threat." Ishmael Reed made the racial subtext explicit a day later in the *New York Times*, excoriating "white progressives" for their lack of patience with the president, as contrasted with blacks and Latinos, who "are not used to getting it all." The novelist's words made vivid a new definition of "white privilege": criticizing a black president because you're used to "getting it all."

King and Reed surfaced an undercurrent I'd felt online: black Democrats, even black progressives, were generally less inclined to angry eruptions about Obama's latest "betrayal," whether on gay marriage or civil liberties or Wall Street or tax cuts. This wasn't merely identity politics; it harked back to some civil rights' leaders caution in abandoning Lyndon Johnson in 1968 over the Vietnam War, because he'd been the country's best president on race and poverty. One of my heroes, Bayard Rustin, argued to stay with LBJ; Dr. King came out against the war. In my lifetime, black voters have been the most loyal Democrats when the Democratic president is white. Still, in the 1990s, I'd seen black liberals and progressives publicly attack Bill Clinton when he crossed certain political lines, whether it involved disrespecting Sister Souljah, backing down on his nomination of Lani Guenier for assistant attorney general after GOP opposition, or endorsing a Republican-backed welfare reform bill. I don't think there was as much progressive African American outrage at Obama's various political betrayals, but I can't be sure.

I also knew that the far right's racism, gun toting, and violent rhetoric renewed some black voters' early fears that the murderous forces of reaction would claim our first black president. The unmistakable upsurge in threatening talk and imagery was like a faded but still disturbing echo of Jim Crow terror, in which the ever-present threat of violence, not just the violent acts themselves, were intended to intimidate Southern blacks out of exercising their basic rights. The outsized, outraged reaction against the first black president, the guns and the bull's-eyes, and the threat to use "Second Amendment remedies" to "take our country back" seemed intended to perform the same kind of intimidation, and it cemented Obama's ties to his African American base.

Yet racial politics got really mixed up when *black* progressives started openly criticizing the president. In June 2011, longtime lefty gadfly and Princeton professor Cornel West attacked Obama as a "a black mascot of Wall Street oligarchs and a black puppet of corporate plutocrats." West derided Obama in tawdry racial terms, claiming he was afraid of "free black men" due to his white ancestry and years in the Ivy League. "He feels most comfortable with upper-middle-class white and Jewish men who consider themselves very smart, very savvy, and very effective in getting what they want," West charged. Oy. The Jews again.

The controversy looked like progressives devouring their own tails. From the left, West attacked Obama for not being black enough; black Obama supporters accused West of being an older-generation leader jealous that he wasn't in Obama's inner circle; in a pro-West backlash, West's allies dismissed black Obama supporters as "elitist" fronts for white liberals and that half-white guy in the White House. People took potshots at some of the players based on their status in Ivy League kerfuffles during the last decade. Preposterously, West attacked Obama's Ivy League background—yes, the president has degrees from Harvard and Columbia—when West himself had been sheltered beneath the cool ivy for most of his career. A West defender continued the theme, trashing West critic Melissa Harris-Perry as "a darker-skinned staple in the white liberal establishment" and an "Ivy League" pro-Obama sellout. Others suggested that Harris-Perry attacked West because they didn't get along at Princeton. Some linked West's anti-Obama animus to the presence of Larry Summers in Obama's cabinet, because West and Summers had clashed back when Summers was Harvard president, and an angry West ditched Harvard for Princeton.

It was farcical. Was our troubled country really supposed to care about who didn't get along with whom in the Ivy League? I guess it represented a kind of progress, given that all of the Ivy League protagonists were black. But with devastating economic problems besieging the country, the right successfully provoked the left into arguing about race in a way that not only divided progressive allies but also united conservative ones. It was depressing.

The racial battles only got stranger during the debt-ceiling debacle. Obama drew out negotiations, looking for his "grand bargain," a big deal to reduce the deficit, offering to consider cost-trimming changes to Medicare and Social Security, sacred Democratic programs, in exchange for closing tax loopholes and maybe even imposing higher taxes on the wealthy (because John Boehner killed the bargain, we never learned exactly what was supposedly in it). Before it all fell apart, the president tried to sell the idea of a big deficit-cutting deal to progressives.

"Get this problem off the table," Obama argued, "and then with some firm footing, with a solid fiscal situation, we will then be in a position to make the kind of investments that I think are going to be necessary to win the future."

The problem was, Bill Clinton had already tried that. Not only did he balance the budget to eliminate Ronald Reagan's deficit, he also endorsed and enacted a welfare-reform plan largely crafted by Republicans. Both bold decisions were supposed to show that Democrats could be trusted to tame the excesses of the Great Society and usher in an era of smart, pragmatic, humane government that combined private sector discipline with New Deal values. If Clinton could get the issues of welfare and bloated government "off the table," he believed, he could set the table for a progressive agenda. It didn't work, and I didn't think Obama's maneuver would, either.

Progressive Obama criticism got louder from all sides after the debt-ceiling deal. The AFL-CIO's Richard Trumka, whose passionate antiracism appeal helped swing white union members to vote for the black Democrat in 2008, denounced Obama's compromise. Members of the Congressional Black Caucus did, too; Emanuel Cleaver called it, memorably, "a sugar-coated Satan sandwich." Representative Maxine Waters told a black audience that the CBC had muted its Obama criticism because "if we go after the president too hard, you're going after us. We're getting tired, y'all," Waters continued. "We want to give him every opportunity. But our people are hurting. The unemployment is unconscionable."

Obama's defenders struck back at Trumka and the CBC. The founder of a fiercely pro-Obama website, "The People's View," denounced Trumka, a former mineworker, as an "elitist" for his criticism. Black pro-Obama bloggers trashed Cleaver and Waters as "starter Negroes"—the kind whom clueless white liberals found inoffensive—betraying their black president to suck up to whites. Both Cleaver and Waters, it was suddenly noted, had backed Hillary Clinton in the 2008 primary. When I criticized the debt deal, it was roundly noted that I had supported Clinton, too, an original sin that apparently made my concerns about the president a case of sore loserdom, although I had come to passionately support Obama. The Nation's Melissa Harris-Perry, a writer I admire, suggested that white liberals' rising Obama criticism might be "a more insidious form of racism" due to "the tendency of white liberals to hold African American leaders to a higher standard than their white counterparts."

When it came to Obama, it seemed, no one got credit anymore for speaking from genuine moral or political conviction; everyone could be dismissed or derided with a nod to their personal background. If you're white, it's your "white privilege" speaking. But if you're black, you're the wrong kind of black: you're old or jealous or angry that you're left out of Obama's inner circle. If you're neither white nor black, you don't understand American race relations, and you should butt out.

It felt like a Nixonian dirty trick. Race had torn apart the New Deal coalition in my childhood; as we kept squabbling, it seemed as if the right would roll back the New Deal itself. I really wondered whether the spirit of Chuck Colson and "rat-fucking" was alive and well online in the twenty-first century, as particularly vicious pro-Obama online trolls went after liberal Obama doubters in harsh personal terms. Could these people really be Democrats?

Maybe this was the logical end of identity politics: each of us winds up locked inside whichever little box we check or whichever box is assigned to us; tiny, fragile, impotent caucuses of one, while Pat Buchanan wins. That's how I felt at the time, anyway.

PART V

WHAT'S THE MATTER WITH WHITE PEOPLE?

25

White males of the 2000s are less industrious than they
had been twenty, thirty, or forty years ago.
                            —Charles Murray, *Coming Apart:*
                   The State of White America 1960–2010

Despite his tireless attempts to woo voters by showing that he
was a man of compromise, Obama's approval rating continued to sink after the debt deal. More than a third of independents, the president's prized constituency, thought he caved to the
GOP too easily and wanted him to fight back, according to opinion polls—and a majority of Democratic-leaning independents
felt that way. Most Americans seemed able to see what our gifted
president appeared not to, for a while: that it takes two to compromise, and Obama had spent most of the summer negotiating
with himself. So he began fighting back. Having gone to the mat
for a deficit-cutting "grand bargain" that was predictably rejected
by Republicans, the president crafted a new jobs bill that was also
predictably rejected by Republicans. Yet this time he was fighting for a tangible goal that would measurably help unemployed
Americans, and his approval rating began to climb.

What changed? Was it really that he'd taken a tougher, more
populist tone on the economy? I'd argue yes, it helped that he got
tougher—and that the GOP got more brazenly stupid.

In fact, Republicans appeared to be trying to alienate a cornerstone
of their party's base: the white working class. When the president

tried to get Congress to pass the section of his jobs bill sending aid to states to avert laying off police and firefighters, Senate minority leader Mitch McConnell derided it as a "bailout," making him the perfect symbol for a party that was fine with bailing out banks but did nothing for the bank's victims. The leading 2012 presidential candidates began regularly demonizing all forms of "dependency" on government with a bitterness they once reserved for black welfare recipients. Newt Gingrich called Obama "the food stamp president," which let him play on that old Reagan-era racism associating the program with black people, but he was able to deny his racial meaning by noting that most of the 46 million Americans on food stamps (as well as the 7.5 million receiving unemployment benefits) are white.

Likewise, when Rick Santorum got into hot water for seeming to say he didn't want to make "black people's lives better by giving them other people's money," he could argue—even if not entirely believably—that he wasn't talking about black people (or "blah" people, as he claimed): "I've been pretty clear about my concern for dependency in this country and concern for people not being more dependent on our government, whatever their race or ethnicity is." All of the candidates came out for cutting or abolishing the earned income tax credit, the low-wage subsidy enacted by President Gerald Ford in 1975 and vastly expanded by President Clinton (in part because they said it made those who paid no taxes a constituency for tax hikes on the rich).

Democrats had come to describe Republicans' coded language about race as "dog whistle politics"; only its intended targets could hear it. Now the GOP seemed to be pioneering a new kind of dog whistle politics: saying negative things about the "dependent" white working class, but hoping their loyal voters within that group wouldn't hear it.

Some 2010 GOP voters seemed to get wise to the ruse after the election, however, when new GOP governors made unexpectedly aggressive moves against labor—and in Wisconsin and Ohio, working-class voters fought back. Wisconsin's Scott Walker and Ohio's John Kasich made public workers the new public enemy, demonizing them as slackers and moochers living off the government, as if they were twenty-first century welfare queens. In November 2011, Ohio repealed GOP Kasich's bill that stripped public sector unions of their collective bargaining rights, and Wisconsin voters began a drive to recall Walker.

Maine elected a Tea Party Republican governor in 2010. A year later, voters overturned a GOP-sponsored law that had abolished the state's traditional same-day registration practice. The states that allowed citizens to register and vote at the same time, a practice that dramatically increases voter turnout, just happened to be the nation's most homogeneous—that is, the whitest—from Idaho to Wyoming to Maine. Yet once Republicans realized that even in the whitest states, same-day voter laws and other easy ballot-access regulations empower citizens who are today more likely to vote for Democrats—students, young people, the lower-income of every race, and yes, the nonwhites—they've fought these voter laws ruthlessly. "Voting liberal, that's what kids do," a New Hampshire Republican said in defense of a bill that would prohibit people from voting with only a college ID—and given his state's demographics, he was mainly talking about white kids. Thus the radical GOP is now rolling back rights white people have long taken for granted—and in Maine, at least, they fought back.

The Ohio collective bargaining victory, the Wisconsin recall, the Maine same-day voter registration backlash: all were evidence of the new activism most widely represented in the Occupy Wall Street (OWS) movement. It had an immediate success: media mentions of the word *inequality* soared as OWS took off. A Tumblr blog, "We are the 99 percent," became the twenty-first-century, DIY version of Michael Harrington's *The Other America*. It put faces and stories to the millions of ways Americans had fallen out of the middle class or failed to climb there—crushing student loans, losing health insurance, a sick child or parent, foreclosure, layoffs—and the role of our political system in keeping them down. *Time* magazine named OWS its 2011 "story of the year," a great honor for an inchoate political movement that was barely twelve weeks old at the time. OWS struggled to remain relevant after its first few months, but the immediate popularity of its "99 percent"

imagery showed a yearning for unity that the fractional sloganeer-
ing and zero-sum politics of the last thirty years never tapped into.

There was even good news for liberals from Pat Buchanan.
Right at the moment when I worried that Buchanan was winning again, that he might always win, as I watched Democrats
fight dead-end battles about identity, Buchanan himself declared
defeat. In his apocalyptic, overwrought *Suicide of a Superpower:
Will America Survive until 2025?* he saw the sun setting on the
white Christian American empire he once ruled. According
to Buchanan, Democrats needn't fret about politics anymore;
demography is destiny. We've won.

"The European and Christian core of our country is shrinking,"
he wrote. "The birthrate of our native born has been below replace-
ment level for decades. By 2020, deaths among white Americans
will exceed births, while mass immigration is forever altering
the face of America." Soon, even whites who supported Obama,
Buchanan warned, "may discover what it is like to ride in the back
of the bus." The architect of Nixon's win-over-whites strategy simply couldn't see a place for himself in a majority nonwhite America.
It's impossible to know how many white people feel the same way,
but the book became a best seller. We know Buchanan has company.

One of the burdens of blackness, W. E. B. DuBois famously
wrote, was facing down an omnipresent question from the wider
society: "How does it feel to be a problem?" I wonder if white
people might soon understand what he meant.

Both the right and left, in the age of Barack Obama, suddenly
had a lot of complaints about white people, particularly the white
working class. In his latest book, Buchanan describes his white
brethren contemptuously at times, as an endangered species oblivi-
ously collaborating in its own demise by tolerating liberal multiculturalism. *Losing Ground*'s Charles Murray, the man who provided
the intellectual basis for Reagan's war on poverty programs, derided
the white working class in terms he used to direct toward blacks
in his 2012 bestseller *Coming Apart: The State of White America*

1960–2010. A rise in single parenthood and a drop in their work ethic was to blame for the declining status of lower-class whites, Murray insisted. But he said white rich people are a problem, too: the white uber-class, whose share of income has soared largely because they stay married and work hard, refuses to impose its own traditional values on their lazy, out-of-control lessers, Murray complained.

To the left, of course, white people have been a problem for a while, of course, thanks to the depth and persistence of white racism. In the Democratic Party, they've been a problem since Buchanan lured working class whites to Nixon. It's now remarkable the extent to which the Republican Party has become a white party. Where that was an advantage back in Buchanan's day, though, it's an eroding base in the twenty-first century. About 52 percent of white voters call themselves Republicans, according to the Pew Research Center, as opposed to 8 percent of blacks and 22 percent of Latinos. In February 2012 *New York* magazine writer Jonathan Chait observed that white voters were all that stood between the Republican Party and "demographic extinction." But since white America itself will soon be demographically extinct, as the dominant racial group anyway, Chait saw the GOP doubling down on its forty-year strategy of fomenting culture war and racial resentment for a "last stand" in 2012 that calls to mind Custer's. Can it work?

It's true: white Americans will technically be a minority by midcentury—although questions about how we count "white people" versus "people of color" (some mixed-race people as well as most Latinos think of themselves as "white") let us crunch these numbers in different ways. However we crunch them, though, Pat Buchanan is right—about the country's demographic future, anyway. Sometime in the twenty-first century this won't be a "white" country anymore. There are signs that some white people, at least, aren't taking it all that well.

Should Democrats pop the champagne corks and celebrate the permanent political realignment? Should supporters of racial justice cheer on the new demographic reality? It's a little early, on both counts. In 2008, James Carville jumped the gun with his triumphal book *Forty More Years.* In 2010, of course, the GOP took back the House and narrowed the Democrats' lead dangerously in the Senate, when the proportion of white and senior voters rose and the share of young and minority voters declined. It could happen again.

But even if time seems to be on our side, there are risks involved in Democrats talking about a counter-racial strategy. Some campaign strategists have suggested that the president worry less about the stubborn white working class in 2012 and double down on the coalition that elected him: young people, the college-educated, unmarried women, and minorities, particularly African Americans and Latinos. The right, in turn, has picked up on such musings and exaggerated them, all to keep that white-hot white resentment burning.

In late 2011, a *Wall Street Journal* columnist announced, "Obama Will Abandon the Working Class." Rush Limbaugh teed off from there, screaming that Obama "publicly writes off white working-class families as advertisement to his base," claiming "the Obama campaign says to white working class families: we're not interested in your votes; we don't care."

The president's crafty strategy, Limbaugh insisted, is meant not only to disrespect whites but also to rev up and turn out his non-white base, which presumably thrills to the notion of reparations and race war. Of course it's Limbaugh and his hard-core listeners who want a race war; the rest of us, of every race, mainly just want to get along.

Still, as I've explained many times in this book, I have a problem with liberals who dismiss the white working class as hopelessly Republican and racist, because they ignore something interesting: in 2008, our first black president got a higher share of their votes than any recent white Democrat in this generation, including John Kerry, Al Gor, and even Bill Clinton. A *New York Times* analysis found that Obama won 46 percent of whites without a college degree who earned between $30,000 and $75,000 a year, to Bill Clinton's 44 percent. He kept John McCain's edge with that group to 6 points, when George W. Bush won them by 35 points against John Kerry four years earlier. And in some swing states, such as Ohio, the "Obama coalition" ultimately included the white working class.

Yes, many of those voters raced back into the Republican column in 2010, when the GOP ran up a 30-point edge in midterm congressional races, and for much of 2011, Democrats talked about a strategy to keep the White House without winning Ohio, Wisconsin, and Pennsylvania, key swing states he took in 2008. But I'm not sure why we'd conclude that those voters' problem was mainly racial, or that they had run back to the GOP for good. Had they shaken off their racism in 2008, only to have it return like a stubborn virus in 2010? Did the president become more black? What if their reaction derived from frustration with Democratic leaders who hadn't pursued an economic turnaround agenda aggressively enough, at a time when unemployment stood at more than 10 percent—and almost 15 percent for whites without a college degree?

The GOP's new dog-whistle politics, trashing white people in coded language once reserved for blacks, opens new opportunities for Democrats—if they can help those white people translate the new GOP rhetoric. In a 2012 debate, then-front-runner Rick Santorum approvingly quoted from Charles Murray's *Coming Apart*, hoping his listeners wouldn't know that this time Murray was scolding white people. After Georgetown University student Sandra Fluke supported President Obama's insurance regulations mandating cost-free contraception, conservatives began trashing the young white law student as a "welfare queen" wanting birth control on the taxpayers' dime.

But "dependent voters" aren't just a problem to the GOP because they eat up our tax dollars. "Republican supporters will continue to decrease every year as more Americans become dependent on the government," Tea Party Senator Jim DeMint wrote in his shrill 2012 book *Now or Never.* "Dependent voters will naturally elect even big-government progressives who will continue to smother economic growth and spend America deeper into debt. The 2012 election may be the last opportunity for Republicans." Wisconsin conservative representative Paul Ryan, he of the "Ryan Plan" to abolish Medicare, divides the electorate into "makers" and "takers."

This is coded language meant to whip the GOP base into a frenzy of fear and resentment. Because for the past forty years, we've all known who the "takers" were, or were supposed to be, anyway: the welfare queens, the urban rioters, the students, the slackers, the various people the Democrats sided with in the 1960s, most of them, in the partisan story-telling, African American.

Yet today, many white folks who are voting Republican don't seem to know one important detail: they are, in fact, the "takers."

We saw white Tea Party supporters demanding the government stay out of their Medicare. We know that much of the GOP's aging white base relies on Social Security.

But the contradiction runs even deeper than that: Dartmouth political scientist Dean Lacy found the more a county receives in federal government payments, the more likely it is to vote Republican. *The New York Times* referred to Lacy's research in its understated but still rather shocking feature "Even Critics of Safety Net Depend On It." As Lacy elaborated to a WNYC reporter: "The counties that are getting more in crop subsidies, housing assistance, and Medicaid payments are a lot more Republican. So it really is about that catch-all category that you might call welfare." Yet because their local congressmen and women tend to defend that type of "welfare," Lacy says, "they have the luxury of voting on social issues knowing that these federal spending programs will be kept in place."

Except those programs won't be kept in place by the new GOP, which is committed to trashing even the economic supports it used to (however hypocritically) defend.

The Democratic Party should even have a chance to make inroads with white seniors in 2012 if they're able to broadcast the extremist Republican crusade even against programs that protect *them*. As long as they give up on the delusion of a "grand bargain," trading Social Security and Medicare cuts for revenue increases, that the president and some of his party allies floated during the debt-ceiling debacle of 2011.

As long as they make it clear they're Democrats, that is.

26

Empathy for one party is always prejudice against another.
—Senator Jeff Sessions, July 2009

I am repeatedly struck by the extent to which conservatives have given up on the America we all grew up with: apparently it costs too much and we can't afford it, and besides, we can't all get along, so we can't enjoy it.

In 2011 *New York Times* columnist Ross Douthat warned Americans that we can no longer provide a strong social welfare state—the kind of society that supports people the way we did from the mid-1930s until the end of the 1970s—because we're too diverse for it. As Douthat argued:

> Historically, the most successful welfare states (think Scandinavia) have depended on ethnic solidarity to sustain their tax-and-transfer programs. But the working-age America of the future will be far more diverse than the retired cohort it's laboring to support. Asking a population that's increasingly brown and beige to accept punishing tax rates while white seniors receive roughly $3 in Medicare benefits for every dollar they paid in (the projected ratio in the 2030s) promises to polarize the country along racial as well as generational lines.

Douthat seemed to fear that the "brown and beige" kids who'll be paying into Social Security and Medicare for the next generation might not look kindly on supporting a population that's disproportionately white. So we may as well unravel our social insurance programs before those tawny kids pull the plug on Grandma? How cynical, how sad.

It's brazen of anyone on the right to warn us that government programs might polarize the country along racial lines, as though we are not already polarized, at least partly because of GOP divide-and-conquer politics. Yet the relationship between American diversity and trust in government is actually an old controversy, with Douthat adding a twenty-first-century right-wing spin. Scholars have long debated whether Americans have a weaker public sector because of our heterogeneity. Some argue that we have less social support and more harried lives than people in comparable nations, at least partly because we don't want to take the chance that increased social spending and a broader safety net will help "other people," those slackers and moochers we've always feared.

In fact, the United States lags behind all industrialized nations when it comes to direct government funding of health care, family leave, child care, and unemployment benefits. In an influential 2004 book, *Fighting Poverty in the U.S. and Europe: A World of Difference*, Harvard economists Alberto Alesina and Edward Glaeser attributed most of the gap in social spending between western Europe and the United States to our unrivaled mix of racial and ethnic groups and the distrust that engendered.

Now, when you add in American social spending on public education, which used to be the highest in the world, as well as employer-provided social supports subsidized by government with tax breaks—health insurance and 401(k)s, to name two big examples—the US welfare state isn't necessarily smaller than that of a lot of industrialized nations. But it's a heavily privatized welfare state, and that strange hybrid has a lot to do with our racially and ethnically polarized political history. Yet even that hybrid is now being threatened as employers insist they can't afford to keep the promises made in an earlier generation. As businesses shed the benefits that used to help keep American workers in the middle class, they imply that those workers are greedy to expect them. They're slackers. Moochers. Privatized-welfare queens.

There is also a fascinating correlation relationship between societies that provide universal government programs—such as Social Security and Medicare, as opposed to food stamps and Medicaid and cash grants only for the "poor"—and societies with high levels of social trust. Which comes first, the trust to provide universal government programs, or government programs that foster a sense of unity and trust?

As the right loses faith in the America we grew up with, it gives the rest of us an opportunity and a clear responsibility. Douthat seems to be saying we can't have a real social compact in a multiracial society; it works only in monochromatic societies. I think it would be the ultimate example of American exceptionalism to prove him (as well as Pat Buchanan and Charles Murray) wrong. We have to be the ones who develop a version of the American Dream that works for everyone.

And yes, that includes the white working class.

So what *is* the matter with white people, anyway?

When I wrote that sentence, I could hear aggrieved whites on the right getting indignant. We can't generalize about any other group like that, why ask such a question about white people!? From the left, suggesting whites could experience something W. E. B. DuBois once wrote about might sound like I'm saying their troubles are comparable to those of black folk. Of course, I'm not saying that.

But if the problem of the twentieth century was the color line, as Du Bois said, in the twenty-first century it's the color *lines*. We don't yet have a new narrative around social justice that makes sense in a world without a dominant majority. We don't quite know what to do with white people.

Of course, whites will remain ascendant economically and politically even after they lose demographic dominance, partly due to the legacy and endurance of racism. But it's clear that times are harder in certain segments of white America. White unemployment and poverty doubled during this last recession, though both rates are only half those of African Americans. Asian American median income is higher that white median income, and growing faster. Asian Americans have higher college completion rates than whites, and the gulf is widening.

In *Suicide of a Superpower,* poor Pat Buchanan seemed to believe that the rapidly growing number of Asian Americans in the nation's top schools had to do with affirmative action. I used to hear the same thing from clueless white people back before the passage of Ward Connerly's Prop. 209 in 1997, which abolished affirmative action. Of course they were wrong—Asian American students were succeeding the old fashioned way, with hard work. Since then, of course, the white proportion of UC students has continued to decline, even without affirmative action.

Living in California it's easy to see subtle and not so subtle signs of white status anxiety, real and imagined. I was intrigued to see, in a recent Pew Research Center survey of intermarriage trends, that intermarriage rates are going up for every group, except for Asian Americans, whose rates have long been among the highest but which are now coming down. Twenty years ago, when I was first writing about California's racial frontier, sociologists explained high rates of Asian "out-marriage" as a kind of status-seeking: "marrying out" was a way of "marrying up." Whites sought out Asian partners, in this analysis, as the closest surrogate for whites and as partners who in some settings might even represent their "marrying up." Whatever the motive behind their pairings, white/Asian couples have the highest income of any pairings, Pew found, including white/white and Asian/Asian, and were far more likely than any other group to have college degrees. But it's noteworthy to me that the Asian "outmarriage" rate has dropped significantly over the past few years; from just 2010 to 2008, the percentage of American-born Asians newlyweds who married whites dropped from 47 percent to 38 percent—a result of a larger Asian population in the United States, as well as a sign Asian Americans may no longer need to marry out to marry up.

I'm not suggesting Asians are becoming the American master race, or that Asian Americans don't still experience racism. But the way we talk about whites versus "people of color" sometimes seems like we're grouping "haves" and "have nots," and making whites the "haves." A growing number of whites aren't "haves," despite our history. And while the country is facing a demographic and generational mismatch, as an elderly white population is supported by a younger, working population in which whites are a minority, it's possible to exaggerate the importance of that mismatch. Upper-middle-class and wealthy kids of every race are doing okay; poor and working class kids, including whites, not so much. The Pew Research Center says that an astonishing 45% of black middle-class children end up "near poor," as do 16 percent of whites—and that data is from 2007, before the recession. The rate for both groups is too high for any society that prides itself on upward mobility. We can't reassure ourselves, if we live in a majority-white area, that we'll be supported by kids who will be doing well. We all have reason to worry, about everyone's children.

It's impossible to generalize about "white people," of course, and almost as hard to make bold, broad statements about the "white working class." There are regional differences and differences in age; distinctions according to whether people are married or have children. The biggest difference seems to be whether you define that group by income, or whether you define it in terms of people without a college degree. The Democrats' current political troubles have more to do with white people who lack a college education than those who lack income. In 2008, Obama lost white voters who didn't go to college by 18 points, but he lost whites who made less than $50,000 by only four points. No wonder Santorum didn't want us to go to college. (Intermarriage rates are also highest among the college-educated.)

Young or old, surveys and polls find that whites without college degrees are the most pessimistic Americans, with a majority saying they expect their kids to be worse off than they are. Are they all like Pat Buchanan, sulking because their country no longer looks the way it did when they were younger, and they are unwilling to share it with people who aren't white? No doubt, some of them are. But the way that white people, particularly the economically vulnerable, react to the browning of America will have a lot to do with how we treat them. Yes, I said *we* and *them*. The forces of social justice have always looked out for the rights and singular insights of minority populations. We're about to have a new one to think about.

I know white people still hold disproportionate wealth and power in this country. They make up an estimated 95 percent of the top 1 percent. But I'm more interested in the more than 99 percent of whites who are excluded from that top group. Whenever I am trying to figure out whether someone is more interested in equity or in racial score-setting, I ask myself, How do they feel about the top 1 percent having 40 percent of the nation's wealth? Is it wrong, whoever the top 1 percent is, or is it only wrong because they're almost all white? Would it be okay if the top 1 percent still controlled their gargantuan share of the nation's wealth, as long as it was racially representative of the US population? It wouldn't be okay with me, or with most Americans, I think.

Some in the white working class are finally, belatedly, waking up to the issue of economic inequality and the fact that they've been sold out by the GOP. We can either say, "Screw you, what took you so long?" Or we can say, "Welcome, let's get to work." You know my preference. I'm sure most people share it.

Clearly, having a black president didn't change everything about race relations in the United States. But did it change anything?

The 2008 campaign and its aftermath convinced me that we need to make more room for curiosity and awkwardness and making mistakes when it comes to race and political debate. We need to move away from the forbidding boundaries of discourse mostly defined in academia, where people of all races can be bigots or prejudiced, but they can only be "racist" if they are a member of the socially, politically, and economically dominant group. In our kaleidoscopic multiracial society, *racism* is a term that, like it or not, has come to be used by every group to cover slights ranging from a peer in one group not liking your group, to someone consistently disrespecting your group, to actual discrimination in education and employment. The idea that whites can't face racism seems silly. In the San Francisco Bay Area, where we have leaders of every race, whites still disproportionately hold political and economic power, although political power is more diffused. Yet your chances of having a nonwhite teacher, boss, coworker, firefighter, beat cop, prosecutor, or judge are pretty high. Grievances can be misunderstood as racial; they may in fact *be* racial.

White privilege remains real. It describes the omnipresent superstructure of advantage that gave whites a head start in this country and that persists today. It shouldn't be used to discourage questions about our president's political priorities, because our president is now black. On the left, now that we've created a culture in which racism is rightly stigmatized, it's unkind, even cruel, to toss the accusation of racism at allies with little or no evidence. Sometimes it has felt to me as if people who behave that way don't yet understand their own power—or else don't believe white people are fully human. James Baldwin once described the multiracial civil rights movement as "the handful that we are" whose efforts might "end the racial nightmare" and "achieve our country." We are still a comparative handful. Why be cruel to one another? Why cast out allies?

We need to acknowledge that our black and white racial paradigm—victim vs. victimizer, the patron and the patronized—is an outdated script, reducing Asians, Latinos, and the growing number of multiracial Americans either to bit players in our national drama or to a vast army of victims (an identity most nonwhite Americans viscerally reject). Many of us cling to the paradigm, though, because we have no other way of talking about race.

We need a better, more generous language of inclusion. Researchers at UC–Berkeley found that white students reacted more favorably to the idea of multiculturalism and diversity if it was made clear that the experiences of white Americans were part of the mix. It also examined subjects' "need to belong"—it has an acronym, NTB, who knew?—and found that whites with a strong need to belong felt particularly excluded by the way we commonly talk about diversity. This is only common sense. Too often, our rhetoric of multiculturalism has a tinge of payback, of retribution, a touch of "We're the future, and you're not." We're all the future. And the future is here.

I'd like to ask more of white people, too. Conservative advocates of a "common culture" love to point to the slogan *e pluribus unum,* or "out of many, one." I love that idea too. The question today is whether white Americans can accept merely being "one, out of many," rather than the dominant American norm to which others are expected to aspire to join. The right acts like "minorities" invented the dreaded "identity politics." But of course white people invented identity politics. It's been our world, and everyone else has had to live in it, coping the best they can.

More white voters also need to realize that in the forty years they've been receptive to the GOP politics of racial resentment, they've let the party take apart the engines of opportunity that built the largest middle class the world has known. Republicans have grown smug knowing they could offer nothing but tax cuts and deregulation as their economic plan, even after the Bush disaster. But they had to double down on racial fear and culture war intimidation, demonizing our calm, centrist African American president in the crudest of terms, to keep the white working class from noticing that their policies never work.

Thus has the GOP become an ever more extreme and dangerous party. In 2012, Mitt Romney had to repudiate his own moderate, market-driven, formerly Republican stands on core issues—the individual mandate for health insurance, the cap and trade answer to climate change, the earned income tax credit for low-wage workers—to appease an ever more conservative, angry, and out-of-touch base. This is terrible for our country, and it's not good for the Republican Party, either. Even white conservatives might want to think about voting Democratic in the next couple of elections, just to save their party from irrelevance and self-destruction.

Of all of the scarce resources in our society today, I think the most precious is empathy. I also think it can be nurtured. I was struck by Alabama senator Jeff Sessions remarking, during Sonia Sotomayor's Supreme Court confirmation hearings, that "Empathy for one party is always prejudice against another." What a crabbed, cynical worldview, I thought. It's as though empathy is finite, like money in your bank account or gas in your tank. There's also an implicit assumption, shared by Douthat and Buchanan, that if nonwhite people get more power and influence, they'll wield it at the expense of white people, the way (many) white people did when the roles were reversed.

Every once in a while, though, the rhetoric from the left can sound that way. Sometimes the cold demographic analysis of the Democratic Party's future seems to come down to waiting for the white working class to die off. But that's dangerous: if they rally to the Republican Party over the next few elections, they can do enough damage to make life very difficult for the Democratic majority that's waiting to emerge—the young, women, black people, Latinos and Asians—and for themselves. Waiting for them to die seems like a risky strategy, and a little mean, to boot. I can't do that; most of my extended family is among them.

At times I've thought my father's "black Irish" story was less a charming fairy tale than a sentimental, ahistorical fantasy. How useful is it, really, to compare the plight of the lowly, persecuted Irish in America to the cruelty of slavery? There is no comparison. Except there's always comparison; all human behavior exists on a continuum from kindness to cruelty, and empathy starts with comparing and with relating. Empathy starts with a story. His black Irish story, I think, was his way of saying "do unto others" or "love thy neighbor," an improvised fable for a perilous time. We're living through another such time, and we need more stories like that.

ACKNOWLEDGMENTS

A book as sprawling and eccentric as this one requires a lot of thank you's. I have many friends and colleagues to acknowledge, but I'm going to start with the crucial books that inspired, sustained, delighted, and sometimes vexed me, as I grew in confidence that the odd social conflicts I experienced personally, which shaped the singular way I see things, have political meaning today. I drew more from these books than a simple text mention can convey.

I immediately recognized the world Rick Perlstein depicted so clearly in *Nixonland:* I had grown up there. Jefferson Cowie's *Stayin' Alive: The '70s and the Last Days of the Working Class* made the tragic clash between the New Left and labor itself come alive again. *Winner Take All Politics: How Washington Made the Rich Richer, and Turned Its Back on the Middle Class,* by Jacob Hacker and Paul Pierson, made vivid to me how the conditions that let the top 1 percent run away with the country's wealth resulted from political decisions, not merely economic change—and that the Democratic Party's alliance with Wall Street hurt the country as well as the party. Tony Judt's final book, *Ill Fares the Land,* convinced me that Americans needed to recognize that we created the post-war social compact, it wasn't handed to us—and that we can create it again.

I deal in passing with epic historical events and bitter controversies that deserve entire books—and in some cases, inspired them. Three in particular helped me appreciate the complexity of Irish and African-American relations in a way I hadn't before: Leslie M. Harris's *In the Shadow of Slavery: African Americans in New York City, 1626–1863;* Ivor Bernstein's *The New York City Draft Riots* and Angela Murphy's *American Slavery, Irish Freedom: Abolition, Immigrant Citizenship and the Movement for Irish Repeal.*

In the legendary realm of civil rights history, I owe a huge intellectual debt to Taylor Branch for his three part trilogy *America in the King Years* and to David Levering Lewis's *W.E.B. Du Bois 1868–1919: Biography of a Race.* Clarence Jones's *Behind the Dream: The Making of the Speech that Changed the Nation* brought home to me the strong bond between labor and the early civil rights movement. And Rev. Martin Luther King Jr.'s *Chaos or Community: Where Do We Go From Here?* is as relevant today as when he wrote it.

On the history of the Irish in the Highbridge section of the Bronx, I thank poet Joan Murray and scholar Kate Feighery for sharing their thoughts. Michael Scanlon, who followed my father through Sacred Heart School and St. Joseph's Normal Institute at Barrytown, N.Y. shared his own writing, thinking and contacts with me. So did George Pallace and Leo Nolan, my father's classmates at Barrytown in the 1940s, two wonderful men—my father's other "Brothers"—who greeted me as long-lost family when we met in 2011. Author Peter Quinn helped me understand the Bronx Irish in ways too numerous to detail; reading *Looking for Jimmy: A Search for Irish America* convinced me to take my own journey more seriously.

I've been blessed with wonderful colleagues for more than a decade at Salon. I thank Kerry Lauerman, Ruth Henrich, Laura Miller, Thomas Rogers, Sarah Hepola, Mark Schone, Glenn Greenwald, Gary Kamiya, Scott Rosenberg, Jeanne Carstensen, Kevin Berger—and the indefatigable David Talbot, the founder who came back for Round Two. Sandy Close and the late Franz

Schurmann at Pacific News Service have warmly and consistently supported my work since I landed in California more than half my life ago. Bruce Kelley at San Francisco Magazine published some of my favorite stories, and Berkeley Mayor (then Assemblyman) Tom Bates gave me an actual job in government so I can say I haven't just stood outside the gates and shaken my fists at the people who do the hard, important work. I still miss Jimmy Weinstein, who believed the most important moral and political forces in American life included the Congressional Black Caucus and labor unions, not unlike my father's lesson to me. And while I'm going way back, I want to thank the late Michael Huth, my unforgettable high school English literature teacher and the faculty advisor to Shorewood Ripples, our newspaper. He made me realize I was more than just glib; I occasionally had something important to say, when I stopped pretending that success came easily and worked my ass off.

I've spent more than a decade on the board of PolicyLink, a research and advocacy powerhouse advocating for racial and economic equity. Its president, Angela Glover Blackwell, is a friend and mentor who continues to make me think new thoughts, as do my fellow board members Jim Gibson, Sheri Dunn Berry, William Julius Wilson, Stewart Kwoh, Geoff Canada, Kate Muther, Manuel Pastor and Richard Baron—and back in the day, the wonderful Maggie Williams. I get much more than I give there.

I spent six wonderful months with the Skoll Global Threats Fund, and came to believe that if anyone can meet the challenge of Middle East politics, water scarcity, climate change and nuclear proliferation, it will be Larry Brilliant, Bruce Lowry, Mark Smolinski, Eric Nonacs, Annie Maxwell, Kate Wilkinson Sylvia Lee, Veronica Garcia, Scott Field and of course Jeff Skoll.

I am such an unlikely television commentator, having broken in at the age of 48. I am grateful to so many people at MSNBC for the opportunity and the fun and the daily camaraderie—even at a 3,000-mile distance. I learned how to debate passionately yet respectfully from my first sparring partner, Joe Scarborough, and my most frequent host, Hardball's Chris Matthews. Ed Schultz, Rachel Maddow, Rev. Al Sharpton, Lawrence O'Donnell, Chris Hayes, Alex Wagner, Mika Brzezinski, Willie Geist, Martin Bashir and Tamron Hall make me smarter every time I'm on with them. I also thank Pat Buchanan for inspiring me in ways he may not have intended, but also for being gracious with time and information even when we didn't agree. John Reiss, Tara Meltzer, Querry Robinson, Erin Delmore, Ann Klink, Michael LaRosa, Rich Stockwell, Gregg Cockrell, Sheara Braun, Arianna Jones, Barbara Fant, Natasha Lebeveda, Dax Tejera, Michele Setteducato are just some of the people who help me daily. I know I'm forgetting people and I apologize in advance. Thanks to the folks at Beyond Pix studios in San Francisco, who make my time there fun.

So many friends and acquaintances who are writers or editors helped me through this process in crucial ways. Rebecca Traister, Lizz Winstead and Anne Lamott were simply always there. I am grateful for advice along the way from John Judis, George Hodgman, Charles Pierce, Howard Bryant, Will Bunch, William Hoagland, John Amato, Melissa Harris Perry, Kerry Candaele, Robert Reich, Camille Peri, David Sweet, Richard Rodgriguez, David Goldfield, Gloria Steinem, David Frum and Claudia Nowicki Cunningham. *Salon* commenters and *Open Salon* writers Clio Tarazi, Mary Kelly, Elaine Theiry, Peter Reed, Dan Foley, Lauren Dillon, Lonnie Lazar, joedavola and Garry Owen stood up for me even when we disagreed.

This book wouldn't exist in the first place without my agent Kathy Anderson, who believed in it when it was just a notion, and hung in there with me for every twist and turn of the story. My editor at Wiley, Eric Nelson, pushed me to be more ambitious, as well as more lucid, in every chapter, and it's a much better book for the struggle.

My closest friends have put up with my obsession and unavailability over these two years with generosity and kindness and love, particularly Debbie Greiff, Bob Davis, Rafiki McDougald, Dean Burrell, Tony Pantaleoni, Don Smith, Jeff

Greenwald, Dwayne Newton, Gia Capadona, Bonnie Fluke, John Elford, David Rubien and Melissa Cox. You're the foundation. Irreplaceable.

I can't begin to adequately thank my family. I have two dozen first cousins and another dozen cousins "once removed" who are there for me in countless ways, even when we disagree about politics (and/or baseball). But I have to single out my cousins Peggy Walsh and Marck Webster because of the way they took care of my daughter once she became a New Yorker. (Much love to Julie Harris, Peggy's better half, and eternal gratitude to Marck's late wife, my cousin Magee Webster, who came through for me in so many spiritual and practical ways.) My Uncle Bill McLaren and Diane Meyers likewise helped me through these last four years, generously making time for me at the last minute if I could take a break from work while visiting New York. My Aunts Sara Walsh, Peggy Regan, Marilyn Webster and Anne Webster Cox have been there for me since I lost my mother. My godfather, Gene Walsh, finds ways to show love and support, openly as well as in hidden ways (that he thinks I don't know about), and my Uncles Dennis and Bill Walsh have fought the miles and the years to connect and to love me.

I couldn't live without my sister Susan: smart, funny, practical, dreamy, and unconditionally loving. My brother's and my relationship remains an unfinished story, one that's terribly Irish. He was my ally growing up in a house that was too often unhappy, and I love him very much. My nephews Patrick, Liam and Aidan—could those names be any more Irish?—keep me excited about our future. My ex-husband Robert DeVries remains one of my best friends and offers me so many kinds of support, while his son Daniel Halpern-DeVries continues to find novel ways to claim me as part of his family, which I am.

And then there's Nora Walsh-DeVries, who taught me how to live in this crazy mixed-up world, and laugh a lot. She makes me happy and proud every single day. I know Nora would like me to acknowledge our dog Sadie, the light of our lives.

This book is for my parents, John Patrick Walsh and Joan Florence Webster Walsh, who gave me the love and advantages they didn't have growing up. They passed along their questions to me, and I have spent my life finding answers. The world would be a better place had they lived a while longer.

INDEX